P9-DFR-270

THE IMMENSE COMPLEX DRAMA

No man,

unless he puts on

the mask of fiction,

can show his real face

or the will behind it.

William Dean Howells

THE

IMMENSE COMPLEX DRAMA

The World and Art of the

Howells Novel

George C. Carrington, Jr.

OHIO STATE UNIVERSITY PRESS COLUMBUS, OHIO

Library of Congress Catalogue Card Number 66–16764

To Ildikó

Preface

THIS BOOK originated in a search for meaningful patterns of form and informing concepts in that sprawling body of fiction known as "American realism." Soon realizing the bulk of the material, I confined myself to the novels of Howells, the leading realist. Not being a Howells scholar or having an emotional investment in Howells, I approached the material with no special preconceptions and no need to make Howells look good. I did have an interest in fiction and some broad critical conceptions that are roughly those of the so-called New Critics; that is, that the important actions of an artist are not in his life but in his work; that the meaning of a work of art resides in the work of art, not in what anyone (including the author) says about it; that the work is ready to tell us its secrets if we observe attentively; that a work of fiction is an elaborate structured gesture, the dynamic resultant of many vectors, each one in turn the product of innumerable words and combinations of words, choices of stress and pace, actions, speeches, figures of speech, points of view, and so on; that this gesture communicates willy-nilly the author's psychic set, existential outlook, Weltanschauung, or whatever fashionable label one wishes to apply to the apprehension of the universe. At the beginning of my research, I had no idea what the structure and meaning of Howells' novels were; in fact, I rather shared the common view that they had little meaning and no structure. My conclusions forced themselves upon me;

I resisted a number of them because I felt that there could not possibly be *that* much in Howells. The study is, therefore, inductive, except for the theoretical background mentioned above; the conclusions emerge from the material (though that is, of course, no guarantee that they are adequate or correct). My attitudes and approaches have made this book different in some basic ways from most previous work on Howells; for a discussion of these differences, see the Introduction below. I do use some ideas from Howells' critical pronouncements and from scholarly analyses, but only for side illumination and for convenience in labeling. The archetypal Howells image and action, for example, I describe in terms of some of Professor Cady's insights; but I worked from the material to these convenient labels, not the other way around.

The main body of my text consists of (1) analysis of Howells' Weltanschauung, as it appears in the novels only; (2) presentation of his underlying formal principles, which arise from his need to objectify his world view in fiction, and of the major literary methods and devices that help him to realize his world view in words; and (3) discussion of his unending concern with perception and with ways of stimulating and examining it. I conclude with a judgment of Howells' flaws and achievements in the light of his novels. Each topic in the text unfolds from the previous one. Within the topics, I often follow a temporal scheme; for even if one avoids a flatly autobiographical approach to Howells, there is no gainsaying the truth that in his artistic life he went through successive periods of experiment, growth, maturity, and decline. The narrowness of my approach should also be clear. One of the most complex, productive, and evasive of the major American writers, Howells can only be discussed satisfactorily by taking him one side at a time—here, the side of the novelist—and ignoring the many other sides (the playwright, the critic, the editor, the man of letters, the literary businessman, the friend of writers, the Christian Socialist, the family man). Readers are warned in advance not to look for things that are not here and are well treated elsewhere in the Howells literature.

My intended reader is not the Howells expert, who needn't be sold on Howells, and who, in my experience, already has decided ideas about him; nor is he the man who knows nothing about Howells and needs first to absorb the Cady biography and the various scholarly studies. This reader has a slight knowledge of Howells, a desire to know what is important in American literature, and, at present, no feeling that it is necessary to expand the former in order to satisfy the latter. This study therefore lacks such elemental props as plot summaries, but is deliberately lengthy in certain places (Chapters III and IV) in which I belabor with examples and discussion those readers who have never felt that the Howells novel has any point (except autobiography or flat recording), or that Howells uses the techniques of language and art like a serious artist. For the same reasons, I have limited my choice of novels to the major ones, which any critic of Howells must deal with if he really takes Howells seriously, to some typical ones, and to a few isolated works crucial to Howells' development. Any knowledgeable Howellsian can at once think of such omissions as *Mrs. Farrell* (or *Private Theatricals*), *The Quality of Mercy*, and *An Imperative Duty*. In defense I can only say that I have read all of Howells' fiction; that choice is necessary if one is to avoid unwieldiness or a series of tiny inconsequential analyses; that I discuss sixteen Howells novels, some at great length, and refer to many others; and that the choice of novels has been made, not to fit a predetermined scheme, but to reveal the pattern found among the novels themselves when they are taken as a whole.

The documentation of the study has been kept as simple as possible. Most references are blended into the text. When a reference can be to only one book, only a page number is given; when there is more than one consecutive reference to a given page, the page number is given for the last reference only. I use abbreviations to refer to the two volumes of Professor Cady's biography, and to the works of Howells that I most frequently quote. These abbreviations are as follows:

Cady, I—*The Road to Realism*
Cady, II—*The Realist at War*
AK—*Annie Kilburn*
ACA—*A Chance Acquaintance*
AFC—*A Foregone Conclusion*
HNF—*A Hazard of New Fortunes*
IS—*Indian Summer*
K—*The Kentons*
LA—*The Lady of the Aroostook*
LLH—*The Landlord at Lion's Head*
LG—*The Leatherwood God*
AMI—*A Modern Instance*
RSL—*The Rise of Silas Lapham*
SD—*The Shadow of a Dream*
SRL—*The Son of Royal Langbrith*
SVQ—*Stops of Various Quills*
SS—*Suburban Sketches*
TWJ—*Their Wedding Journey*
TA—*A Traveler from Altruria*

GEORGE C. CARRINGTON, JR.

Acknowledgments

I OWE A GREAT DEBT to Professor William Charvat of the Ohio State University, who shepherded me patiently through the doctoral dissertation that forms the basis of this study, and whose suggestions helped make the study meaningful to a larger audience than myself. I would also like to thank Professors Robert M. Estrich, Claude Simpson, Howard Babb, and Albert Kuhn, of the Ohio State University, for helpful comments over a period of some years.

The Case Research Council provided a grant that allowed me to begin the study; the Department of Humanities and Social Studies of Case Institute of Technology provided funds for the typing of the manuscript. My thanks to both.

My intellectual debts are many. In my text I offer implied acknowledgments for many of them; here I would like to offer special acknowledgment to Professor Edwin Cady for some important ideas and for a sustaining picture of Howells the man.

I gratefully acknowledge permission to quote from the following works:

From *Howells and the Age of Realism* by Everett Carter. Copyright 1954 by Everett Carter. Published by J. B. Lippincott Company.

From *The Poetry of Experience,* by Robert Langbaum. Copyright 1957 by Robert Langbaum. Published by Random House, Inc., and Chatto and Windus, Ltd.

From *The Road to Realism* and *The Realist at War,* by Edwin H. Cady. Copyright 1956 and 1958 by the Syracuse University Press. Published by Syracuse University Press.

From *William Dean Howells: Representative Selections,* edited by Clara Marburg Kirk and Rudolf Kirk. Copyright 1950 by the American Book Company. Published by the American Book Company.

GEORGE C. CARRINGTON, JR.

Contents

Introduction

THIS BOOK is a limited study, an examination of William Dean Howells as an artist and of his novels as works of art, revealing meaning through the complex relationships of theme, subject, technique, and form. It is written by one who is primarily interested in novels as works of art, not as depositories of ideas, or applications of creeds, or reflections of their authors' reading and conversations, or opportunities to apply elaborate critical or philosophical systems, or incidental products of men important for other things. This study is an answer, a partial answer, to such questions as, Given the novels of Howells, what happens if we look at them with the irreducible minimum of external reference, and examine them for meaning? What do their structures tell us? What are their characteristic elements? Is there significance in the use of these elements? The frequency of their use? The patterns of their use? I think that we can gain immensely in our understanding of the novels of Howells through this approach, which should not be taken as a programmatic application of the so-called New Criticism, myth criticism, or any other critical method, fashionable or unfashionable.

My approach must be set against the existing approaches to Howells as revealed in the body of Howells scholarship and criticism. I am not going to do this in order to find fault, or to prepare for vast claims of originality, but to place my method in a proper perspective. First consider the method farthest from my own: the method of conventional scholarship, developed in the nineteenth century and passed on through the graduate schools. In theory, according to its detractors, this method can lead to blind accumulation of facts, the only principle of unity being that the facts are all from the same subject; in practice, the method leads to sound but limited knowledge. In these terms conventional scholarship has done very well by Howells. Because of his prodigious output of novels, plays, travel books, biographies, reviews, autobiographies, criticism, occasional essays, and letters, and the immense amount of spoken and written comment on him by contemporary friends and enemies, and because Howells was genial, respectful of culture, and industrious (traits admired in academic life), he has an inherent attraction to scholars. They have thoroughly studied Howells the historical figure who, like a model president, clearly set forth his aims and then realized them in acts (novels, in Howells' case). Clara and Rudolf Kirk are the major active figures among the traditional scholars of Howells; they are the "old pros" of the field, as Professor Edwin H. Cady has said.[1] In a long introduction to *William Dean Howells: Representative Selections,* in the "American Writers Series," the Kirks summarized everything known about Howells in 1950, and also summarized the approach of their school: "Since practically all of Howells' writing is ultimately autobiographical, our study must be biographical in order to be properly critical. . . . [His novels] are only to be understood against the background of his life." [2] (One should ponder the implications of *must* and *only*.) Together and separately, the Kirks have applied these principles many times (for example, in Mrs. Kirk's thorough study of Howells' Christian Socialism, *W. D.*

[1] Review of Clara M. Kirk and Rudolf Kirk (eds.), *Criticism and Fiction and Other Essays by William Dean Howells* (New York, 1959) in the *New England Quarterly*, XXXII (1959), 403.

[2] Clara Marburg Kirk and Rudolf Kirk (eds.), *William Dean Howells: Representative Selections* (New York, 1950), p. vii. Hereafter referred to as *Representative Selections.*

Howells, Traveler from Altruria, 1889–1894 [New Brunswick, N.J., 1962]; their brief critical biography, *William Dean Howells* [New York, 1962]; and their reissue of *Criticism and Fiction and Other Essays by William Dean Howells* [New York, 1959]). In *The Road to Realism* and *The Realist at War* (Syracuse, N.Y., 1956, 1958), Professor Cady applied all the traditional methods of scholarship to produce the definitive biography of Howells. In his analyses of the Howells novels, Professor Cady modified the rigid biographical approach to criticism and used some "modern" methods, notably analysis of symbols; but his approach still makes literature a function of biography. A pleasant literary biography, full of sharp observations not pursued, is Van Wyck Brooks' *Howells: His Life and World* (New York, 1959). Robert L. Hough's *The Quiet Rebel: William Dean Howells as Social Commentator* (Lincoln, Neb., 1959) and James L. Woodress, Jr.'s *Howells and Italy* (Durham, N.C., 1952) are full treatments of smaller aspects of Howells' work and world. Other scholars have edited Howells' major novels with introductions, or brought out anthologies of criticism of him.[3]

It would be absurd to carp at the research that scholars have done on Howells. Every investigator of any aspect of Howells owes a debt to these scholars, whether he uses their discoveries directly or not; for it is the scholar who defines the world that the critic works in (or against). Nevertheless, there has been some restlessness with the limitations of the scholarly approach to Howells the man and the strictly autobiographical approach to his work. In the 1940's and 1950's, some new approaches became popular. Closest to

[3] Important editions are George Warren Arms (ed.), *A Hazard of New Fortunes* (New York, 1952); George Arms (ed.), *The Rise of Silas Lapham* (New York, 1949); and Edwin H. Cady (ed.), *The Shadow of a Dream* and *An Imperative Duty* (New York, 1962). The anthologies are Kenneth E. Eble (ed.), *Howells: A Century of Criticism* (New York, 1962), and Edwin H. Cady and David L. Frazier (eds.), *The War of the Critics over William Dean Howells* (New York, 1962).

conventional scholarship is the "American-civilization" approach, in which American works of art and their creators are assimilated to American culture, or more narrowly to the history of ideas in America (by which is usually meant the United States considered as a semi-independent offspring of northern European culture). "Ideas" and "culture" here refer in some cases to supposedly archetypal ideas operating, often in Hegelian fashion, in the minds of every American who has left a verbal record of his ideas or his responses to ideas. In this vein are the earlier studies of Howells by Parrington and Kazin and Arvin and Trilling, all colored to some extent by the desire to find material "usable" for a liberal tradition. An able recent article, in a non-political version of this vein, is Richard Foster's "The Contemporaneity of Howells." [4] Foster defines Howells' realism as " 'cultural' " (p. 54 n.), a way of studying what we now call "the 'dissociation' of modern sensibility" (p. 56). Howells' characters, in Foster's view, stand uncertain and anxious between two worlds, "the commercially structured present" and "the traditional past" (p. 55); their isolation suggests "the displacement of the intellectual as the traditional spokesman for intelligence and responsibility in the arena of public action" (p. 55). Foster concludes, "The final effect of Howells' fiction, then, is to create an aura of hazardous moral ambiguity which subtly conveys a controlled sense of the moral confusion that constituted the actual world he wrote about" (p. 77). In one sense we are a long way now from the conventional assumption that the Howells novel is ultimately autobiographical; but at the same time, we still have the traditional scholar's idea that Howells' novels are instrumental. In Foster's analysis Howells' characters (to take one aspect of his work) are instruments in a grand design aimed at revealing "the predicaments of what we have learned to call 'the modern world' " (p. 55). In

[4] *New England Quarterly,* XXXII (1959), 54–78. Other references to this article are in the text.

essence Foster's brilliant essay, which is so penetrating when he talks about the Howells "aura," is not so different from the essays of the 1930's in which Howells was praised or damned for attacking what the given critic was interested in.

Another flourishing modern division of Howells studies is that which, for convenience, I call "scholarly criticism." The workers of this school study Howells' novels primarily; discussions of external matters are not separate or even parallel, but contained in the treatments of the novels. But this structure is deceiving. If we look beyond it, we find that as in the conventional scholarly works, the novels are held to depend on and illustrate the external factors of sources, environmental influences, and biography. The relationship holds true no matter how rich and long the analyses of the novels. A great deal of solid and helpful work has been done within this genre. The earliest critics of Howells are still among the best —for example, Delmar Gross Cooke, *William Dean Howells: A Critical Study* (New York, 1922), and Oscar W. Firkins, *William Dean Howells: A Study* (Cambridge, Mass., 1924). Both Cooke and Firkins separate their analyses of biography and theory from their criticisms of Howells' actual methods and practice. Cooke had the important insight that Howells was often a romantic, but unfortunately, he did not develop the point into an informing principle. Firkins was and still is good on the usual grace and occasional weariness of Howells' style, and the whimsy or grotesqueness of his humor; but, like Cooke, Firkins does not explore the significance of what he finds or seek a synthesis of findings.

Two contemporary examples of scholar-criticism are: George N. Bennett's *William Dean Howells: The Development of a Novelist* (Norman, Okla., 1959), and Olov W. Fryckstedt's *In Quest of America: A Study of Howells' Early Development as a Novelist* (Cambridge, Mass., 1958). "Development," a key word in both titles, suggests that Howells' work and methods grew consciously, that he deliberately carved out a career; and as it turns out, this is the Howells of these two books. Fryckstedt analyzes "the slow growth of Howells' ability to portray America" in terms of Howells' expressed theory and his application of that theory. The "America" of this Swedish scholar is rather a Platonic absolute than a concrete world, but within its clearly defined limits, this work is definitive. Bennett's Howells is more a working literary man, responsive to the pressure of friends, editors, and audiences, and, during the 1860's and 1870's, gathering strength in the creating of character and plot. Bennett's accuracy of observation is unquestionable, but his interest in analysis and synthesis is small. Reviewing Bennett's book, Professor Cady, the kindest of reviewers, well defines the manner and limits of Bennett's approach: "The tone of his writing is that of the old 'judicial' critic who approaches literature from the outside and makes flat, authoritative statements about it, often from a height of adverbial superiority." [5]

Still the best scholar-critic is Everett Carter, whose book fulfils its initial promise to present "the history of the growth of sensibility of a man and an age and part of the biography of ourselves" and "the story of the growth of the mind of William Dean Howells." [6] It remains to define "sensibility" and "mind" as Carter uses them. We can sense his approach when we read, "Those traits conventionally assumed to be American traits, concern for fact, pragmatism, optimism, were the basic attitudes of Howells and the movement in letters called American realism. . . . What this work is going to do is sympathetically to re-examine these attitudes as they appear in the work of Howells and those writers of his convictions [such as Twain, De Forest, Eggleston, and Tourgée]" (pp.

[5] Review of George N. Bennett, *William Dean Howells: The Development of a Novelist* in the *New England Quarterly,* XXXII (1959), 401.

[6] *Howells and the Age of Realism* (New York, 1954), p. 13. Subsequent references are in the text.

21–22). Here again is programmatic realism, consciously propagated by an expert wordsmith as the organizing concept for novels that he is certain will embody them 100 per cent. Carter also makes sources and influences into first causes. During the 1870's, Carter says, Howells was led by "his large early admiration for Turgenev" (p. 126) to write neat novels about small groups (*The Lady of the Aroostook,* for example). Carter's readings of Howells' major novels are always unexceptionable, within the limits of Carter's focus. *The Rise of Silas Lapham,* for example, succeeds in Carter's view as a neat structure, but fails over-all because the big theme of private vs. social morality is too large for that neat small structure. Carter's analyses of Howells' symbolism (such as the intaglio ring in *A Hazard of New Fortunes*) and his placing of Howells in relation to the later naturalists are important milestones in Howells criticism.

But the critical vision of these scholar-critics is still limited, to the point that new advances must be made along new lines. The preoccupation with matters extrinsic to the fiction—programmatic realism, cultural concerns, historical phenomena, parallels and influences—makes it difficult for these critics to grasp Howells as an artist and to see the Howells novel as a work of art. Carter, for example, says that Howells' late novel *The Kentons* is about "the pleasant troubles" (p. 224) that arise when a small-town couple has a marriageable daughter. Now *The Kentons* is assuredly a small novel, a minor effort, but the troubles of Ellen Kenton and her family are the opposite of "pleasant"; in fact, the novel is a paradigm of Howells' representations of helpless innocence in the grip of gratuitous evil. Looking at the American qualities of Howells, these critics miss many of his general human qualities, although it is only fair to say that Carter, in particular, frequently circumvents his self-imposed limits. Studying sources also creates invisible but strong blinkers; sources and influences come to be accepted, in the worst cases, as causes rather than as catalysts or parallels or even results, and the identification of parallels comes to be an end in itself. Bennett emphasizes a similar external matter, the publishing history of Howells' works, to the point that explanations in this area apparently satisfy him as explanations of the works themselves. Bennett says that the lost child incident at the end of "A Day's Pleasure," a slight but interesting tale in *Suburban Sketches* (1871, 1872), is simply Howells' device for "eking out his material." [7] The point is fully documented, but it does not begin to explain the meaning of the incident or its relation to the sketch (and as I shall try to prove later, the little added incident does have meaning, and reinforces the larger meaning of the sketch).

The world of the scholar-critic, then, is a pre-Freudian one (despite Cady's use of the term *libido*); it is a world in which fictional events (plots, characters, and the like) follow from conscious intention and programs, and can be analyzed quite subtly but are more likely to be taken at face value and in isolation from one another. Sometimes the result is error on a minor level. Carter's analysis of *The Octopus* (pp. 236–37) reveals insensitivity to tone and to relationships. He is not bothered by the placing (at the very end) and the explicitly assertive bareness of Norris' famous statement of optimism, and does not seem to be aware that the statement's relationship to the novel is more than one of mere intellectual contrast; apparently, Carter feels that Norris can do what he pleases without being held to account for destroying the emotional effects of hundreds of pages of fiction. Readers of *The Octopus* will also recall Norris' device of alternating snatches of chatter at a society dinner with the moans of the dying Mrs. Hooven and her child. To Carter, who again takes Norris at face value, this device "made an almost unbearably affecting contrast" (p. 236); elsewhere, Carter says that *The Octopus* "stunned the reader" (p. 237). Few will doubt that

[7] *Op. cit.*, p. 13.

this was Norris' intention, but that the book had that effect then or now on "the reader"—that is, every reader—remains to be proved.

This tendency to take things (especially pronouncements) at face value and in isolation from other things (and other pronouncements) becomes a serious error when the critics get to the subject of Howells' general achievement. Here the central point involves Howells' idea of "real life" and his actual practice as a "realist" who is "imitating" the "reality" of "American life." Too many critics have been ready to accept Howells' aims and claims at face value, to equate *his* "real life" with real life, *his* "realism" with realism, *his* "American life" with the whole culture, *his* "imitation" of reality with a total imitation of reality. Carter, for example, accepts the formlessness of the big Howells novel—he is discussing *The Quality of Mercy*, but it could be one of many others—but he does not do so because he feels that the formlessness has an aesthetic purpose (or is an aesthetic failure, which would be saying the same thing from another point of view). Carter feels that this formlessness is "something very close to the texture of life itself" and therefore more suitable for Howells' purposes than "the medium of the well-formed dramatic novel" (p. 313). Here Carter assumes that Howells is imitating "life itself" and that "life itself" is a universal and universally understood concept. But can one reach these conclusions so quickly? Aristotle, who originates the imitative theory, does not confuse mimesis with reality or with an imitation of all of reality; *Oedipus Rex* is mimetic in part and whole, but it does not subsume reality. In *Mimesis: The Representation of Reality in Western Literature*,[8] Erich Auerbach showed that "reality" and "the imitation of reality" have changed in meaning again and again from the time of Homer to the present. Howells is no exception; his reality in his fiction is *his* reality, shaped by his concerns and by his

[8] Garden City, N.Y., 1957.

ability to objectify those concerns in fiction; and the slice-of-life theory is no more final an explanation of his novels than it is of a Thomas Wolfe novel or *I Am a Camera.* In addition Howells' reality, as I hope to show, is not only his own but is problematic as well; his fiction is both an attempt to find out what reality is, and a revelation of what it is like to be forced to live in the world and find out what it is at the same time. Carter rightly points out that the literary tendency known as realism "found meaning and value to reside in the world of physical appearances" (p. 265) but does not realize that one can agree with that and still ask: What is that meaning? What is that value?

As a result of postulating the Howells novel as a slice of life, the scholar-critics give us a flat Howells, a writer without meaning; for meaning follows from selection, arrangement, and emphasis. Bennett, as I have said, correctly points out that a given incident was tacked on to a given Howells story in order to make it long enough, but goes no further. The point here is that Bennett *cannot* go further. His theory does not allow it. He cannot deal with the notion that the given incident must have been selected (whether consciously or not is unknowable and beside the point anyway) from other incidents, any one of which would have done a satisfactory job of adding wordage; nor can Bennett deal with the proposition that, tacked on clumsily or not, the added incident is offered to the public as part of the sketch and has certain relationships—for which Howells can be held responsible—to the other parts of the sketch. Rather than the concept of *meaning,* which is entangled with relativity, the conventional critic of Howells stresses *truth,* an absolute that naturally follows from "real life," "life itself," and the rest of the credo of the slice-of-life school. In the course of a shrewd, useful discussion of myth and symbol in Howells, Carter says that there are "false and evil myths as well as good and true ones" (p. 220), Carter's claim being that Howells gives us "true" ones. The Kirks conclude that "Howells' novels and his critical essays together reflect the first major battle to take place in this country over the novelist's right and duty to tell the truth." [9] Truth as the artist's inspiration is acceptable, but to confuse it with his achievement is the ruin of criticism.

The scholars and scholar-critics claim too much for Howells and drive readers away, or claim the wrong things, and drive more readers away. Modern readers and critics accept relativity; they know very well that Howells is not universal, and would be ready to admit Howells' world view as one among many if they were not told that Howells is not writing about *a* world (his own, and an interesting one), but *the* world, and that, by inference, other writers are wrong. Also, scholars tend to project their professional interests into their material, to look in that material for qualities that will test their training or hold their interest or confirm their prejudices; this is a natural human tendency. The Howells researcher is so engulfed in secondary material, and finds the primary material so enticingly close to that secondary material, that it is fatally easy for him to overemphasize programs and influences, to conclude that characters are simple photographs of real individuals or cultural types, and to value achievement in those spheres (the close resemblance of a plot to one of Turgenev's, or of a character to a Boston type, being defined as an achievement). But readers are not interested in this scholars' Howells any more than they are in the Howells who is said to embrace all of "real life." The achievements of the scholars' Howells do not touch readers, any more than the achievements of Professor Fenton's skilled journalist-Hemingway interest the reader of "Big Two-Hearted River." The reader of Howells scholarship and scholarly Howells criticism —I am referring to *reader,* not *student*—has been asked to do something that everyone dislikes—admire something that bores him, or admire something potentially admirable for reasons that bore him. Readers have responded by silently

[9] *Representative Selections,* p. cxxxviii.

disappearing. Now, even respectable scholars writing for staid journals do not feel it impossible to mention their feelings of apathy toward Howells. In the *New England Quarterly,* Professor John Lydenberg, no establishment-baiter, says, "Howells at best awakens our admiration; passionate engagement we do not feel. . . . He wrote from his head, not from his subconscious, and we must respond correspondingly, with our heads, our understanding, rather than with our whole being." [10] Professor Lydenberg concludes that the Howells "revival," so often announced, is academic only.[11] It is ironic that Howells himself was harsh about the pretense surrounding the classics; in one of his widely read "Editor's Study" essays in *Harper's Monthly,* he said that "at least three-fifths of the literature called classic, in all languages, no more lives than the poems and stories that perish monthly in our magazines. It is all printed and reprinted, generation after generation, century after century; but it is not alive; it is as dead as the people who wrote it and read it. . . . A superstitious piety preserves it . . . but nobody really enjoys it." [12] Both men express feelings that the reading public has long had about Howells, and what many academics now feel (and are perhaps too polite to say). But one large question remains to be answered: this classic Howells, this "realist," is he the real Howells or just the scholar's?

One might think that Howells himself could and would answer that question, but he does not answer it satisfactorily; his pronouncements, on himself and others, are interesting, but do not get us much closer to the real quality of his fiction than the analyses of the scholars and scholar-critics. To begin with, there is so much criticism by Howells that only in a major book could one adequately disentangle the various

[10] Review of Edwin H. Cady, *The Road to Realism* and *The Realist at War* (Syracuse, N.Y., 1956, 1958), in the *New England Quarterly,* XXXII (1959), 395, 397.

[11] *Ibid.,* p. 395.

[12] *Harper's Monthly,* LXXV (1887), 641, in *Representative Selections,* p. cxlii.

Howellses and synthesize his deepest opinions. For my purposes, Howells' theories are adequately summarized by the Kirks, whose volume in the "American Writers Series" is more widely available than the scattered material that they efficiently pull together. They rightly emphasize that Howells' opinions "were not mere theories devised by an editor in need of copy; they were the outgrowth of many years of novel reading and novel writing." [13] The Kirks conclude that "the five component parts of Howells' theory of realism ". . . are his defense of the commonplace as the source of novel material, his insistence that character is more important than plot, his attack on the romantic writers, his attitude towards idealism and morals, his belief in realism as the expression of democracy." [14]

The scholars' Howells is, apparently, close to the Howells that he himself knew, or, perhaps, the Howells that he himself wanted to know. Realism to this Howells was "the truthful treatment of material," [15] and romanticism was not "the absolutely unreal, the purely fanciful in all the arts," but the "thing which asks to be accepted with all its fantasticality on the ground of reality." [16] Howells seems to distinguish not so much between realism and romanticism as between trivial art and "serious" art (which could include elements of romanticism). Idealism to Howells is false sentiment, the opposite of common sense. Given this point, I suggest that realism to Howells meant much more than just copying "reality" (whatever that might be); it involved attitudes toward reality; it meant having the proper, the pious attitude toward the facts, toward Being (the exact nature of the latter being undetermined and perhaps indeterminate). The question of "morals" brings us to Howells' sexual squeamishness,

[13] *Representative Selections,* p. cxxxix.

[14] *Ibid.,* pp. cxxxviii–cxxxix.

[15] *Criticism and Fiction* (New York, 1891), p. 73, in *Representative Selections,* p. cxliii.

[16] *My Literary Passions,* 1895, pp. 216–17, in *Representative Selections,* p. cxliii.

the target of three generations of criticism. Though Howells admired Zola and Tolstoy, he kept their frankness out of his own work, because he felt it dangerous, as he implied in his introduction to *The Coast of Bohemia,*[17] and as Professors Carter and Cady show at some length [18] in terms of Howells' era and Howells' neurotic fears.[19] Howells, however, does not suggest that his fiction may in part be about this fear of sex (or libido, to use the more flexible modern term substituted by Professor Cady).[20] The close identification of "realism"—the "commonplace," the "everyday"—with democracy at once suggests the central, American tradition of Emerson ("the meal in the firkin; the milk in the pan") and Whitman, and strengthens my feeling that realism is an attitude, the opposite of frivolity. But this is my idea; Howells does not interpret his approach as "an" art. And nowhere does he tell us plainly what his books do, in themselves and in relation to his theories. Here and there he does imply a good deal, however. At the age of seventy-nine, he wrote, "No man, unless he puts on the mask of fiction, can show his real face or the will behind it. For this reason the only real biographies are the novels, and every novel, if it is honest, will be the autobiography of the author and biography of the reader." [21] At first glance, this statement looks like reinforcement for the Kirks' argument that Howells' "novels are only to be understood against the background of his life." But the phrase "the mask of fiction" and the reference to the "biography of the reader" suggest irony and symbolism rather than simple transposing from personal experience to the printed page. Howells also put his finger on the confusion about "truth" when he advised

[17] See *Representative Selections,* pp. cxlvi–cxlvii.

[18] Carter, *op. cit.,* pp. 139–52; Cady, II, pp. 122–28. (For a complete listing of abbreviations used throughout the text and notes, see page x of the Preface.)

[19] See Edwin H. Cady, "The Neuroticism of William Dean Howells," *PMLA,* LXI (1946), 229–38.

[20] Cady, II, p. 128.

[21] *Years of My Youth* (New York, 1916), p. 127. Quoted by Bennett (*op. cit.,* p. 36), who fails to see any significance in the statement.

young writers, "Do not trouble yourselves about standards or contempts or passions; but try to be faithful and natural; and remember that there is no greatness, no beauty, which does not come from *truth to your own knowledge of things*"[22] (my italics), implying a basic difference between a devotion to one abstract "truth" and the knowledge that one either has or is searching for his own truth.

I agree with Howells that we must go to the novels to find "his real face" and "the will behind it." Knowing so much about Howells the man and the writer, we may persuade ourselves that, in knowing that much, we know a great deal about his fiction (and I think that many critics have so persuaded themselves). But look at the novels. Why are they so full of comment and generalizations and expressions of uncertainty (like "perhaps")? Why do his characters do so little and spend so much time analyzing and conjecturing? Why do they suffer continual petty humiliations? Why do we hear so little about the details of their professional activities if Howells was the kind of realist he is claimed to be? Why, in "the" record of "the" world (and that world one of commonplace events) are there so many unnatural or gratuitous acts of violence, and so many brief, startling disturbances? Why are his narrative and moral centers so often undermined and made to seem absurd? Why is *A Traveler from Altruria* told in the first person? Is the house-hunting episode at the beginning of *A Hazard of New Fortunes* really too long, or is there meaning in it and its length?

Critics are beginning to answer some of the smaller questions about Howells' novels. William Wasserstrom has grappled with the problem of Howells' young heroines, who seem to be so fresh and innocent, yet are so often checked or disappointed or sent away (as Penelope Lapham is whisked off to Mexico at the end of *The Rise of Silas Lapham*).

[22] *Harper's Magazine,* LXXV (1887), 641, in *Representative Selections,* p. cxxxiii.

Wasserstrom concludes that Howells publicly admired but privately loathed "the American girl" of Victorian mythology because her innocent flirtations led directly to marriage, and marriage led to sexual relations; she and her sisters were "depraved innocents,"[23] the phrase linking Howells to Hawthorne and James. Howells "saw in family life a kind of metaphor of the life of society at large," saw woman at the center of the family, but could not deal squarely with woman, and therefore "his fiction does not multiply its effect but instead dissipates it."[24] Wasserstrom makes some small errors in his readings of Howells,[25] and he certainly is no New Critic; but he does work from the novels back to the biography and critical programs, and not the other way around. A better example of the newer Howells criticism is William McMurray's "Point of View in Howells's *The Landlord at Lion's Head*."[26] McMurray's Howells is a true artist: a man who manipulates the techniques of fiction in order to create meaning and present, not "realism," but his vision of reality (and in McMurray's view of fiction, "techniques" is not limited to the Jamesian definition of the term). Howells, says McMurray, saw "human existence as a complicity of self and other, an organic inclusiveness in which self and other interacted to create a multiple reality in a changing and continuing experience."[27] The unobtrusive symbolic center for this world in this novel is Lion's Head, the New England mountain that never looks the same from one hour to the next and looks different from every angle, and

[23] "William Dean Howells: The Indelible Stain," *New England Quarterly*, XXXII (1959), 494.

[24] *Ibid.*, p. 494.

[25] As an example, he stops his interpretation of *The Shadow of a Dream* at the point in the novel where Nevil and Hermia agree to part, and ignores Nevil's decision to follow March's advice and again lay siege to Hermia (this happy development being abruptly ended by Nevil's horrible death in a railroad accident—a point that reinforces Wasserstrom's theory).

[26] *American Literature*, XXXIV (1962), 207–14.

[27] *Ibid.*, p. 212.

that the novel's center of intelligence, the painter Westover, can record not once to his satisfaction. Anticipating *The Ambassadors,* whose hero is based on Howells, the latter demonstrates "that the act of seeing (and judging) is relative to the person who does the seeing," [28] by giving Jeff Durgin, who grows up in sight of the mountain, the enigmatic power of a mountain and a lion, and by making him a separate mystery to every other character in the novel. Without any fuss, this is modern criticism at its best: the meaning generates the literary work, and the work generates the meaning.

This is the approach that I take in this book. It is an approach that moves from the world of technical criticism into Howells' fiction and sometimes beyond, into the world of programs and historical facts—an approach that supplements the conventional movement from the latter world into Howells' fiction and occasionally a little beyond into the former world. I postulate that Howells lives as an artist or not at all; and without being intentionally rigid about it, I apply the working hypothesis that the Howells novel is quasi-lyric, a complex gesture revealing attitudes toward his existence as a man.

This Howells is, to be sure, a limited Howells—"my" Howells, so to speak—and it would be presumptuous to claim anything more. (I deliberately set aside two promising Howellses: the dramatist of ideas,[29] and the minor turn-of-the-century experimenter with proto-Freudian ideas.[30] My Howells is quite different from the scholars' Howells, though he ultimately derives from the insights of scholars, especially Professor Cady, the analyst of Howells' neuroses, and though many of my points have been made by earlier students, who saw little or no significance in them. In relation to the

[28] *Ibid.,* p. 209.

[29] See the remark of Cady in his review of *Criticism and Fiction and Other Essays,* p. 405.

[30] See Cady, II, pp. 242 ff.

scholars' Howells, mine is a kind of "ur-Howells," that part of the man who responded immediately to the reality he knew before his cautious, scrupulous consciousness could rationalize and control the responses. This Howells is not just "American," but human, and "American" in synecdoche (while, from another point of view, remaining decidedly high-Victorian American). He is not a public figure who wrote novels that are interesting because a public figure wrote them; he is rather a group of novels telling us something through their qualities and internal relationships and their relationships to each other, and signed by one "William Dean Howells," who is interesting because he wrote those interesting novels. He is a conditional Howells, built up from application of the thesis that a man deserves to be taken as the sum of his actions in his proper sphere—that is, he is an artist. This Howells is an artist of the uncertain and of the problematic; he acts out and projects in action (which includes comment as well as event) the personal concerns—Foster's "dissociation," for example—that critics see him discovering like an anthropologist and then covering with a clothing of fiction.

Adding this hypothetical Howells to the Howellses of the scholars and scholar-critics, one can see that Howells *is* an artist; that his artistic growth is primarily regulated by internal forces (influenced, of course, by external events); that he is not merely representational, his often-derided "teacup-realism" not just the passive record of a bloodless seismograph or an Emersonian eyeball, but an artistic device working with other devices to create meaningful forms (or meaningful formlessnesses); that the commonplace in his work is potent and sometimes threatening, and is at any rate plentifully offset by violence, horror, "blackness," and the other gothic traits admired by present-day critics. We realize that his fear of sex (now probably his most controversial trait) is for Howells the artist not at all a limiting flaw but simply a *donnée* from which art may or may not follow, depending on

the skill of the artist rather than the subject matter of the *donnée*. (In this respect Howells started on equal terms with James.)

The over-all aim of my study, then, is to offer some hypotheses that will lead to theories helpful both to readers of Howells and critics of Howells. For the former, it will be helpful to be able to "read Howells," as one "reads Dostoevski" or "reads Faulkner"—that is, to read the separate works with an appreciation of their immediate qualities, but at the same time to be aware of the voice and the sensibility present in all of the novels. This Howells can be read for the same reasons that, for example, Thomas Wolfe is read by adolescents, Hemingway by more mature readers, and Faulkner perhaps by readers more mature still: these books satisfy a need; they objectify recognizable and important human situations in ways that at the same time satisfy the reader and expand his horizons, thus leaving him ripe for more complex art. I had better not claim too much for Howells, though; he is not a major artist or one of broad appeal (and he is a flawed artist). His appeal is perhaps more to middle age or to the outlook we consider appropriate to middle age than to any other human situation. (This point may be involved in Howells' low reputation among younger critics and graduate students.) Everett Carter has aptly compared Howells to James Gould Cozzens,[31] a modern writer who also tells us that life is complex and problematic, great efforts accomplish little, the best people grow tired and anxious, libido is dangerous, and caution is the watchword.

An attempt to find a thesis uniting the Howells canon may also give Howells studies a fillip—one much needed, I think. The field of Howells studies has never gone through the "take-off era," the stage of shock and sass and ferment that has characterized the early years of contemporary studies of

[31] *Op. cit.*, pp. 267 ff.

Melville, James, and Faulkner, to name three of many. Where is *Howells' Quarrel with God*? or "Come Back to the House, Silas, Honey?" Where is the book that will briskly solve the problem of Howells' "young American girl" by "proving" that she is a Lesbian? The free-swinging, undisciplined but fresh young minds have not been attracted to Howells, have equated him with their own (or sometimes their professors') quick reading of Howells according to a priori standards, or with their reactions to a hasty glance at some of the Howells scholarship. In search of large opportunities and demands, the seminal minds gravitate toward other writers and toward methods of study ("new" criticism, myth criticism, tracing of Jungian archetypes, etc.) that seem "naturally" to demand application to almost anyone but Howells. It is symptomatic that in the introduction to *Love and Death in the American Novel,* Leslie Fiedler announces that he is not going to discuss Howells at all, and that in his text Fiedler mentions Howells only in a passing slight. Of course it is absurd to claim too much for Howells as a field of study; we then wind up like the scholars who announce the periodic Howells revivals to an indifferent world. But one can claim that Howells is a phenomenon well worth examining, and can offer preliminary explanations of that phenomenon.

This inductive method makes use of all kinds of critical tools whenever they are needed, but is not based on any one "critical method." Such a general approach as I have is expressed most clearly in the "Polemical Introduction" to Northrop Frye's *Anatomy of Criticism.* In addition I have used his ideas on satire as a major critical tool. I can best express my debt to Frye's ideas and clarity of expression by quoting some of his statements without comment. These statements define some major aspects of critics and criticism, and, by application, some errors of omission and commission of Howells scholars and scholar-critics.

My approach is based on Matthew Arnold's precept of

letting the mind play freely around a subject in which there has been much endeavor and little attempt at perspective.[32]

. . . There is still a lingering notion that it is somehow ridiculous to regard the critic as the final judge of its [a literary work's] meaning, even though in practice it is clear that he must be. The reason for this is an inability to distinguish literature from the descriptive or assertive writing which derives from the active will and the conscious mind, and which is primarily concerned to "say" something. (p. 5)

The dialectic axis of criticism . . . has as one pole the total acceptance of the data of literature, and as the other the total acceptance of the potential values of those data. This is the real level of culture and of liberal education, the fertilizing of life by learning, in which the systematic progress of scholarship flows into a systematic progress of taste and understanding. On this level there is no itch to make weighty judgements. . . . Comparative estimates of value are really inferences, most valid when silent ones, from critical practice, not expressed principles guiding its practice. (p. 25)

It occurs to me that literary criticism is now in such a state of naïve induction as we find in a primitive science. Its materials, the masterpieces of literature, are not yet regarded as phenomena to be explained in terms of a conceptual framework which criticism alone possesses. They are still regarded as somehow constituting the framework or structure of criticism as well. I suggest that it is time for criticism to leap to a new ground from which it can discover what the organizing or containing forms of its conceptual framework are. (pp. 15–16)

The absurd quantum formula of criticism, the assertion that the critic should confine himself to "getting out" of a poem exactly what the poet may vaguely be assumed to have been aware of "putting in," is one of the many slovenly illitera-

[32] Northrop Frye, *Anatomy of Criticism* (Princeton, N.J., 1957), p. 3. Subsequent references are in the text.

> cies that the absence of systematic criticism has allowed to grow up. This quantum theory is the literary form of what may be called the fallacy of premature teleology. It corresponds, in the natural sciences, to the assertion that a phenomenon is as it is because Providence in its inscrutable wisdom made it so. That is, the critic is assumed to have no conceptual framework; it is simply his job to take a poem into which a poet has diligently stuffed a specific number of beauties or effects, and complacently extract them one by one, like his prototype Little Jack Horner. (pp. 17–18)

Even more debatable than these general remarks are Frye's essays in critical "organizing [and] containing forms," though detractors should note that Frye plainly disclaims perfection. He has a native impulse to organize, usually into tetrads and sextets, and to parallel and interlock such organizations. Waiving the question of absolute correctness, I have found much of use in Frye's definition of satire and his organization of kinds of literary satire. For him, "satire is militant irony: its moral norms are relatively clear, and it assumes standards against which the grotesque and absurd are measured" (p. 223). Two things are essential for satire: "wit or humor founded on fantasy or a sense of the grotesque or absurd" and "an object of attack" (p. 224).

Frye distinguishes six stages, from the lightest comic satire to the grimmest tragic satire. His initial form postulates a dominating, immovable, humorous society ("humorous," of course, having its Renaissance meaning). The unconventional here is gaily accepted (see Dickens' lovable eccentrics) or quietly observed and when necessary resisted by prudent, pragmatic observers, or *"eirons"* (p. 227), in Frye's term (Basil and Isabel March are Howells *eirons,* especially in Howells' early novels). Works in this first form make their satiric thrust indirectly, in the sense of futility and nightmare that they leave behind them. In Frye's second kind of satire, the conventional itself comes under fire. By bringing up the inconvenient data that system-makers omit, works on this level tell us that experience is bigger than any explanation of it and that explanations may do more harm than good. Here the classic form, or anti-form, is the picaresque novel, with *Don Quixote* a principal archetype (note that Cervantes was not merely Howells' favorite writer, from childhood on, but his hero; he once thought of writing a biography of him).[33] The third level of satire questions not only the data of experience, but experience itself and the means of experience, perceptions and perception (the latter a favorite theme of Howells). Here perspectives are violently shifted in order to destroy them and faith in them (Howells, like Swift, does this frequently). Rabelais, Apuleius, and again Cervantes are models of this third level; the wild Rabelaisian use of language is a symptomatic technique (conspicuously and significantly lacking in Howells). The fourth division brings us closer to "the ironic aspect of tragedy, and satire begins to recede" (p. 236). This phase is associated with "sincere, explicit realism" (p. 237), with man as a suffering person (not animal), with firm but understanding rejection of inflated heroics (as in the ending of *Hamlet,* seen as a muddle rather than as towering tragedy). In the fifth phase, writers emphasize "the natural cycle, the steady unbroken turning of the wheel of fate or fortune" (p. 237) stoically endured. Much of the mature Howells reflects this attitude. In the sixth and last phase, life is seen as "largely unrelieved bondage" (p. 238), a hell on earth, as in *1984* and *In the Penal Colony*. There is no possible end to this hell for man in general, and no possible end (except for lucky accident) for man in particular, because the dominant figures (rulers and their assistants, random psychopaths) are insatiably sadistic, and relax their tortures only to return refreshed. In this phase authors often use parodies of religion and romance: anti-heroes like Faulkner's Benjy, atonements and other religious actions turned upside down, villains who are chillingly unlike the straw figures of melodrama, courtships that become the

[33] See Cady, I, 25, 51; II, 223.

occasion for gratuitous tortures. A Freudian or proto-Freudian sense of the id and its power can lead to satire on this level and is especially effective because the given hell is located entirely on earth and originates in men themselves; in some late Howells works (*The Kentons, The Landlord at Lion's Head, The Son of Royal Langbrith, The Leatherwood God,* for example), this element, which Frye does not mention, is quite strong. In any given work the six levels can intermingle and a technique or character can reflect more than one level; Frye's orderly structure exists only in the abstract world of the science of criticism, and must not be crudely applied to a single work. His structure is, nevertheless, immensely useful in studying aspects of Howells novels and the general trend of Howells' sense of life as seen in his fiction; the brief applications of Frye's points that I have made above will be considerably expanded later.

CHAPTER I

THE PSYCHIC SET: HOWELLS AND ALIENATION

. . . Was existence all a miserable chance, a series of stupid, blundering accidents? We could not believe that; for our very souls' sake, and for our own sanity we must not.

CONSIDER a Howells novel, a mediocre one, not one of the big novels of Howells' peak years (*A Modern Instance, The Rise of Silas Lapham, A Hazard of New Fortunes*) with their important subject matter and strong ethical and social themes. Consider *A Foregone Conclusion* (1875), Howells' first full-length work of fiction that is wholly dissociated from the essay and the travel book (*A Chance Acquaintance,* published only two years earlier, is still entangled with these two forms, especially the latter). *A Foregone Conclusion* is so minor that it offers us a chance to catch Howells off guard and follow his own advice: "The sincere observer of man will not desire to look upon his heroic or occasional phases, but will seek him in his habitual moods of vacancy and tiresomeness" (*TWJ,* pp. 86–87). On the simplest level, the novel is a love triangle. The scene is Venice, still occupied by the Austrians, in the 1860's. A miscast priest (Don Ippolito), and an American painter (Ferris) acting as the American consul, both fall in love with a young American girl, Florida Vervain, who is accompanied by her widowed mother.

Not one of the three major characters really belongs to Venice; the priest, a native of the place, is so miserably at odds with his world and his occupation that he is as alien to it as the two Americans. Not one of the three can communicate with the others and thus get on with his life; they are all continually together, but continually at cross-purposes. Even the two young Americans are held away from each other.

Communications and revelations come awkwardly and spasmodically and are tinged with absurdity. The priest is an inventor, we learn, but this impressive title comes to us in a context of perpetual-motion machines, and cannons that blow themselves up. The novel moves in a desultory fashion, with much strolling to and fro and many chance encounters. In one of the central episodes, a long-planned excursion by boat, all meaning and pleasure evaporate in a confusion of misdirected small talk and changing moods, ending with the girl's spiteful rebuff of the priest's friendly inquiries. On the way back to Venice after the long catastrophe of the day, the three have a frightening brush with the Austrian customs officers. Slithering about in deep mud, the gloomy priest heaves their gondola off a shoal while the girl explains their midnight presence in the lagoon to a trigger-happy Austrian sentry. Later in the novel, the priest plans to leave the church and Venice, and clumsily tells the girl of his hopes and his love for her; she rejects him in instinctive disgust, but then takes pity on him and embraces him like a mother comforting a baby. The consul observes this ambiguous scene from behind a tree, assumes that the priest and the girl are lovers, and rushes off, to be united with Florida only after a chance meeting in a New York art gallery years later. At the end, the pair discuss Don Ippolito as if he had never been real.

The approximate center of this awkward fiction is the consul, Ferris, but it is soon obvious that he is not a Jamesian illuminating center, but a source of further confusion. He falls in love with Florida Vervain, but he does not understand her. After he sees her embrace the priest in the deluding light of the moon, he is miserable; but he cannot define his condition, and he cannot be sure the event or his condition is real. He is not even sure that he himself is real. He cannot see Don Ippolito as a man, but only as a function determined by his dress, an "inhuman, sacerdotal phantasm" (p. 195). The priest's avowal of love for Florida so upsets Ferris that ordinary people on the Grand Canal "are all like sights in a mirror, or things in a world turned upside down" (p. 194). Ferris hopes to do a good deal of painting in Venice, but gets entangled with the priest and the girl, and floats helplessly and confusedly along in that situation until an outside force —Don Ippolito's passion—breaks through and precipitates the crisis. Ferris is so little in control of his feelings that after a tiff with the girl, he not only cannot sustain his anger but cannot remember why he was angry. The world, then, presents itself as a weird, blank mystery to Ferris. The other characters, almost entirely seen from the outside, are mysteries from beginning to end.

What does a reader get from *A Foregone Conclusion?* If a lover of the picturesque is looking forward to set-piece descriptions of Venice, he soon realizes that setting is used only as a projection of the characters' feelings or as a foil to them. The romantic, who wants a love story—any love story, whether favorable or "tragic" in outcome—will be put off completely. The priest is ludicrously clumsy as a lover, and the two Americans seem to avoid straightforward love scenes or even open avowal of their feelings to themselves. The reader who wants to kill time with an interesting story, whether a love story or not, will be irritated by the Brownian movement of the plot and will find the huddled, tacked-on ending more irritating than satisfying. A reader in search of the Howells "realism" may well ask if real people are as consistently confused, or often as deeply confused, or act as melodramatically, as the three major characters of this novel; he might also wonder what principle dictated the creation of Mrs. Vervain, an addlepated Army widow, who named her daughter Florida because she was born in that state. Evidently, *A Foregone Conclusion* is neither well-made entertainment nor a slice of life.

What the book does, and what any Howells novel does, is represent Howells' apprehension of the universe and of man's life in the universe. With its confusions and absurdities, its "sacerdotal phantasm" of a priest, its bumbling lover and sullen, baffling *jeune fille,* its bungled crises arising from uncertain perceptions, *A Foregone Conclusion* presents a structure of meaning that is not qualitatively different from the structure of meaning of any other Howells novel. In this structure the universe and life are not conceived of in a surface sense; Howells is not a recorder or behaviorist. He is fundamentally interested, not in the petty facts and actions for which he was once notorious and is now ignored, but in the situation that reveals itself first behind those facts, then in the relationships between man and those facts, and finally during the actions. In Howells the archetypal human situation is the condition of an observer, the role of his genuinely human characters.

This condition is alienation. Howells' universe is post-Cartesian; his feelings about it combine the satiric and the romantic. The satiric feeling of alienation is always present in Howells; it dominates his first books, in which he finds it amusing to be an outsider, and provides a basis for his mature work, as I will later show at some length. The romantic side of his alienation is equally essential. There is no Byronic Satanism in this feeling; it is closer to the sense of alienation and loss found in the early Wordsworth, but is not set at an aesthetic distance as in *The Prelude* and the Intimations Ode. In Howells there is an underlying apathy arising from a sense of strangeness and puzzlement accepted without argument as the condition of life. With the Anglo-Saxon poets of "The Seafarer" and "The Wanderer," Howells shares a dignified endurance of *wyrd;* in Howells, however, dignity is not repose, but a precarious balance. When the balance slips, as it does in *A Foregone Conclusion,* Howells becomes panicky, in the ancient and literal sense of that word. Then life becomes not only a fundamentally mysterious and blankly unknowable object, but a terrifying source of destructive energies that operate confusingly, sometimes at random and sometimes with apparent malice. This side of Howells brings him close to modern "existential" writers. Indeed, with his strong sense of man's "thrownness" in a world he did not make, and with his fundamental concern, not with static facts, but with man's dynamic mode of existing among such facts, Howells foreshadows the explicitly existential modern philosophers. The almost paranoid fear of mysterious energies; the use of exaggerated scenes in well known settings; the dependence on coincidence; the occasional presence of sinister villains (see Chapter III below); the feelings of despair and ecstasy; the sense of the "fantastic" and the "grotesque" (to use some characteristic Howells diction)—these qualities, which apparently constitute "faults" in novels like *A Foregone Conclusion,* link Howells to the stage melodrama, that characteristic Victorian form, and to melodrama in general, a Weltanschauung that we are beginning to realize is basic to art, the projection of a radical way of apprehending the universe.[1]

For Howells, then, alienation and melodrama were more than literary, and more than products of experience (as, for example, Hemingway's "separate peace" was); they were evidences of a fundamental cast of mind, built into Howells from the beginning. In *The Road to Realism,* Edwin Cady has shown how this quality of Howells' nature influenced his whole life. In his boyhood Howells suffered from debilitat-

[1] My approach to melodrama follows Eric Bentley's treatment in *The Life of the Drama* (New York, 1964). In addition to the qualities of melodrama that I infer above, Bentley brings out another that makes "realism," that often-derided movement, of fundamental importance to the history of modern fiction. Referring to Zola's use of apparent "banalities," Bentley says, "What Zola is really doing is recharging the battery of fear which had been allowed to run down in the Victorian stage-melodrama. The substitution of a banal (that is, recognizable) milieu for a 'romantic' (that is, unacceptable) milieu is to play on the spectator's anxieties" (p. 211). A little thought will show that Howells' similar attempt to find and present the portentous in the ordinary makes him a legitimate successor of Poe, Hawthorne, and Melville, and a forerunner of the great modern American naturalists (Hemingway, Faulkner, *et al.*). Bentley's final claim for melodrama, though modified elsewhere, is strong and, I believe, justifiable: "The melodramatic vision is in one sense simply normal. It corresponds to an important aspect of reality. It is the spontaneous, uninhibited way of seeing things. . . . The dramatic sense is the melodramatic sense. . . . Melodrama is not a special and marginal kind of drama . . . ; it is the quintessence of drama" (p. 216).

ing neurotic phobias and obsessive anxieties. He was morbidly afraid of dogs; he was sure that he would die at sixteen (Cady, I, 35). He had to leave a promising newspaper job in Cincinnati because he could not face the crudity of life as a reporter must know it (Cady, I, 65 f.). He was incapacitated by vertigo in 1858 (Cady, I, 67); he broke down while he was writing *A Modern Instance,* one of his most important and revealing novels (Cady, I, 210).

Howells' use of the significant expression, "The bottom dropped out," referring to a psychological "vastation" of 1884, was derived from personal experience with the disasters that commonly followed the collapse of canal banks in his native Ohio. His two earliest memories, recorded in *A Boy's Town* and prominently noted by Cady, were of a peach tree in bloom and a one-legged man sliding into the Ohio River: "The man tried to step aboard [Howells' steamboat], missed, and slid silently into the muddy river with, in the boy's memory, the same meaningless finality as the splash of the rain. Beauty and terror, clothed in vivid imagery, were paired at the threshold of his memory" (Cady, I, 13). Significantly, both the beauty and the terror are merely *there,* dissociated from any structure of rational meaning and causation.

Howells' lifework is the symbolic representing of this earliest vision, and the record of man's repeated failures to penetrate such a vision. The expression "The bottom dropped out" and the image of the helpless man falling through the placid surface of the Ohio do in fact reveal the structure of Howells' world view. In the Howells novel, an apparently stable and often agreeable situation changes, suddenly and pointlessly, into a welter of confusion, terror, or even death, and then returns to the initial state of placidity. A similar archetype is the eruption of Pan (or an analogue) into a pastoral scene. In American literature the classic parallel to Howells' "bottom" or river surface is Melville's sea, calm and genial until someone falls into it or until something—evil squid or inscrutable whale—erupts from it, and again calm and genial afterward. (Recall Moby-Dick's climactic breeching, followed by his swimming placidly in the turbulence he had created.) Melville and Howells, then, brooded on the same things: evil and its qualities, man thrown into a world of explosive violence. Both presented their visions in symbolic actions, but unfortunately for Howells, his symbols are so close to everyday life that one is liable to see only the literalism or "realism" and miss the meaning.

The most clearly symbolic treatment of Howells' world view appears in an out-of-the-way place, a poem, "Society," in the neglected volume of poems *Stops of Various Quills* (1895). Here the narrating "I," a familiar Howells device, sees a pastoral vision of frolickers "in a flowery plain" but on looking closer, realizes that the lovely plain is really a squirming mass of people and the "red of flowers" is blood gushing forth. The poem is of course immediately applicable to Howells' social feelings of the eighties and nineties,[2] but the greatest meaning lies on the deep level where the image becomes Howells' archetype: the deceptively pleasant surface, the demonic energy breaking through, the pointless movement to and fro, the observer's symbiotic relationship to the object as moving perceiver, first deceived and then enlightened.

II

. . . like sights in a mirror, or things in a world turned upside down.

Howells' sense of life is expressed most clearly in the mature and late works: *A Modern Instance* (1882), *A Hazard of New Fortunes* (1890), *The Shadow of a Dream* (1890), *Stops of Various Quills* (1895), *The Landlord at*

[2] See Clara Marburg Kirk, *W. D. Howells: Traveler from Altruria*, chap. i.

Lion's Head (1897), *The Kentons* (1902), *The Son of Royal Langbrith* (1904), *The Leatherwood God* (1916). These are the works that I shall discuss the most fully. But Howells' feeling of alienation and the complex of images and actions surrounding the idea of surface—these are constant; they appear in his earliest works, occasionally with a different tone. In Howells' first book, *Venetian Life,* the fascinating old city is a "fantastic vision at the best" (p. 125). After a few months there, Howells is forced into a mood of dreaminess and alienation from reality (*VL,* 37–39). The opening paragraph presents the surface concept humorously, for this is the young Howells. The surface here is the thin film separating illusion and reality in the theater. Thanks to the unusual perspective of a stagebox, reality breaks through this film to show Howells and his wife "the shabbiness of the theatre" and "the unreality of the properties" (p. 9). This interaction between illusion and reality, history and the present, expectation and reality, lies at the core of the book. In *Suburban Sketches* (1871; expanded, 1872), Howells begins to move awkwardly away from the playful treatment of his theme toward his mature problems and tensions. The alienation is no longer from Venice (always a never-never land anyway), but from everyday American life, the world that Howells must grasp if he is ever to grasp any world. In an essay on horsecars, Howells notes that a friend finds romances there, but that he himself has "beheld for the most part only mysteries" (*SS,* p. 92) such as the boorish behavior of supposedly genteel Americans on crowded horsecars (again the image of violence striking through a placid surface). The rapid emergence of the Irish, Chinese, and other strange elements into American life fills him with Know-Nothing forebodings, though he finds foreigners picturesque and innocent in their own settings. Strangeness and change in one's own world, one's own refuge, is inherently unpleasant for Howells, it seems, and as we shall see, this worry forms the theme of one of Howells' most revealing novels, *The Kentons* (1902).

The most significant of these sketches is "Scene," a crisis in Howells' artistic development. In this vignette, death, the ultimate alien and alienator, breaks through "the tender serenity" (p. 190) of an autumn morning in Charlesbridge (Howells' term for Cambridge). While strolling in the manner of Howells' observers early and late, a magazine writer simply called "the contributor" (partly a Howells persona and partly a whipping boy) sees the body of a pregnant Irish girl (a suicide by drowning) brought home in a wagon driven by "two Americans, unperturbed by anything, concerned merely with the business of the affair," and surrounded by "a guard of ragged urchins" (p. 193). Shaken out of his pleasant mood, the contributor thinks of how "her woman's heart must have been shocked from death could she have known in what a ghastly comedy the body she put off was to play a part" (pp. 193–94). While the boys "broke out with wild yells, and danced madly about" the wagon, and "the red shawl hanging from the rigid feet nodded to their frantic mirth," the hovering narrator (who is distinct from the contributor) concludes, ". . . and the sun dropped its light through the maples and shone bright upon the flooded flats" (p. 194). The little sketch foreshadows Howells' later grim satire on man's simple-minded expectations (of continuity, for example). Here the tension between a beautiful, placid surface and erupting, overwhelming horror is for the first time made the focus of Howells' art. The narrative technique (fallible observer and hovering narrator) also foreshadows the later Howells, especially the novels involving Basil and Isabel March.

In *Their Wedding Journey* (1871) the theater image again encompasses alienation and surface:

> So the play of which they were both actors and spectators went on about them. Like all passages of life, it seemed now a grotesque mystery, with a bluntly enforced moral, now a farce of the broadest, now a latent tragedy folded in the disguises of comedy. All the elements, indeed, of either were

> at work there, and this was but one brief scene of the immense complex drama which was to proceed so variously in such different times and places, and to have its *dénouement* only in eternity. The contrasts were sharp: each group had its travesty in some other; the talk of one seemed the rude burlesque, the bitter satire of the next. . . . (p. 70)

The sense of "grotesque mystery" extends to the most ordinary aspects of life. As the newlywed Marches travel, we are not allowed to forget the fear and tension that underlay the gilded elegance of travel by Pullman and steamboat in the 1860's. The author himself tells us of Pullman travel that "the knowledge of your helplessness in any circumstances is so perfect that it begets a sense of irresponsibility, almost of security" (p. 18), and that because of "the fantastic mood which possesses you . . . the stoppages of the train have a weird character" (p. 19). (The effects and functions of alienation, clearly suggested here, will be discussed later.)

With the surface image, Howells associates the idea that life is an illusion, a dream. Whereas Twain makes dreams a solution to and escape from the miseries of life, for Howells the dream-feeling is fundamental; the explicit emphasis on the theme in *The Shadow of a Dream* (1890), *Questionable Shapes* (1903), and other late works only intensifies Howells' basic set. In "A Day's Pleasure," one of Howells' early sketches included in *Suburban Sketches*, the characters observe a lost child who has strayed into their house while they are gone.

> His helplessness in accounting for himself was as affecting as that of the sublimest metaphysician; and no learned man, no superior intellect, no subtle inquirer among us lost children of the divine, forgotten home, could have been less able to say how or whence he came to be just where he found himself. We wander away and away; the dust of the road-side gathers upon us; and when some strange shelter receives us, we lie down to our sleep, inarticulate, and haunted with dreams of memory, or the memory of dreams, knowing scarcely more of the past than of the future. (SS, p. 165)

The Wordsworthian overtones of "lost children of the divine, forgotten home" has less relevance than the gratuitousness of the whole comment. This easily moving sketch does not call for such deep remarks. The fictional situation has triggered some basic feeling in the author, as the shift from the past tense to the present tense suggests, and the child becomes a symbol of man lost in an alien world.[3]

The image of the dream appears again and again. Sometimes the author interrupts to present it. In the early novel *A Chance Acquaintance,* the pensive heroine "went on turning substance into shadow,—unless, indeed, flesh and blood is the illusion" (p. 98). At other times the characters speak of it. Journeying from backward New England to Venice, Lydia Blood, another Howells heroine, says, "But it seems to me as if I had died, and this long voyage was a kind of dream that I was going to wake up from in another world" (*LA,* p. 210). The Reverend Mr. Peck, the grotesque but perceptive minister of *Annie Kilburn* (p. 168), stresses the need for intention behind deeds, "otherwise the moral world is no better than a crazy dream, without plan or sequence."

III

. . . hopeless mazes of error.

Howells' alienation changes little; his feelings about it change greatly. In his earliest work, he not only accepts alienation—he embraces it, exploits it, finds it the major source of pleasure in art. This phase coincides roughly with Howells' first book, *Venetian Life.* In the late 1860's and

[3] As George N. Bennett has pointed out, in *William Dean Howells: The Development of a Novelist,* this ending was tacked on so that "A Day's Pleasure" could be "stretched to three issues" (p. 13) of the *Atlantic.* But this fact only makes the ending the more significant, on the Freudian—and common sense—ground that materials chosen "at random" or "just to fill up space" may uncover deeper areas of the psyche than materials chosen consciously to fit into some pre-existing logical scheme.

early 1870's (the time of *Suburban Sketches* and *Their Wedding Journey*), Howells begins to realize the disadvantages of alienation for man and to explore them in his art.[4] Explaining the good and bad sides of alienation, and the relations of various combinations of good and bad, occupies Howells' middle years, from the early 1870's to the late 1880's; in this time he wrote solid classic novels like *A Modern Instance, The Rise of Silas Lapham, Indian Summer,* and *Annie Kilburn*. In the late 1880's, Howells' fictional world darkens.[5] No longer merely a passing nuisance (another fact to be noted), man's separation from the world is the essential quality of life, and something to be endured rather than changed. From *A Hazard of New Fortunes* (1890) on, Howells' novels reveal the ever-growing difficulties of endurance. The novels of around 1900 (e.g., *The Kentons, The Son of Royal Langbrith*) show man to be helplessly bound to what is now not merely a condition but an active quality, evil. After *The Son of Royal Langbrith,* Howells no longer has anything new to say; in fact, there is nothing for him to do but turn away from this impossible world toward reminiscence, travel sketches, and other make-work. In two late books, *A Boy's Town* and *The Leatherwood God,* Howells returns from contemporary life, and in a sense puts a seal on his feelings about it by showing that the boyhood world, the frontier of the 1840's, was no different in essence from the world of the 1900's. The condition of life was universal and inescapable.

But for Howells the young man of the 1860's, alienation was something to dally with in words. We have seen with what pleasure Howells greeted his sense of alienation, and his awareness of it, in Venice. In a later discussion of Howells'

[4] This is the shift discussed in terms of "realism" by John K. Reeves, "The Limited Realism of Howells' *Their Wedding Journey*," *Publications of the Modern Language Association,* LXXVII (1962), 617–28.

[5] Howells' own difficult emotional situation in this period is well explored in Cady, II, Chapter III ("The Black Time").

techniques, I will take up some of the ways that Howells plays with reality in Venice to make it yield more meaning than it can alone; here, the important point is that the youthful Howells experiences only pleasure in that play. The pleasure may be full of amazement or surprise or romantic shivers, but pleasure it is. The opening essays in *Suburban Sketches* are similar, but one soon catches a different note. The strolling observer is shown to be cut off from the world, and sometimes to be in trouble because of that separation; Howells or his observer is more and more aware of the *quidditas* of things and people. In "Jubilee Days," an account of the Boston Peace Jubilee of 1869, the crowds and later the deserted fairgrounds are as interesting to the strolling "I" as Venice was, but they are essentially baffling and often grotesque in their being. Howells even says of one side-show performer, "Who was he? what was he? why was he? The mind played forever around these questions in a maze of hopeless conjecture" (p. 217). This tone of intensity is largely foreign to *Venetian Life,* but strikingly foreshadows the quality of Howells' mature work (such as *A Modern Instance*) and exactly states the quality of such gloomy late works as *The Shadow of a Dream* and *The Son of Royal Langbrith.* In "A Day's Pleasure" and "A Romance of Real Life," early attempts at consecutive fictional narrative, the world changes from merely being there to a reactive agent. It is not an aggressive world, but it resists efforts to order it. In *Suburban Sketches* Howells still emphasizes the pleasures of discovery, even if the discoveries give promise of leading toward unpleasant confusion.

In *Their Wedding Journey,* with its exploration of places (New York City, Niagara Falls, Canada), subjects (railroad passengers, heat waves), and techniques (the observed team of observers, the travel fiction), the emphasis is again largely on the pleasures of the new. The book contains famous passages on "realism" on which three generations of critics have built their view of Howells. Howells says, "Ah! poor

Real Life, which I love, can I make others share the delight I find in thy foolish and insipid face?" (p. 67), and, "It was in all respects an ordinary carful of human beings, and it was perhaps the more worthy to be studied on that account. . . . Yes, it is a very amusing world, if you do not refuse to be amused; and our friends [the observer team] were very willing to be entertained" (p. 87). The feelings here are, as we shall see, more properly defined as those of a satirist than of a realist, but at this time it is enough to note the emphasis on pleasure and entertainment. The mystery of life does intrude, though, in one small but significant scene, the first quarrel between the Marches. "In a moment it had come . . . as all such calamities come, from nothing" (p. 209), and a little later, with reference to March, "the pathos of the case having yielded to its absurdity, he was helpless" (p. 211). Suddenness, mystery, pathos, absurdity, helplessness—five major qualities of Howells' mature treatment of alienation. The quarrel quickly passes, and in the usual early Howells fashion "it gave a wonderful zest and freshness" (p. 213) to the Marches' touring later that day.

Howells' first novels explore the unpleasant effects of such splits between and among people, and dwell less and less on the exciting aftereffects. In *A Chance Acquaintance* (1873) and *The Lady of the Aroostook* (1879), two representative novels of the 1870's, young people of different cultures fall in love and want to communicate, but can do no more than tentatively reach out to each other. In the first novel, the lovers separate; in the other, they are reunited, but only by desperate contortion of the plot. In the major novels of the 1880's, alienation and the sense of separateness can no longer be explored for humor or local color; the characters not only suffer from their isolation and their misunderstandings of man and reality, but are often beaten in their efforts to control situations that cannot be controlled. Silas Lapham loses his money and his social position after clumsy efforts to increase both; Halleck, the rich neurotic in *A Modern Instance*, tortures himself into collapse, while Bartley and Marcia Hubbard destroy each other. Annie Kilburn almost wrecks her life and the lives of others in trying to identify herself again with her old home town. *Indian Summer* is a minuet of misunderstandings, loveless engagements, and cross purposes; it superficially resembles an Austen novel, but Austen miseries are comic and Howells miseries are not. Colville, the hero (or in modern terms, the antihero) feels that he is caught in a "grotesque and terrible" situation (p. 282); he cannot decide whether he is good or evil (p. 287); he is sorry to see a young girl sacrificing her life for him, but he feels "powerless" to alter the situation and can only "grieve" and "submit" (p. 303); her behavior he cannot "penetrate at any point" (p. 337); finally, he sees his situation "whirling away beyond his recall in hopeless mazes of error" (p. 355); but the impasse is happily resolved by a carriage accident, one of Howells' useful and gratuitously horrible catastrophes.

"Bondage" is a good term to describe this feeling of helpless entanglement that grips Colville and most of the later Howells characters. The conventional term is "complicity," which has been fully analyzed by Howells scholars, especially in connection with Howells' Christian Socialist phase of the 1890's.[6] But for my purposes, the word "bondage" is superior. It suggests the helplessness of men, and their union in helplessness; it refers us not to specific reform movements but to existence in general. The term, like "complicity," has its authority from Howells. In the sermon entitled "Complicity," from *The Minister's Charge* (1887), Howells' mouthpiece, Sewell, speaks from the text of Paul: "Remember them that are in bonds as bound with them."[7]

Truly the later Howells characters are in bondage—to their natures as men, to their own qualities, to their social situations, to their families, to their responsibilities, sometimes to

[6] See Cady, II, 6 f., 110–13, 247–49; Clara Kirk, *W. D. Howells: Traveler from Altruria*, chap. i.

[7] This significant sermon is discussed in Cady, II, 6 f.

evil people. In all of this there is no conscious planning, as "complicity" suggests; the conscious planning, in fact, is generally directed toward escape from the maze, and most consciousness, especially in the Howells spokesmen, is awareness rather than directed thought (planning). Even in *A Traveler from Altruria,* in which a Mr. Homos describes his utopian homeland to an American summer colony, the emphasis lies on the realized existential situation of Americans rather than on simple social analysis. The social milieu of this novel is firmly and accurately realized, as one expects in Howells; his bankers and flirts are without question the American bankers and flirts of the early 1890's. Yet these characters are not figures in a sociological survey. They are men and women projected by the Howells sense of things, and they are helpless and entangled. The banker cannot help being greedy; the flirt cannot help dancing herself into neurotic exhaustion. The setting, one of Howells' most carefully contrived, reinforces the feeling of bondage. The huge summer hotel, which the narrator aptly compares to a great steamboat, dominates the landscape and the mountain peasants, but at the same time is isolated and absurd. The narrator notes first that "the hotel seemed idling at anchor on the swell of a placid sea" (p. 22); but this figurative sea acquires Melvillean portentousness, and later the narrator compares the hotel to a ship "anchored off some strange coast," its steward bartering with the natives, while the passengers carefully ignore them (p. 109). This echo of Conradian mystery is reinforced by the behavior of one of the natives in selling off the timber on a ridge facing the hotel. The ugly scar and the ugly hotel face each other, not just in complicity within a social order, but in mutual helpless bondage to the human situation.

In these late Howells works, beginning with *A Hazard of New Fortunes* (1890), man is isolated and humiliated, and his condition, like the world itself, is a pointless mystery, to be endured patiently. The characters tend not only to work at cross-purposes, but to exist in closed spheres, which may make contact but do so without meaning. In *A Hazard of New Fortunes,* for example, Howells develops his social dance from the confused minuet of *Indian Summer* to a crowded shuffle around a common center, the magazine that Basil March edits.[8] This plan seems to promise a sound structure, until we realize the nature of the center. For the reader, *Every Other Week* is a vacuum; it is never seen clearly. The characters talk about it in general terms, but the thing never comes to life. Thus the characters cannot reach each other through their mutual work on the magazine. Neither do they talk well to each other at other times. They meet constantly, and Howells has so arranged his sequences that, as in a French play, there is someone in each scene from the preceding scene. But in the scenes themselves there is little communication, because there is no community. We can see this only on the social level,[9] or we can take it on the symbolic level and say that man's fate here is not to communicate. There is less talk at cross-purposes here than in *Indian Summer,* for example, because the characters are not facing the same things; and to be at cross-purposes, people must be within the same area or reaching out into it. In *A Hazard of New Fortunes,* two *nouveau riche* Ohio girls attend a formal "at home," and we expect social comedy of the sort seen in the dinner-party episode of *The Rise of Silas Lapham.* Here there is no such comedy because the girls are perfectly tranquil in their opinions (that they awe the New Yorkers with their wealth), and the New Yorkers are perfectly tranquil in their own opinions (that they awe the provincials with their social polish). Isolation here is part of life.

At a slightly lower social level, the same conditions prevail. A Mrs. Leighton and her daughter come to New York from a small town and open a rooming house, to which comes an

[8] The concept of the magazine as center is developed by Cady, II, 104.

[9] See Cady, II, 100 ff.

elderly southern gentleman, Colonel Woodburn, with his daughter Madison. The little house soon becomes a buzzing world. It is crowded in the evenings as Fulkerson, the magazine's promoter, and Beaton, the magazine's artist, court the two girls. Yet there is little community even here; the grouping is accidental and leads to nothing. Everybody is wrapped in his own concerns: Colonel Woodburn is lost in his dream of restoring the slave system and extending it to the North; Fulkerson talks across the Colonel to Madison; the Colonel and Beaton refuse to speak to each other; Beaton and Alma spar and eventually part in bafflement and bitterness. Each person is isolated in a way that recalls the crucial scenes of *A Foregone Conclusion*. At the house of the newly rich Dryfooses, all is the same. They are cats; they ignore each other, unless they get in each other's way, and then they claw and snarl. The thematic climax occurs in one of Howells' frequent satiric treatments of a formal social occasion, here an honorary dinner for old Dryfoos and his magazine. The hollowness of the magazine as center, the impossibility of community, and the lack of much desire for it, are all revealed in this episode. The dinner moves from a cautiously correct opening to a shambles in which personal hostility and contempt for polite convention triumph over the well-meaning efforts of March and Fulkerson to preserve a minimum of decorum.

New York appears in the late Howells as the symbol of chaos and loss of community, yet it is not only there that men are isolated even in company. In *The Landlord at Lion's Head* (1897), the Boston Brahmins are represented by young Bessie and Alan Lynde, the one an aimless flirt, the other an alcoholic; they talk at each other, but cannot help each other. For these orphans, the world of authority is a bumbling and (significantly) deaf aunt, and the world of society is endless balls at which mirthless gaiety goes on and on while everyone wonders why he doesn't go home. The poems of *Stops of Various Quills* (1895) also reflect this sense of the pointlessness of polite social gatherings. In "Twelve P. M.," the strongest treatment of this theme, Howells speaks of the relief of emerging from "the not unkindly fatuousness" of his friends, taking off his "perfunctory smile," and confronting "the eternal Verity" of "one's sheer self again."

This kind of existential isolation is not so bad in itself, because the individual soul in Howells is generally quite tough, if not hard, and can well stand up to its situation. But in these later novels, man is not just bored or alone in the crowd; he is humiliated, by others and by himself. With some justice, the aggressive, evil characters, whom I shall discuss later, are often the victims of their own diabolical energies; but the well-meaning, mild people so typical of Howells are often their own victims, too. In *A Hazard of New Fortunes,* Basil March loses his job because he is so loyal to an employee that he stands up for him against Dryfoos, the owner of the magazine. Only the most delicate finagling by his friend Fulkerson can get March back into his editor's chair. In the meantime March feels disgusted with himself as much as with Dryfoos and the world. "He felt the misery of the man who stakes the security and plenty and peace of home upon some cast. . . . His indignation was shot with abject impulses to go back and tell Fulkerson that it was all right, and that he gave up" (II, 137–38). With this feeling goes the expected sense of humiliation: "He realized, as every hireling must, no matter how skillfully or gracefully the tie is contrived for his wearing, that he belongs to another, whose will is his law" (II, 138).

In *The Shadow of a Dream* (1890), Howells' treatment of isolation and humiliation reaches a high point (except for a few poems in *Stops of Various Quills*), and adds a new theme, the bondage of man to the dead. The title of the novel accurately suggests the situation. After dreaming that his wife is marrying his best friend, a dying man allows the dream to destroy his faith in himself, his wife, and the friend, and leaves the doubt behind him to poison the later love of his widow and the friend. In a pointed, symbolistic way, curiously evocative of Hawthorne, Howells presents a world in which there is and can be no surety or confidence in self, situation, or perception. The situation in the novel parallels *A Foregone Conclusion* but is even grimmer and much more pointed. The pain of a heart attack and the helpless misery of the bystanders are strongly expressed:

> I glanced round at his face: it was a lurid red, and, as it were, suffused with pain: his eyes seemed to stand full of tears; his lips were purple, and they quivered.
>
> It was an odious moment: we could not speak or stir; we suffered too, and were cruelly embarrassed, for we felt that we must not explicitly recognize his seizure. (p. 21)

Years later, after numerous miseries and separations, the friend and the widow arrange to get married; but then she tells him about the dream, and he rebuffs her. The narrator, March, with difficulty persuades Nevil to change his mind. With everything apparently settled for the last time, Nevil sees March off on the train, steps backward off the platform of the Pullman car, and is caught and crushed between the train and the wall of a tunnel. The scene is one of Howells' typical coincidences, but it is also his most gruesome one; when struck, Nevil's body emits "a hideous, crashing sound" and, when dead, Nevil still stands upright with "a strange effect of patience in his attitude" (p. 214).

It is no wonder that March punctuates his narrative of these miserable events with gloomy comments. "Was existence," he broods, "all a miserable chance, a series of stupid, blundering accidents?" (p. 108). And he adds, significantly for us, "We could not believe that; for our very souls' sake, and for our own sanity we must not" (pp. 109–10). The Howells man must make his own meaning, if he is to have any; the profuse references to God in the Howells canon are seen to be what one often suspects: forms of psychological self-defense. Later in the novel, as the affair becomes even more confused, March is even more bitter:

> It seemed to me intolerable that I should be made the victim of it: that this gossamer nothing . . . should have power upon me . . . seemed to me atrocious. . . . Faulkner appeared to me a demoniac presence, at the end of the lurid perspective, running back to the scene in the garden by the sea—implacable, immovable, ridiculous like all the rest, monstrous, illogical, and no more to be reasoned away than to be entreated (pp. 145–46).

There is no stronger statement in Howells of the sense of demonic persecution than this jerky, repetitious outburst by the character who, throughout Howells' career, was closer to him than any other.

As a type, the "demoniac" character is so important that I give him a section to himself below. Here I should look at him from the viewpoint of his victims. The sense of pressure, of being haunted and badgered by these "implacable" creatures, dominates Howells's major novels of the turn of the century: *The Landlord at Lion's Head,* (1897) *The Kentons* (1902), *The Son of Royal Langbrith* (1904). In *The Landlord at Lion's Head* and *The Son of Royal Langbrith,* the decent characters, who are trying to build quiet normal lives, painfully win only partial victories. In the first, Westover, the center of consciousness, manages to keep out of the way of the demoniac Jeff Durgin and marry Durgin's castoff girl; in the other, the son of a devilish businessman learns the truth about his long-dead father, rejects him, and marries the daughter of the man driven to opium by the father. In each book, though, the victory is only partial and an optimistic interpretation is possible only if one avoids looking at the whole novel. The painter, Westover, and his wife are safe only because Durgin is not interested in them. A single-minded hotel owner, he is ruthless in pursuing his aims of expansion, genially contemptuous of Brahmin society, and happily ignorant of morals, good manners, and culture. In *The Son of Royal Langbrith,* the union of the young people is paralleled ironically by the miserable efforts and failure of the boy's mother and the local doctor to fulfil their old love. These weak, middle-aged people are ridden by guilt and anxiety, and haunted by the malevolent disembodied presence of Royal Langbrith, who seems all the more sinister for our ignorance of the details of his evil actions. Using on Mrs. Langbrith a method that recalls James's *The Sacred Fount,* Howells shows quite perceptively how a small, painfully hoarded pool of psychic energy can be quickly exhausted in a crisis and constantly drained by the steady efforts of a "demoniac presence." "That scoundrel has had power to corrupt you, even now," groans Anther (p. 90), who, like many Howells doctors, is a center of perceptiveness and intelligence. And, speaking of Hawberk, the partner whom Langbrith had driven into opium addiction many years before, Anther says, "He holds the man in bondage now much more securely than he could have held him living" (p. 82). Later Anther must admit of himself, "He had been beaten in the struggle. The dead hand had been too strong for him" (p. 275).

In this novel, the victims, all too aware of what they are doing, actually help the criminal persecute them, to his delight; and the grim irony of the situation is increased whenever we are reminded, as we constantly are, that the criminal is long dead. After gazing long at a smiling portrait of his father, James Langbrith (who has never been told the truth) decides to put up a plaque in his father's memory on the library that Royal had given the town (with money he had swindled from it). After much wringing of hands, the older characters can do nothing but assist in this grotesque project and keep silent. The miseries of their indecision fill much of the book and create a general sense of strain relieved only when Royal's crotchety brother, John, tells young James the truth. But by this time it is too late; Anther is dead, and those in the know decide to keep quiet. As Anther says, "A wrong like that seems to gather a force that enslaves those who have done nothing worse than leave it unacknowledged through a good motive" (*SRL*, p. 82). The opium addict, the inventor who made Royal's success possible, is of course literally enslaved; nightmare-ridden, green-faced, and yet grimly humorous, he is one of Howells' last and best efforts in the line of utter victims that begins with Nevil in *The Shadow of a Dream*.

But it is in *The Kentons* that Howells gives us the most concentrated and forceful symbolic presentation of man as victim and life as humiliation and bondage. As the title suggests, the novel focuses on a whole family. At the beginning of the book, the long and careful presentation of this family should make us realize that they are not "just folks" (which they resoundingly are), but also symbols and a symbol. The Kentons personify, not perfection, but a viable norm, that of *decency*. They are not perfect, or noble, or intellectual, or worldly; but they are well-intentioned, and any harm they do arises only from their kind, anxious bumbling. As Civil War colonel, retired judge, and local historian of a leafy Ohio town, Tuskingum, Mr. Kenton represents the American ideal, one still viable even if only in nostalgia; in particular, he represents the pre–Civil War virtues inherited from the Federalist days and reconfirmed in battle. His shrewd wife, dignified older son, solemn older daughter, truculent adolescent daughter, and gawky fourteen-year-old son are apparently a group straight from the world of Norman Rockwell *Saturday Evening Post* covers—but only apparently, for Howells does not caricature and sentimentalize the Kentons. He treats them with irony and simplicity.

The devil bursts into Tuskingum-Eden and turns it into a hell. The devil is a young reporter, Bittridge, who seduces Ellen, the older daughter; he seduces her spiritually, not sexually (though sex hunger is clearly related to the spirit), and then ignores her. At Ellen's request, the family flees to New York. They are followed by Bittridge, who humiliates them again. Next, they go unwillingly to Europe, only to meet more Bittridges: a thoughtless young minister who teases Ellen cruelly, and a young "Cook's tourist" who badgers the fourteen-year-old, Boyne, into a scrape with the Dutch police. During these troubles, the parents helplessly observe their children and their own helplessness, and search uselessly for ways to get rid of the villains or enlighten the victims. Fortunately—and accidentally—everything turns out all right. Bittridge is horsewhipped by the older brother (who, typically, is sickened rather than relieved by his successful outburst of demonic energy). Boyne is rescued from the police and the Cook's tourist vanishes. Breckon, the young minister, who is well endowed with the saving Howells gifts of decency and perceptiveness, realizes his cruelty to Ellen and marries her. The Kentons then return to Tuskingum and to equilibrium, but not to innocence.

The scenes of humiliation here are the most pointed that Howells ever wrote. Using his most characteristic manner, analysis, he summarizes in one scene the Howells vision of life at its darkest. After a wretched winter in New York, Judge Kenton comes home alone on a pretext, sits down in his deserted house, and realizes his situation:

> He had always supposed himself a happy and strong and successful man, but what a dreary ruin his life had fallen into! Was it to be finally so helpless and powerless (for with all the defenses about him that a man can have, he felt himself fatally vulnerable) that he had fought so many years? Why, at his age, should he be going into exile, away from everything that could make his days bright and sweet? Why could not he come back there, where he was now more solitary than he could be anywhere else on earth, and reanimate the dead body of his home with his old life? He knew why, in an immediate sort, but his quest was for the cause behind the cause. What had he done, or left undone? He had tried to be a just man, and fulfil all his duties both to his family and to his neighbors; he had wished to be kind, and not to harm any one; he reflected how, as he had grown

> older, the dread of doing any unkindness had grown upon him, and how he had tried not to be proud, but to walk meekly and humbly. Why should he be punished as he was, stricken in a place so sacred that the effort to defend himself had seemed a kind of sacrilege? He could not make it out, and he was not aware of the tears of self-pity that stole slowly down his face, though from time to time he wiped them away.
>
> He heard steps in the hall without, advancing and pausing, which must be those of his son coming back for him, and with these advances and pauses giving him notice of his approach; but he did not move, and at first he did not look up when the steps arrived at the threshold of the room where he sat. When he lifted his eyes at last he saw Bittridge lounging in the door-way, his hands in his pockets and his hat pushed well back on his forehead. (pp. 44–45)

To confront extreme misery directly with its cause is unusually melodramatic and symbolic for Howells, but the method is successful in this context. The judge becomes a Job, and Bittridge a devil. There are no comforters here, though; isolation is the condition.

In the other major scene of direct humiliation, Howells uses a striking bit of drama, again unusually symbolic for this author. No sooner does Judge Kenton return from his miserable trip to Tuskingum than Bittridge shows up at the hotel in New York with his half-witted mother. Using her as a social front, Bittridge arranges a date with Ellen, and then kisses her in the hotel corridor. (This kiss can be taken, of course, as figurative rape.)[10] In the hotel lobby the next morning, Bittridge laughingly tries to make it up with the furious judge, but the spluttering old man tells him to go away. " 'Oh, I don't think,' said Bittridge, and suddenly, in the wantonness

[10] See Everett S. Carter, "The Palpitating Divan," *College English,* XI (1950), 427–28, and Kenneth E. Eble, "Howells' Kisses," *American Quarterly,* IX (1957), 441–47.

of his baffled effrontery, he raised his hand and rubbed the back of it in the old man's face" (p. 89). Boyne swings wildly at Bittridge, who knocks him down. Then, in what "seemed the gathering of neighborhood about Kenton, where he had felt himself so unfriended, against the outrage done him" (p. 90), the bellboys seize Bittridge and the desk clerk ousts him. As a symbolic action, this rubbing the back of a hand in the judge's face succeeds in bringing together a cluster of motifs—arrogance, cruelty, gratuitousness, on the one side; helplessness, humiliation, public embarrassment, on the other. The judge's prompt rescue tells us something else about Howells. He cannot go all the way to present openly a world of total helplessness, a world in which those who are not evil are indifferent or silently approving. Howells could imagine this world and embody it in language in the semi-privacy of a few poems like "Society" in *Stops of Various Quills,* but Howells the novelist could not do so. He could not foresee the modern fragmented and vulgarized urban crowd-society, or the modern totalitarian state; it would be absurd to elevate him as a forerunner of Orwell and Kafka and Riesman and Genet and other touchstones of the mid-twentieth century. Yet his books remain faithful representations of the alien world as he knew it in the transitional society between the Civil War and World War I, and in this faithfulness, partly justify his reputation as a "realist."

CHAPTER II

ALIENATION GIVEN FORM: THE HOWELLS NOVEL AS SATIRE

. . . habitual moods of vacancy and tiresomeness.

I HAVE BEEN DESCRIBING Howells' sense of things in isolation, but of course it really exists in a context, in a condition of use. In order to understand the Howells novel itself, it is necessary to see how the world view is put to use. If we know how Howells uses it, then we can understand what the Howells novel is and why it is the way it is: awkward and confused (apparently), full of comments and generalizations. To get at the essential nature of the Howells work, we must free ourselves of the accepted terminology. When applied to Howells, the term "novel," used for everything that is more fiction than anything else and not poem or essay, simply makes for trouble. In recent years critics have begun to object to the restrictive stiffness of the term as it is generally used. Richard Chase, for example, advances the thesis that "novels" in American literature are subdivisions of a larger group that also includes the romance, and shows that "realism" and "romance" can dwell together peacefully as strategies toward a common end.[1] Studies based on anthropology and dynamic psychology have cut across established dividing lines; conversely, it is more and more apparent that something is wrong with a terminology that lumps together *Tristram Shandy, The Ambassadors,* and the *Pickwick Papers* under the same heading.

The Howells works are "novels," in the sense that they are not short and contain more narrative fiction than anything

[1] Richard Chase, *The American Novel and its Tradition* (Garden City, New York, 1957), pp. 2 ff., 16–28, 236.

else. But if a critic is content with such a term and such a definition, he finds himself nudged inevitably into the current of traditional literary discussion, where quantity outweighs cause and function, where facts have absolute value and context can be ignored, where the expression

$$a(x^2 + 3x + 4x^3 - x^4)$$

can be dismissed as just a collection of x's, rather than a quantity modified throughout by a. If we are ever to get beyond the factual surface of Howells' works and see what they are and what they mean, some approach, some seminal term, is needed that will lead us toward what R. S. Crane has called the "power" of a literary work, the cause of its being what it is.[2] After forming and discarding other hypotheses, I have concluded that the most useful term to open up Howells—but certainly not to finish him off—is *satire*. In general usage this term is even more woolly than *novel*. There are many histories of satire, and some analyses of it, but no generally accepted definition of the term. The literature in this field is, in fact, of very little help to the student.

For Howells, the most fruitful working definition of satire is found in Northrop Frye's *Anatomy of Criticism,* in the ideas that I have already discussed at length in my Introduction. I will use Frye's ideas not as dogma (Frye himself has a bent in that direction that must be resisted), but as tools. He considers satire a condemnation of deviations from a real or ideal norm. In the satiric process (viewed abstractly), the satirist first establishes his norm, then shows that the thing to be condemned is different from the norm, and finally, makes the condemned thing absurd or grotesque in order to attain its rejection. In reality, of course, the steps in the process can be shifted, telescoped, or blurred. Any instrument—fiction (vignettes, episodes, stories, novel-length actions), case histories, comment, discussions, parody, are only some examples—will do in satire if it serves one of the purposes of satire; any

[2] *The Languages of Criticism and the Structure of Poetry* (Chicago, 1963), pp. 140 ff.

combination of instruments, any combination of their use, will produce satire if the underlying aim of attacking deviations from norms is present. As for types of satire, Frye (who has a classifying obsession) presents six types, ranging from comic darts at trivial foibles through brisk attacks on human behavior and institutions to black picturing of a nightmare universe. As for form, anything goes as long as it is functional; but one form peculiar and natural to satire is the "Menippean satire" or "anatomy," a sweeping world view using any device of letters. It is hardly necessary to say that the anatomy, like free verse, is a trap for the sloppy and complacent, and that it must be judged in terms of the heedfulness and efficiency with which the author uses his liberty.

The Howells canon forms an anatomy of the Howells world. In his fictions Howells does several things at once: he establishes a norm (or refers one to an established norm) that I briefly call *decency,* embodied best in the Kentons; he presents a world that is alien and that deviates from his norm; and, largely through his constant emphasis on perception, he attacks efforts to deny or ignore the alien and incomprehensible nature of life. In each work he uses a battery of devices—such as the fictional *exemplum,* comment, generalizations, indications of uncertainty, the symposium, the observer team—that I will discuss later in more detail. During Howells' long career, he changes gradually but decidedly in his application of the two kinds of satire (attacks on deviations and attacks on imperceptiveness). Howells was fundamentally alienated from the world that surrounded him, but at first, as I have shown, he was content with whimsical satire on the foibles of men and the universe; and it was only after he was fifty that he presented a grim and grotesque world, a place at odds with all our preconceptions and hopes, a place to be endured, not known or used. The second kind of satire must be approached through classification, not chronology. Howells saw that there are various ways of handling "codes," my short term for systems of organizing the facts of perception, thus falsifying them, and then getting into trouble. These attempts to level the maze, to evade the radical confusions and mysteries of life, take three forms, given in order of increasing error: passive and usually weak adherence to a pre-existing and usually inherited code; attempts to force an existing code upon a fluid situation; and attempts to create a code and act upon it, usually by coercing others. This neat tripartite division, of course, falsifies the reality of the Howells novel, which resists neat analysis and, in fact, exists in part to show the impossibility of neat analysis. Applying to protagonists, observers, communities, and readers, these forms of false dealing combine with character and accident (the contribution of the inscrutable universe) to produce action in the Howells world. The contribution of character is strongest in Howells' early work; of manipulative methods, in his middle period (roughly, the 1880's); of accident, in his later novels.

Remember that these distinctions and classifications are in part arbitrary. In Howells, man and the world, observer and observed, are entwined in an endless disordered dialectic. Likewise, the two kinds of satire are intertwined in context. When Howells shows us that the world is not the same as our normative idea of the world, he often shows us that truth through the eyes of an observer who is being satirically handled at the same time. In the conventionally fictional works of Howells, this observer is some character, often Isabel or Basil March, or sometimes the hovering amateur himself. In the early sketches, from which Howells' fictions developed, the author or his persona is the observed observer, himself a subject of the sketch (as in "Scene"). But paradoxically, this concern for the relationship of nature and man, observed and observer, reinforces the feeling of separation between the two; for every time the Howells man looks at nature, he is reminded afresh of his ambiguous relationship to it.

In Howells' case this essential ambiguity makes the antithesis of "realism" and "romance" misleading. He is a realist in the simple sense of holding that only in this world, and in the relationship of man to this world, is there any meaning. (His hovering "I" and his characters deny this point right and left, but the patterns of his books confirm it.) Yet Howells is not a materialist. The term "teacup realism," applied to Howells by Frank Norris, a Byronic romantic, suggests a leaden matter-of-factness that does exist in Howells but as a strategy, not as an end in itself. (Howells sometimes conveys a leaden despair, but that is another matter.) Apparent matter-of-factness in Howells is actually charged perception (and it is here, if anywhere, that Howells foreshadows modernists like Hemingway). The mere perception of exterior reality carries for Howells a voltage of alienation,[3] or, to use the term appropriate for this chapter, a voltage of satire, based on the contrast between the expected qualities of reality and perception and the actual qualities, which are always different.

Even in his theoretical moods, Howells clearly shows that he is accumulating data not blindly ("because it is there"), but for a purpose: to satirize the world and wrong ideas about it. The well-known passages on "real life" in *Their Wedding Journey* are a case in point. As the Marches are riding in a day coach up the Mohawk Valley, the author's hovering "I" takes over to praise the suitability of the passengers for the "true artist." They are suitable because they are "ordinary" (p. 86). This term looks flat, but a glance at the context shows that it is charged with satiric meaning. We are told of the ordinary man's "habitual moods of vacancy and tiresomeness," "his vast, natural, unaffected dullness," "his shallow and feeble thoughts," "his dumb, stupid desires," "his stunted inspirations," "his foolish prejudices," "his obtuse selfish-

[3] Recall Eric Bentley's point that by emphasizing the "banalities" of everyday life, naturalism (which in this context includes realism) recharged "the battery of fear" that the improbabilities of conventional romantic melodrama had "allowed to run down" (*The Life of the Drama*, p. 211). This "fear" is the panic terror of the unknown and the potential hostility lurking in the unknown; in Howells' case it is the force, or what I here call "voltage," produced by his feelings of alienation.

ness."[4] "Yes, it is a very amusing world," the narrator concludes, "if you do not refuse to be amused; and our friends were very willing to be entertained" (p. 87). The common man's faults are then developed at length.

This is not random or photographic realism, but satire based on a norm possessed by the "I" and the Marches, and supposedly also by the reader, who is tacitly assumed not to be ordinary or, for the time being, to dissociate himself from the crowd. The author does everything he can to make his point clear; the method is heavy, in fact, and the attack unfair. After a few paragraphs, one begins to feel sympathy for the yokels who are serving unwittingly to entertain the bored travelers (and in later life Howells came around to this viewpoint himself). But regardless of the matter of degree, the matter of kind is indisputable. To call this only "realism" is to mistake matter for meaning, to reduce criticism to cataloguing. Terms like "amusing," "shallow," and "dullness" are not photographic—that is, neutral and scientific—terms; they are judgments, implying a thinking observer with a set of standards, an object, and a relation (superiority) between judge and object. There is another matter, intention or function, which in daily life is scattered or hidden or irrelevant, but which in aesthetic work must be present. In this case satire functions clearly as Crane's "power," the final reason for the quiddity of an artifact.

II

. . . a spectator awaiting some entertainment,
with a faint inclination to be critical.

From the early sketches to the end, this principle of satire operates throughout Howells. Even in *Venetian Life,* which

[4] Even these strong phrases are milder than those in Howells' original manuscript, as John K. Reeves has shown in "The Limited Realism of Howells' *Their Wedding Journey.*"

is colored by youthful enthusiasm for travel and which contains long cribbed descriptions and historical passages, the satiric sections are important, are carefully worked out, and occupy major positions. I have discussed the book's important opening paragraph, in which Howells dwells on the results of seeing a play in terms of the tension between its illusion and its reality. A page later Howells discusses the contrast between illusion and reality in Venice itself.

> But after all, though I find dry land enough in it, I do not find the place less unique, less a mystery, or less a charm. By day, the canals are still the main thoroughfares . . . And by night, they are still as dark and silent as when the secret vengeance of the Republic plunged its victims into the ungossiping depths of the Canalazzo!
>
> Did the vengeance of the Republic ever do any such thing?
>
> Possibly. (pp. 10–11)

This sequence satirizes not only the conventionally "romantic" approach to Venice, but also the conventionally "realistic" approach, and more subtly attacks one of Howells' life-long targets, the eternal human yearning to tidy up reality, to put it in definite static terms. Though Howells is a competent stylist, he does not usually gain effects so exclusively through effects of style and typography as he does here. The swift transition from judicious analysis to parody of goggle-eyed romancing effectively jars the reader back and forth from one viewpoint to another and thus cuts him loose from both; then, the paragraphing and the flat use of "possibly" (where we expect "no") increases the emphasis on the dynamic relating of viewpoints. Thus the reader is told again that the magic of Venice lies not in its facts (buildings, pictures, and the like), but in the ambiguity of their relationships and effects, and in the subsequent liberating mood of uncertainty developed in the observer. In the Howells world, to be fixed is to be dead, or dishonest and existentially dead; to be uncertain is to live. The facts of reality, then, are not ends in themselves but catalysts for creating uncertainty.

Howells does not reach this view all at once. As we have seen in the case of the Marches in *Their Wedding Journey,* the early Howells character uses surface reality, not for the serious purpose of penetrating its relations, but for amusement. Howells rapidly outgrows this attitude. *Their Wedding Journey,* with its many frivolous passages, is in fact a regression; for in his previous book *Suburban Sketches* (itself an apprentice work), Howells is already attacking the amused observer for his blindness and inhumanity, and at the same time, presenting his alien world and thus satirizing the reader's expectations. Natural casual inclination, not organized purpose, dictates the satire in these sketches, and this naturalness makes the satire all the more significant. "A Pedestrian Tour" contains touches of this kind of satire. The "I" of this ramble through Charlesbridge is one of Howells' bad artists, an arrogant shaper rather than a humble, passive receiver of reality; he rejoices that the town is "a vast space upon which I can embroider any fancy I like as I saunter along" (p. 61). Strolling past an Irish cemetery, he reflects on the "dreadful fact" that memorials are all we can give to the dead, whom we would rather see, and that memorials are "a mere conventionality" anyway (p. 65). Then he contemplates some Irish women wailing over a fresh grave, while Irish urchins singing obscene songs go skipping by. The narrator notes that had he seen this in Italy, he would "have been much more vividly impressed by it, as an aesthetical observer; whereas I was now merely touched as a human being, and had little desire to turn the scene to literary account" (pp. 65–66).

This little scene has been cited by John K. Reeves as typical of Howells' early addiction to romance (see note 4), but I see it as an example—a rather clumsy early example—of Howells' satire on the selfish observer. From the beginning of the sketch, the narrator has been presented as self-consciously superior and whimsical. The little passage about memorials reveals a conventional sensitivity to the grotesque ironies of life, so that the following section about the weeping Irish women and the urchins must be taken as the author's irony, or the narrator's self-depreciation, signaled by the word "merely." In either case Howells has made the observer's withdrawn, abstractly philosophical attitude sterile and unsympathetic. The observer fails to grasp the essential grotesqueness of the contrast between the mourners and the obscene boys; his definition of the term "literary" has been so debased by the cult of the picturesque that he cannot hope to begin to be a true artist.

"Scene," the little sketch about the drowned Irish girl, develops the same idea, but here the fictional technique is more complex and more advanced; the author and the character are clearly separated. The entire sketch is devoted to the one satiric point, and it is impossible to miss the object of the irony. As in the episode from "A Pedestrian Tour," Howells develops what seems to be an everyday, "realistic" Charlesbridge setting, but a little thought shows that the setting has been selected and arranged for a purpose. The sketch begins,

> On that loveliest autumn morning, the swollen tide had spread over all the russet levels, and gleamed in the sunlight a mile away. As the contributor moved onward down the street, luminous on either hand with crimsoning and yellowing maples, he was so filled with the tender serenity of the scene, as not to be troubled by the spectacle of small Irish houses . . . or to be aware at first, of a strange stir of people upon the streets. . . . (p. 190)

This is the "loveliest" day, not an ordinary day. The dynamic uncontrollable force of nature ("the swollen tide") is present and has been active, but is quiescent, or so it seems, until the contributor comes back down to earth and realizes what is going on. The hovering author uses dry phrasing to underscore the contributor's dreamy, "literary" evasion of the human scene; even the title "contributor" seems ironical, for what will such a man ever have to contribute to anything?

Into the static scene bursts a horror—again death—the corpse of the drowned pregnant girl brought back in a wagon surrounded by yelling boys (imps in more than one sense). The contributor observes the spectacle, and the author observes the contributor. The style is deliberately flat, so that the contrasts between the bland beauty of nature and the bland horrors of nature, between the seriousness of death and man's reaction to it, are allowed to reveal their own unpleasantness and remain distant. The contributor is directly chastised in a manner that seems wrong for the "novel" (Jamesian dramatic fiction) and so natural for the anatomy-satire. This "literary soul," the author tells us, "fell at once to patching himself up a romantic story for the suicide, after the pitiful fashion of this fiction-ridden age, when we must relate everything we see to something we have read. . . . Nothing could have been more trite or obvious [than this suicide of a typical "fallen woman"]. . . . He could not consider himself other than as a spectator awaiting some entertainment, with a faint inclination to be critical" (p. 191).

Here is the core of Howells' attack: the "literary" approach widens the gap between man and reality rather than bridges it, and at the same time, dehumanizes the culprit. Later, when the contributor thinks of the girl's life, "the history was of fancy, not of fact in his mind . . . of her hopes and her fears, who could tell him anything?" (p. 192). The attitude is a little healthier here, but the damage has already been done. Howells has tacitly referred the contributor to the reader's accepted norm, and the contributor has been shown to be seriously wanting. At the end of the sketch, the contributor disappears and the author intervenes to describe what he calls the "ghastly comedy" of the affair (p. 194). This typically Howellsian oxymoron makes the point that we are not reading a sentimental sketch, but a satire on our expectation of sentimentality. We believe that a beautiful natural scene should continue, and should not be shattered by horror and evil; we believe that death should be treated with decorum. In both cases we tend to assume—and Howells needed no Freud to tell him this—that the desired result *will* follow. The sketch shows that neither expectation makes sense. In the last sentence the author, returning to his cold imagistic manner, clinches the point of contrast:

> As the cart jolted through their lines, the boys could no longer be restrained; they broke out with wild yells, and danced madly about it, while the red shawl hanging from the rigid feet nodded to their frantic mirth; and the sun dropped its light through the maples and shone bright upon the flooded flats. (p. 194)

Just as in "A Pedestrian Tour," the observer in the scene still misses the point; but now the author provides it, and in doing so, not only shows us that man and nature, expectation and reality, are at odds, but that man is at odds with himself if, like the contributor, he ignores the truth, or, like the boys, he abandons himself to the uncontrolled natural forces suggested again in the last words of the sketch.

From "A Pedestrian Tour" to "Scene," Howells evolves from loose, satiric picaresque toward a satiric fictional action, small but complete. In the next sketches, "A Day's Pleasure" and "A Romance of Real Life," he further complicates his fictional actions, but, as he will throughout his career, continues to subordinate them to satire. Howells is not just presenting a certain view of life; he is using that vision to show us that our norms, our expectations and beliefs, are often wrong, and are often far removed from reality. Thus the sketches are didactic; their value as entertainment is instrumental; they are *exempla* in an endless sermon.

In both sketches the only conflict is between man and reality, and the characters change only in their grasp of reality. Man pushes at nature, and nature, like a compressed spring, pushes back, especially when man drops his guard. The alien world is not only *there;* it is charged with force and ready to use it. At this point in Howells' career, this force is mild; later, it will be dangerously vigorous. Here too the demands on nature are mild, so that the spring is not compressed much, and cannot fly back violently. In "A Day's Pleasure," the characters, a suburban family, ask only that nature co-operate passably with them in their effort to have an enjoyable holiday at the seaside near Boston. When the characters act on that expectation, their reasonable demands meet with both passive and active resistance. They remember to take everything they need, but their necessaries are, as it turns out, encumbrances at every instant of the journey. They miss one boat because it has been chartered; they miss another by a minute and must wait five hours for the next one. While sitting quietly on a pier, they are suddenly surrounded by swarms of obnoxious children, all suffering paroxysms of whooping cough directly in the faces of the helpless family. Drinking claret with their picnic lunch on the boat, they are persecuted by a woman who appears from nowhere, sits opposite them, and glares pointedly at them and the wine. When they finally reach Nantasket, the weather, warm up to this point, suddenly turns cold. They decide to stay on board and return to Boston. The boat promptly goes aground. Dragging themselves home late at night, they find even that haven upset by the presence of a lost little boy. Restoring the boy to his parents leaves the family totally exhausted. It is midnight when they finally go to bed. The story sounds helter-skelter, but it is not; there has been a movement forward in what counts for Howells: the realization of the nature of things, and the development of methods for making others realize it. At the end Howells has the paterfamilias step forward—he even has this character refer to "advancing to the footlights" after his "little comedy"—and announce that although "nothing I had meant to do had been done, yet the man who had ended at midnight by restoring a lost child to the arms of its father, must own that in spite of adverse fortune, he had enjoyed A Day's Pleasure" (p. 170). Howells says, then, that if man can realize his predicament, and, even better, if he can help his fellow sufferers in that universal predicament, he has advanced as far as a man can expect to advance; he has stood up to chaos and thumbed his nose at it. (The confidence of this ending may be compared to the weariness and puzzlement at the end of Howells' later, major novels.)

"A Romance of Real Life" is a more complex work. It is not only a satire on false expectations and interpretations of life, but a dissertation on perception, always one of Howells' central interests (see Chapter IV). Here the central figure is again "the contributor," watched closely by "I," the hovering narrator. At a late hour, the contributor is visited by a sailor looking for his family. Returning alone after some futile casts about the neighborhood, the contributor learns from a convenient passer-by that the people he wants live nearby. In the morning the sailor does not return, but the contributor goes to the indicated house alone. He learns that the "sailor" is a convicted bigamist just out of jail, and that his family is trying to avoid him. With Howells' help and criticism, the contributor analyzes the little episode. Nature first makes the contributor cover himself with ridicule as a penalty for his romantic ideas and then reassures him with events more interesting, because more puzzling, than anything to be found in books. Again we see that what fascinated Howells about "realism" was the opportunities it gave not just to render the bland surface of things, but to imply the mystery hidden under the blandness. As the contributor broods on, he concludes that the ex-convict is not to blame for making up a story, but was forced into deceit because men, wrapped in their frozen attitudes toward "convicted Error" (p. 189), would not help a criminal, no matter how just his claims. (Society's indifference is underlined by one of Howells' typical whiffs of cruelty: the sailor's daughter, listening in boredom to a woman describing her father, "having deftly caught a fly on the door-post occupied herself in plucking it to pieces" [p. 185].) Thus society, as well as the sentimental "literary" artist, is attacked satirically for deviating from the norm and making someone look ridiculous. Here, in embryonic form, is Howells' doctrine of complicity, or, from my point of view, bondage, since all men are involved to their mutual disadvantage. Howells pooh-poohs the contributor's feelings, but he does so in a way that the latter's phrases, such as "a dark necessity of misdoing" (p. 189), elicit more sympathy from us than do Howells' criticisms.

III

> *"What was my reason for not being explicit with her; for going away from her without one honest, manly, downright word . . . ?"*

After *Suburban Sketches,* Howells moves toward the novel —or, to put it more accurately and more awkwardly—toward the long anatomy-satire in which a long fictional *exemplum* is the major but dependent device of revelation and persuasion. He retains the basic elements of the early story-sketches: the characters' awkward attempts to control reality, the recoil of reality toward those who push it, the emphasis on life's mystery (in satiric contrast to know-it-all explanations), realization of the human condition as the final goal and the reason behind the satire. *A Chance Acquaintance, A Foregone Conclusion,* and *The Lady of the Aroostook* are typical of these early novels. I have already said something about *A Foregone Conclusion,* and it is necessary here to consider the novel only as satire. The major male characters—Mr. Ferris, the American consul, and Don Ippolito, the priest—are at fault, and therefore become objects of satire, because they try to force their worlds to assume foreign shapes. Don Ippolito tries to make himself into a modern practical man, a kind of Venetian Connecticut Yankee. But first he succeeds in making himself into an ass with his preposterous "inventions" (here is the mild satire of the absurd); then, by rejecting the church and Venice, he alienates himself from the only world he has and can ever have. At last, he alienates himself from himself, and the satire loses its humor and becomes the Howells nightmare. Finally, he undergoes the Howellsian catharsis of self-realization and self-acceptance, but by that time he is dying. Within a few years, he has suffered the final indignity, according to established human standards and hopes: he has been forgotten as a man; and to the other characters, he is an abstraction, "a mere problem" (p. 264). Florida Vervain, the young girl, does not try to shape life; she therefore never gets herself into trouble, though she suffers from the follies of the men in her life. After its many miseries, the novel ends on a feeling of calm, with Ferris and his new wife accepting and realistically examining life, and therefore living as happily as people can.[4]

In *A Chance Acquaintance* and *The Lady of the Aroostook,* Howells uses the Boston Brahmin as the target of his satire on rigid "codes." In each novel an ordinary courtship action is complicated not by the classic external hazards, like grumpy fathers, but by a Brahmin's errors in judgment and behavior based on his rigid and faulty code. In each case, again, the girl is a simple provincial with no proper social training and hence no mental barriers against reality. She is decidedly not a Daisy Miller, however, for she is perceptive, with all that that adjective implies in the Howells world. Both Brahmins are accepted by their girls, after many complications. In *The Lady of the Aroostook,* the young man keeps his girl and goes off to California with her, thus rejecting codified error and returning to the state of nature and natural flux,

[4] Howells did not originally plan to continue the novel beyond the garden scene, in which the priest confesses his love to the girl while Ferris watches in horror; but at the request of his publishers, he added the present ending (see Cady, I, 190–91). This ending must, however, be taken into account: Howells did write it, and if we are to take him seriously as an artist, we must be able to take into account anything he wrote. (That the added ending has certain meanings and a certain tone is fortunate for my argument, but this point is secondary.)

symbolized by the West of the 1870's. In *A Chance Acquaintance,* the Brahmin stupidly loses the girl at the end, and returns to Boston, the fount of rigidity and error. In both novels the characters meet accidentally while on a trip; thus Howells presents the quintessence of an open, fluid situation and relationship, the better to allow his characters free play for their denseness or perceptiveness. In each novel, as in the early sketches, Howells concludes in his own voice with recapitulations and evaluations, thus re-emphasizing perception and reminding us that the preceding fictions are *exempla* in satiric sermons.

Although—or perhaps because—these two books are so much alike, the first one, Howells' first genuine work of fiction, is much more pungent and vigorous than the other. Arbuton, the rigid Brahmin of *A Chance Acquaintance,* is more carefully developed than Staniford, his counterpart in *The Lady of the Aroostook.* Generally a kindly author, Howells employs unusually cold irony in his treatment of Arbuton. The young Brahmin, having viewed his fellow-passengers on the river boat, concludes "that probably the journey would require the full exercise of that tolerant spirit in which he had undertaken a branch of summer travel in his native land" (p. 16). To the priggishness of Arbuton's thoughts, Howells thus adds the ironic evaluative effects of his own style. Arbuton's rigid artificiality is further suggested by a series of clothes images. He wears his clothes with "scrupulosity" (p. 15), and, as Kitty Ellison notes, his clothes look like him and respect him as he respects himself. His manners, like his clothes, "seem to have been put on him instead of having come out of him" (p. 149).

This bipartite structure of rigid, brittle surface and unknown interior parallels Howells' vision of life as a generally smooth surface covering mysteries and horrors, and opposes Howells' ideal personality structure (or antistructure), which is fluid, receptive, unpretentious, homogeneous. Also, from the brittleness of this surface and the pressure put upon the hidden qualities by that brittle surface arises the typical Howells action: an explosive intrusion of reality, a violent period of conflict and confusion, a simmering-down period characterized by much discussion and readjustment, and then a renewal of the surface, leading, by and by, to the next explosion. The Howells action is essentially cyclic and limitless, in the tradition of Emerson and Whitman, not formal in the Jamesian architectural sense.

Action and symbol fuse in *A Chance Acquaintance* when Arbuton intercepts a savage dog about to leap on Kitty, gets his coat torn, rips it off, immediately loses "all the cold doubts and hindering scruples which he had felt from the first" (p. 175), and realizes that he loves Kitty. After the first rapture, the lovers enter upon a period of discussion; meanwhile, Arbuton's surface hardens again. The final crisis, and the crucial effect of Arbuton's surface, have already been foreseen by the perceptive Kitty when she says that nine times out of ten his manner is coldly perfect, but the tenth time "he may say something so rude that you can't believe it" because "his training doesn't hold out, and he seems to have nothing natural to fall back upon" (p. 149), "natural" implying a Rousseauistic innocence. This final crisis arises, appropriately enough, because of Kitty's unfashionable clothes, which embarrass Arbuton so much before some Boston friends that he cuts Kitty dead rather than introduce her to them and thus acknowledge her acquaintance. Finally seeing through Arbuton's and her own pretense, Kitty rejects him. His code of surfaces has rebounded against him and defeated him. Kitty goes off temporarily saddened but permanently a gainer; she now knows more about life than she did, and, what is more important, she knows that she knows.

In *The Lady of the Aroostook,* both young people reach this ideal Howellsian state of self-knowledge. The conflict here is simpler and harsher than in *A Chance Acquaintance;* there is no intrusive social background at all—just a young man and woman on a sailing ship bound from Boston to

Venice, with some conventional supporting characters. Only Staniford's conviction that no nice girl would go to Europe alone prevents his embracing reality and the girl. His code is all wrong. But significantly, he is "fittingly dressed in rough blue" (p. 53), which he wears casually; his surface offers little obstacle to the passage of reality, and it is only by resort to a shameless use of coincidence that Howells keeps the young pair apart until he has a book of regular length. What most handicaps this young hero is his habit of analyzing people. "He was one of those men who cannot rest in regard to people they meet until they have made some effort to formulate them" (p. 90), says Howells, in one of his typical generalizing comments. Staniford is a mild example of Howells' bad artists, the people who err through predisposition rather than through use of a conscious code energized by sadism. Unlike some of these characters, whom we shall meet later, Staniford has the saving quality of self-analysis. He becomes a Howellsian success when he shouts at his friend, "What was my reason for not being explicit with her; for going away from her without one honest, manly, downright word; for sneaking off without telling her . . . ?" (p. 235), and when he tells her, "It began the moment I saw you on the wharf, there, and when I came to know my mind I kept it from you only till I could tell you here. But now I wish I hadn't! Life is too short, . . ." (p. 315). The close association of "downright" and "manly" (in its pre-T.R. literalness) reveals the importance that Howells attaches to honesty.

IV

"Ah, I don't know! I don't know!"

These novels of the 1870's are well enough in their small way, but their simplicity and their conventional plot lines (which do not entirely accord with what Howells is trying to do) make them exercises for the novels of the 1880's. In *A Modern Instance, The Rise of Silas Lapham,* and *Annie Kilburn,* Howells swings away from his belief that being "downright" is a primitive and natural talent, toward the belief that it is the precarious product of a precariously balanced training and vision. Codes, then, are necessary, up to a point defined with difficulty; beyond that point lies trouble. Such a swing toward ethical conservatism is common enough as one grows older. It is Howells' special achievement, however, to avoid turning his novels into special pleading for a simplistic vision. What we still find in these big novels is Howells' mysterious world, and what we find on the surface of that impenetrable mystery is a vast, heaving tangle involving every one, good or bad, who acts in the world. Earnest plainness and correctness of perception do not guarantee success or immunity in such a world. The whole muddled business is seen and presented by the satiric narrator, who shows us the absurdity, and even the monstrosity, of our expectations and standards.

The most complex of Howells' big novels, *A Modern Instance* is probably Howells' most difficult book, not excepting *A Hazard of New Fortunes.* As the title suggests, *A Modern Instance* is an anatomy based on an *exemplum,* and it is truly an "instance," a part of an action rather than a complete action. In one sense this instance is the situation arising from the marriage of Bartley Hubbard and Marcia Gaylord, and involving a number of people in several places. This situation stands for the whole of human history; it is "one brief scene of the immense complex drama" having its "*dénouement* only in eternity" (*TWJ,* p. 70). At the same time, the modern instance is Bartley Hubbard himself. His story is a strong satire on deviations from the correct, accepted moral standards that I have roughly summed up as "decency." If that were the only level in the book, it would long since have become another obsolete Victorian sermon. But the book also attacks the spokesmen who righteously and rightly condemn Bartley Hubbard, the standards by which they condemn him, and the belief (in these characters and in the reader) that these standards operate in real life. The public condemnation of moral errors is thus itself partially condemned—partially, not wholly. This is an agnostic's book, not an atheist's; a moral atheist could not write satire that presents an edge no matter how one looks at it. It is significant that the last words of the book are "I don't know!" (*AMI*, p. 514).

To give a full analysis of this long and long-winded novel would take a very long time. Not only are there many characters and events; there are the even larger numbers of relationships, and it is the relationships that matter in satire. A look at chosen incidents will suffice to develop the major satiric effects of the novel. The key section is the opening. We see Bartley Hubbard, a clever young reporter, conquering the isolated northern New England town of Equity, and then being ejected by the same people who once admired him; we see Marcia Gaylord, daughter of the leading citizen of the town, being pursued by Bartley and then pursuing him. Throughout the episode, Bartley suffers from the common Howells disease of believing that the world (beginning with Equity) is comprehensible, that he comprehends it, and that he can impose his own views on it. In the old-fashioned sense of the term, he is "smart"—talented and pushy—and the author shows us and tells us about that smartness at wearisome length. The town seems to accept this pushiness. When Squire Gaylord says, "I don't know . . . as I ever heard that a great deal of morality was required by a newspaper editor" (p. 23), the local bigwigs laugh. Bartley's courtship of Marcia, the leading belle, is condoned and approved. But eventually, the harsh facts of reality shatter the pleasant surface. Bartley's tubercular assistant picks a quarrel with him over a local wench and theatrically dashes a piece of paper in Bartley's face. Slapped in return, the youth falls and suffers a concussion. The town immediately freezes Bartley out, and his only compensation is that Marcia chases after him to become his wife and his burden. Thus Bartley is properly shown up and punished.

But at the same time, Howells satirizes the town and the world as strongly as he satirizes Bartley, and for the same reasons: they are corrupt, and they are out of touch with reality—indeed, they are corrupt *because* they are out of touch with reality. Squire Gaylord admires Bartley's lack of deference because the squire (and, we must assume, the other leading citizens) has no deference himself. The local church has become a social club, to which Bartley contributes his geniality, not unmixed with heartily appreciated sarcasms. The town encourages his "free, joking way" (p. 22) with girls, and it is this habit that leads to the fatal clash with the assistant editor. Marcia Gaylord herself is so simple-minded in her glowing reaction to Bartley's cynical courting that she is more comic than tragic. Then the town, and Marcia, too, for a while, turn on Bartley with swift cruelty. The genial modern surface disappears, and the corrupt Puritanism beneath it comes forth.

With unusual care, Howells makes this pretentious society into a closed world, and makes it symbolize the world. Before we meet Bartley and Marcia, we see the town, in one of Howells' most pointed and economical openings. The first paragraph of the novel begins, "The village stood on a wide plain, and around it rose the mountains" (p. 3), and goes on to establish this influential natural background, a symbolic prison. From this large scene, Howells moves into the town. It has only one street, a natural stage, and every time that Bartley and Marcia go in or out, they must run the gauntlet of prying eyes. Howells then presents "the women who sat with their work at the windows on either side of the way" looking with "starved curiosity" (p. 5) from houses "where the smell of rats in the wainscot and of potatoes in the cellar strengthened with the growing night" (p. 6). In this description the method of "teacup realism" allows Howells unobtrusively to insert images that are sober enough in one sense, but also have the symbolic suggestiveness of the details of Poe's House of Usher. The rats and the night are the people themselves and their situation. A thin diet of moldy moral potatoes cannot keep them from starving.

Even when Bartley goes out to the country, he cannot escape temptation and suffocating corruption. While happily sleighing with Marcia, he collides with the sleigh of Hannah Morrison, the red-headed trull who works in Bartley's office and who is his later undoing. The scene is a neatly symbolic bit of presentation, not unusual in Howells. After his downfall, Bartley seeks refuge in a lumber camp, but is remorselessly sought out and seduced (in the figurative sense, of course) by a visiting flirt.[5]

But behind character and environment is always the alien universe, the dark mystery under the surface, and it is the appearance of this force that makes *A Modern Instance* more than "realism," or a study of certain interesting themes, and puts it into the continuum of Howells' works. Bartley Hubbard has something devilish about him. Sleekly rapacious, he belongs to the class of Howells' demonic characters.[6] Also, there is the mystery behind Bartley's downfall in Equity. We know that this follows directly from his slapping Henry Bird, his assistant, even though the punishment greatly exceeds the crime. The incident occurs because Bird resents Bartley's sarcasms about Hannah Morrison, whom Bird loves, preposterous though it may seem (Hannah is the town trollop, and Bird is a meek consumptive). Why does Bartley make these remarks? Because he is grumpy; he has just been berated by Hannah's drunken father for "makin' up to my girl" (p. 74). In the light of the town's loud admiration of Bartley's "free, joking way" (p. 22) with girls, Morrison's attack is preposter-

[5] The corruption of Equity, and of Boston as well, is discussed by Cady (I, 209–11), for purposes different from mine.

[6] The basic details of Bartley's devilishness are also brought out by Cady (I, 214), who sees in them reminders of Howells' Swedenborgian background.

ous. At any rate, whenever Morrison is drunk, he gets after Bartley to raise Hannah's wages; these scenes are an office tradition, and we tend to side with Bartley when Morrison suddenly becomes sincerely angry. The underlying question, then, is the source of Morrison's liquor. Equity is a dry town; even the loggers working nearby cannot get liquor; the apothecary is afraid to sell it. But "Morrison never failed of his spree when the mysterious mechanism of his appetite enforced it" (p. 72). Bartley's immediate motive for striking Bird is "the demons, whatever they were, of anger, remorse, pride, shame" (p. 79). The chain of causation, if pursued beneath the surface of events in any promising direction, thus disappears at once into mystery. The pattern of the book conforms to Howells' governing image of a thin surface covering a deep drop into frightening mystery.

Even if the small town is not a sound moral base, Boston, where Bartley and Marcia settle, should be. It is, of course, the center of American culture and morality. But as the novel continues, we find that even the finest Bostonians are not as strong or as morally authoritative as they should be, or as they think they are, or as we think they are. The Bostonians divide into several groups, representing several subcultures. On a low level is Witherby, Bartley's employer, whose sleazy moral standards and bad taste make his paper an accurate premonition of modern yellow journalism. In this newspaper world only Ricker, a brisk and able editor, has high standards; and he can do nothing more effectual to Bartley than cut him socially.

On the high social level, where morality can be backed up with prestige and power, are the Hallecks, representing the solid mercantile class, and the lawyer Atherton and his rich friend (and later wife), Clara Kingsbury, representing the Brahmin professional and society groups. All of these people become involved willy-nilly with Bartley and eventually judge him, but all are skilfully robbed of final authority. The elder Hallecks, shy people of small-town background, are the closest to authority; but since they are baffled and imperceptive, they cannot be spokesmen in the Howells world. Their son, Ben Halleck, has strong opinions about Bartley, his college classmate, as do Atherton and his wife, but they are thoroughly undercut by the author. Halleck is crippled—literally, by a childhood accident, and figuratively, by his neurotic suppression of his love for Marcia. Like her, he is a humor character, distorted by demonic forces he cannot control or understand, and like her, he is continually put into miseries and embarrassment by Howells' remorseless manipulation of circumstances. The sensitive Halleck, of course, suffers and reacts more to his bondage than the simple-minded Marcia does; and he would win our sympathy were it not for the exaggeration of his reactions, which carry him beyond the norms of the Howells world into a series of baroque moods and actions. He even begins to doubt his own identity, and nothing, for a Howells character, can be more significant than that. Being of the same small-town Puritan background as Marcia, he sees himself as a sort of latter-day Dimmesdale, outwardly genteel and inwardly corrupt; here again is the image of surface and mystery. At one point he flees to the South American jungles for two years, to return more miserable than ever. Even though in the abstract he is right, in the world of existence he is of no account. Sharing the linguistic structure of his name with the author and the other major male character (Halleck, Howells, Hubbard), he symbolizes the civilized half, the surface half, of Howells, and contrasts with Hubbard, his alter ego, the uncivilized, "natural," demonic, hidden half of the author.[7]

The last authority in the novel is Atherton, the lawyer. He comes off better than Halleck, but he too is made to suffer by

[7] In *Expression In America* (New York, 1932) Ludwig Lewisohn argues shrewdly that Howells identified with Hubbard, but Lewisohn's reasons (briefly, that Howells was a timid old maid obsessed with sex) are too simplistically Freudian, in the loose popular sense, to assist the literary critic.

indirection. In the first place, he, like Halleck and Marcia (and Hubbard too, for a while), becomes a victim of Aphrodite, a possessed man. He falls in love with and marries Clara Kingsbury, a Brahmin heiress. (There is an absurd parallel, which doesn't help Atherton, between this marriage and that of Bartley and Marcia. Bartley wants to become a lawyer, and Marcia is a small-town heiress who wants to become sophisticated.) Miss Kingsbury is genial—and rich—but she lacks every quality of good sense. She is flighty, gushing, and gauche, as Howells tells us at unnecessary length, and soon takes her place as another of the humor characters in the mad world of the novel. Atherton's marriage to her is a necessary convenience to the author, but is damaging to Atherton's reputation with the reader. Secondly, Atherton's moral condemnations of Halleck and Hubbard are so lofty, so firm, and so lengthy that they become a bore. He attacks the possessed Halleck in the most unreserved manner, so that Halleck eventually breaks off with him. Howells' intentions behind these diatribes are not fully clear; as his biographer shows, he was suffering from the aftereffects of a nervous breakdown, probably connected with problems put into and arising out of the novel, when he wrote the part of the book (after Chapter XXXI) developing Halleck's obsession and Atherton's preachings.[8] At any rate, the reader experiencing the novel will tend to sympathize with Halleck for all his tiresome faults, and brand Atherton as a prig.

At the very end of the novel, in one of Howells' typically analytical conclusions, Atherton delivers, with Clara as audience, a disquisition on the Hubbards that must remain the final word on the subject. Atherton concludes that the Hubbards are untrained, uncontrolled, and dangerous animals. His facts are indisputable, and his verdict fits the Howells dimensions; but we are concerned here with Atherton as a standard, not with the Hubbards. Dismissing the

[8] Cady, I, 210, 213 f.

latter, we want to know, as we read their judgment, if these Brahmins can be accepted as ideals. In the abstract we would answer yes, but fiction does not take place in the abstract (even if its effects are used in satire). In the actual scene, Howells so manages Atherton that he looks smug and priggish.[9] The lawyer does not talk with his wife—he orates at her during breakfast, not a generally accepted time for orations. The scene is interrupted continually by the petty needs and actions of eating, and concludes, after an eloquent attack on " 'implanted goodness' " with the following action: "Atherton lifted, with his slim, delicate hand, the cup of translucent china, and drained off the fragrant Souchong, sweetened, and tempered with Jersey cream to perfection" (p. 472). I will discuss the technical qualities of this scene later. Here it is enough to say that by handling of details of style—in fact, quite literally by "teacup realism"—Howells makes Atherton look smug and self-righteous. The path of righteousness leads to a cup of tea, drunk delicately by an overbred bore. (What one might call the Mark Twain in Howells, the Midwestern village boy, is lurking behind this outsider's description of the private behavior of rich big-city folks.) When Atherton a bit later remarks, "This whole thing is disorderly" (p. 474), he begins to sound querulous and self-pitying, despite his insight; and we may recall the Brahmin hero of *A Chance Acquaintance*, who was made to suffer so by his forced acquaintance with barbarians. By the end of the book, a few pages later, the reader has been well prepared for Atherton's epitaph to the whole "instance": "Ah, I don't know! I don't know!" (p. 514). It is actually the reader who

[9] In *The Victorian Mode in American Fiction, 1865–1885* (East Lansing, Mich., 1965), Professor Robert Falk also uses this final passage to show that Howells is "careful to qualify the authority of Halleck . . . and of Atherton" (p. 128). But Professor Falk concludes that "Howells's realism suffers somewhat from employing the Atherton and Halleck episodes both as objects of satire and as qualified vehicles for the expression of his own ideas" (p. 129), whereas I conclude that "realism" as such is not the issue, that the complexity reflects Howells' world view.

does not know, who cannot understand why the events of the book happened, who is guilty, who is to judge and to be judged, what the structure of existence is, whether or not there is a structure, how we can go about finding the answers to our questions, whether we have a right to ask questions and expect answers, whether we are any better than, or any different from, the people in the novel. Like *Pierre* and *The Confidence Man,* this book blurs everything. Howells can be excused for having a nervous breakdown while he was writing *A Modern Instance,* for his "intellectual failure to *think through* to their last conclusions the ideas for which the main body of the novel's drama stood" (Cady, I, 208). How can one think his own destruction and remain sane? Even Melville could not solve this problem, and became silent.

V

"Seems sometimes as if it was a hole opened for me, and I crept out of it."

Howells' other big novels of the mid-eighties reveal a certain relaxation of satiric tension and a hint of new tensions. *The Rise of Silas Lapham* (1885) and *Indian Summer* (1886) have the same basic theme as *A Modern Instance*—the error of trying to codify the world—and in *The Rise of Silas Lapham,* there is the same debunking of Brahmins as in *A Modern Instance.* But in each book Howells reduces the consequences of error, and in fact makes the major characters better off after "defeat" (the loss of pretensions and pretentiousness) than before. Silas Lapham, the self-made "Paint King," loses wealth and status; but the one was rickety and the other hollow, and his honest poverty at the end of the book is for him the only decorous state. Mrs. Corey, defender of the Brahmin code, loses her fight to keep her son from marrying a Lapham daughter, but the loss is presented to us as a gain, a restoring of social fluidity. In *Indian Summer* the aging Colville and the adolescent Imogene give each other up after the most preposterous kind of mutual and personal pretense, and turn to contemporaries for love. Because the initial situation here is so distorted, the return to reality produces a feeling of physical relief.

Another kind of emphasis also makes these novels more comforting than some of the earlier ones. The central characters are steadily satirized for their foibles and stupidities, but at the same time they are all given a strong sense of responsibility and a feeling for decency. In Lapham and Mrs. Corey and Colville and the others, there is none of the indifference of Arbuton and Staniford and none of the malevolence of Bartley Hubbard. Evil does exist in the world of these characters, but it is not in them.

This movement of evil away from the foreground begins to produce the pattern of the later Howells novels. As I have said, this pattern consists of a decent person or persons struggling against an alien, mysterious, and sometimes cruel world (which includes certain people). In the early Howells novels, the bad people are either not there or are in the foreground; the world in the background may be silly (as in *Their Wedding Journey*) or corrupt (as in *A Modern Instance*), but it is not frightening. With *The Rise of Silas Lapham,* we are not yet in the world of *The Kentons,* but we are heading in that direction. Thus *The Rise of Silas Lapham* is reassuring in some ways—the central characters are silly but decent—and troubling in others—the world they live in is not a secure place. The Coreys build themselves a complete, graceful world, apparently based on solid investments and the hope of proper marriages for their children. But the investments mysteriously shrink; their daughters are homely and unsought; and their adored son marries the pert offspring of a Paint King. Lapham also builds what he feels is a complete, safe world; but he himself destroys part of it out of vanity (his lavish house), guilt (his clumsy retributory involvements with his ex-partner), and carelessness (he accidentally sets fire to the unfinished new house). The mysterious forces that rule the world take the rest: a depression weakens him, competitors crowd him, and the only bidders for his last bit of property are so obviously the devil's emissaries that he refuses their offers and allows another financial group to swindle his interests away from him. Thus the hubris in man and the malevolence in the world combine nicely to destroy mental structurings of reality.

In *The Rise of Silas Lapham* (and in *Indian Summer* too) Howells integrates satire, action, and plot to an unusual degree. Technically, we are at another mid-point in Howells, far from the awkward boy-meets-girl stories of the 1870's and also far from the looser satires of the 1890's. In the two books of the mid-eighties, Howells satirizes blandly optimistic views of life, the foibles of the pretentious and the striving, and the "literary" idea that life corresponds to human rules. All of these varieties of satire are involved in the action of *The Rise of Silas Lapham.* This action works out of the situations created by life and human error; in this process man is purged of and punished for his errors. The "literary" and unperceptive approach of the characters creates misunderstandings, which then create confusion and more misunderstandings. As in Howells' early sketches, the action is like the compression and rebounding of a spring. The characters try to control life; the harder they try and the more they need to keep their gains, the harder it is to keep what they have or to compress the spring more tightly; finally the situation escapes from control, and life violently reassumes its usual relaxed shapelessness. The mysterious world adds its integral contribution. The entanglement of the Laphams and the Coreys, a nuisance for both sides, follows, the characters think, from Mrs. Lapham's kindness to Mrs. Corey when the latter is seriously ill at a small Canadian resort; but such a small event could never in itself create a lasting intimacy between Brahmins and *nouveaux riches*. Mrs. Corey's intense feelings of obligation, which override her natural contempt for the Laphams and lead her to fatal courtesies toward them, are the result of a casual remark made by an outsider, a doctor, who "said that but for Mrs. Lapham's timely care, the lady would hardly have lived. He was a very effusive little Frenchman, and fancied he was saying something very pleasant to everybody" (*RSL,* p. 32). The obscure notion of an anonymous passer-by thus determines the fate of eight people; the mysterious forces behind the surface of life are ultimately responsible, as in *A Modern Instance.*

This alien and touchy world does offer comfort to those who repent and accept it. Both Lapham and Colville do so, and receive their just rewards. Colville accepts middle age and marries Mrs. Bowen, the charming widow whom he could have married years before. Lapham is apparently given less. Having lost his money and position, he is last seen pottering around the rocky family farm in northern Vermont; his shabby clothes suggest the change from pompous merchant to marginal farmer. Yet his triumph is the greatest a Howells character can have, and amply justifies the word *Rise* in the title. He has not only acted and risen morally, but he is aware of what he has done and he is consciously humble before the dark forces of the world. "Seems sometimes as if it was a hole opened for me, and I crept out of it" (p. 515), he muses to Sewell, the Boston minister and acting representative of the author. Here again is the surface image, this time from the point of view of the man who fell through and was allowed to climb out. As a farmer, Lapham is now passive, an assistant to the workings of alien nature, rather than its opponent; but he squarely faces, understands, and accepts them, and he is therefore an existential success.

Annie Kilburn in part parallels *The Rise of Silas Lapham* and in part advances toward *A Hazard of New Fortunes.* The Paint King tries to apply a code to that aspect of the world that society offers him for occupation: seeking success through business. The earnest young Annie tries to codify her own little corner of things—doing good in her small native town (Hatboro, Massachusetts—a commuting and industrial town with a summer colony at one edge, a complex Equity brought into the outer orbit of Boston). Both characters fail, and both are redeemed despite and because of failure. Being a Victorian lady with solid investments and no interest in business, Annie Kilburn cannot be made to suffer through her pocketbook as Lapham suffers. She suffers in her pride, as she finds herself, through her bungling efforts, becoming alienated from, or even worse, pitied by, her friends and by the people she wants to save. The world of *Annie Kilburn* is, moreover, a much grimmer place than the world of *The Rise of Silas Lapham* and *Indian Summer*. This world is now almost totally alien. Annie, returning to Hatboro after years abroad, is a stranger to her own home town. Of course, it has changed, and she has changed; but the alienation is much more than the commonplace variety arising from absence. Annie is newly born into what was once an Eden, and finds it an anti-Eden, hostile, snobbish, and rapacious—a sad commentary on the universal human dream of return. Errors here are punished brutally. In *The Rise of Silas Lapham,* deviators suffer ridicule, misery, loss of money and status. In *Annie Kilburn* they may cause or suffer death. When Annie, acting on her code of good intentions, tries to save a poor sick child by sending it to the seashore, away from its mother, the child dies, and the crazed mother tacitly accuses Annie of murder. The socialite's gracious presumptuousness has been swiftly punished. It is no good to point out, as the Job's comforters in the novel do, that the child would have died anyway. Annie is fully implicated in this typically Howellsian situation. She is an accomplice of death; here is the conventional idea of complicity. Even more, she is the helpless accomplice; she is in bondage to the mysterious world, and she has made her bonds all the tighter by trying to act as if they do not exist.

She makes herself look ridiculous by being so imperceptive and bumbling, and likewise, she makes the world reveal its horrors. Thus the satire operates on two levels: light satire on human foibles, and harsh satire on our views of the world.

VI

"I feel like I was tied hand and foot."

This kind of harsh satire dominates *A Hazard of New Fortunes*. The satire is implicit; it is aimed at the reader, at his views and his consequent desires and expectations. There is little satire here on people, or perhaps it would be more accurate to say that although the absolute quantity of ridicule of persons is great, it becomes insignificant alongside Howells' black indictment. The book is thus Howells' richest anatomy-fiction. In a manner more assured than that of *A Modern Instance,* Howells quashes one expectation and standard after another until we can be sure of little more than that the sun will continue to rise on the Marches, the Dryfooses, the painter Beaton, and the other characters. The book is not a comedy, though if we look at it with one eye shut, we can see scenes of social comedy, and we can distort the Marches' career in New York into a success story. But the social comedy is not so comic after all, and the Marches' success is soft-pedalled. The book is not really tragic, either, for the tragic possibilities are blurred and satirized. Even Beaton, the self-pitying artist who bungles a suicide attempt, realizes "that his case was not to be dignified into tragedy" (II, 326).

What kind of world is it that is presented here as an implied satire on what we expect and want? First, it is in ironic contrast to the author's own explicit morality. When Basil March says of Conrad Dryfoos' accidental death, "All that was distinctly the chance of life and death. That belonged to God, and no doubt it was law, though it seems chance," and implies that this "law" was "that old doctrine of the Atonement" (II, 252), he is giving a moral meaning to events and at the same time abandoning any attempt to find meaning in human terms. The author's spokesman picks up the whole, vast, unwieldy problem and throws it across the gap into the alien and unknown, thus "solving" the problem. At the same time, March's analysis is silently and thoroughly overruled by the almost six hundred pages of confused misery that have preceded it, and the reader would need to be another Basil March to accept his bland disposal of those six hundred pages. Also, March, like Atherton in *A Modern Instance,* is not presented as the most clear-sighted of analysts. A basic artistic norm—the belief that art can explain or at least order life—is thus satirized while it is stated.

In the structure of the book, the reader's yearnings for form and completeness are also ridiculed. The action is not that of a complete novel; there is no "ending," not even the sense of change leading to stasis that Howells gives us in the *The Rise of Silas Lapham.* The characters merely go on living in their usual ways, after certain vicissitudes. Because the only marriage of the book involves two secondary characters, Howells cannot use this traditional device for giving a pleasing tidiness to an otherwise open-ended action. The core of the action, the magazine *Every Other Week,* does change hands, but does not itself change. (Even the title of the magazine takes no stand; it refers neutrally to its time of publication.) Fulkerson and March start the magazine near the beginning, develop it into a quiet success, become the proprietors and then go on as before, doing the same work and living the same lives. (Fulkerson's marriage does not change him.) At the end the author uses a conventional present-tense summary of later events to reveal the literally inconclusive nature of the action. Some other characters are killed or disappointed in love or driven to Europe, but again, none of these changes leads to any central meaning or conclusions. Like *A Modern Instance,* the book is a lot of things that happened and were observed by major characters who were in turn observed by the author; the point of the novel is the careful analysis of the pointlessness, and the book is an anatomy-satire.

The book itself does revolve around the magazine, and we should see what that means (cf. Cady, II, 103). This structure affects not only the theme of alienation, but the satire. Because the magazine is not realized, the characters are busily revolving around nothing—a Chaplinesque touch. This revolving structure also means that the characters do not confront each other directly but look at each other indirectly through the medium of the magazine. Howells thus satirizes the modern industrial and commercial organization, in which direct relations, whether they are for good or for bad, give way to isolation and alienation. The circular arrangement around the magazine resolves itself, if we omit the magazine, into a circular lock step, making the characters in *A Hazard of New Fortunes* physically close and mentally distant. Howells so arranges the entrances and exits that the sense of meaningless, circular shuffle is reinforced; and we are left with the ironic awareness that life is not the meaningful, linear progress we have been made to think it is. Chapters and episodes are hooked together by the appearance of common characters; for example, the nine chapters of Part Third are linked by the movements of characters as follows:

1. Fulkerson, March, and Dryfoos.
2. Fulkerson, March, Dryfoos, and Mrs. March.
3. Dryfoos, Beaton, Mrs. Dryfoos, Christine Dryfoos, Mela Dryfoos.
4. Beaton and Alma Leighton.
5. Beaton and Margaret Vance.
6. Margaret Vance and Mrs. Horn.
7. Margaret Vance and Mr. and Mrs. Dryfoos.

8. Mr. and Mrs. Dryfoos.

9. Mr. and Mrs. Dryfoos, Margaret Vance, and Mr. and Mrs. March.

Here the Marches are the beginning and also the end of a chain. In this way the book is given a complex non-structure, and life becomes an absurd, solemn bustle, busily going nowhere.

This endless round leads the characters into a similar round of confused personal relationships. These are so involved with business relationships that the book's presentation of a dreadful business world becomes the presentation of a dreadful human world. *A Hazard of New Fortunes* is much more, however, than a work of economic and social criticism. The book criticizes existence, for which society and the economy are synecdoches. The economy is a mess because that is the nature of things. Economic forces, in fact, are part of those alien forces that erupt through the thin Howellsian surface and disturb or destroy men. The streetcar strike in *A Hazard of New Fortunes* is such an event. Coming after several hundred pages of muddling, growing feuds and generally rising tension, it explodes with indifferent ruthlessness, precipitates decisions and changes, and makes it impossible for any one to go back to the old situation. With impartial random efficiency, the strike destroys both Conrad Dryfoos, the gentle idealistic son of March's publisher, and Lindau, the bitter anarchist. Wealth in this novel also erupts: it comes from natural-gas wells, and wrecks the order of society by making impossible the human relationships on which that order depends. In a long, portentous speech, Fulkerson, the boyishly enthusiastic promoter, describes the sensational flames and explosions in the Ohio gas fields. Later a miniature derrick is the centerpiece at an unfortunate dinner party for Dryfoos; as the characters squabble and the party breaks up, the derrick collapses.

The universal bondage to the terrible, more-than-economic forces is clearly revealed. Not only do the downtrodden—the workman and the white-collar worker—complain about their lot; so does the fabulously "successful" capitalist, and much more strongly than Silas Lapham, who only grumbled from time to time. In a manner suggesting the universe of Kafka more than that of Marx, Basil March summarizes his feelings: "No one is sure of finding work; no one is sure of not losing it. I may have my work taken away from me at any moment by the caprice, the mood, the indigestion of a man who has not the qualification for knowing whether I do well or ill" (II, 253). Dryfoos lacks March's perceptiveness and literary gifts, but in his bewilderment he expresses even more poignantly the sense of being victimized:

> If I was to give all I'm worth this minute, we couldn't go back to the farm, any more than them girls in there could go back and be little children. I don't say we're any better off, for the money. I've got more of it now than I ever had; and there's no end to the luck; it pours in. But I feel like I was tied hand and foot. I don't know which way to move; I don't know what's best to do about anything. The money don't seem to buy anything but more and more care and trouble. We got a big house that we ain't at home in; and we got a lot of hired girls around under our feet that hinder and don't help. Our children don't mind us, and we got no friends or neighbors. But it had to be. I couldn't help but sell the farm, and we can't go back to it, for it ain't there. (I, 309–10)

These characters, then, are generally passive. The Stanifords and Laphams of the earlier novels were confused and absurd, but had distant goals in mind and had trust (even if it was misplaced) in man's future and their own; they moved through worlds of utter openness (the sea) or neutral compactness (Boston). This later Howells world of New York is cramped and crowded; there is no elbow room; the characters trip over each other and their environment at every turn.

Time also has closed in. Except as a dimly sensed area of continued burdens and confusion, the future hardly exists. (It is significant that March feels little joy and hope when he leaves his boring job in Boston and commits himself to a project existing in New York and in the future.) It is almost all a man can do now simply to dig in and hold on to what he has, not only to his property, but to his dignity, his honor, and his picture of the world. But just to live and observe is impossible. Willy-nilly, men are involved with each other and with the alien world. They must act and react—and, when off guard, they often find themselves liking action—but when they act, the world mocks their dignity and their laboriously acquired pictures of reality. March's humiliation, which provokes the bitter comment just quoted, follows from his action, his attempt to impose his own code upon reality. In this case the code is that of honor, and March tries to apply it to business: he refuses to let Dryfoos go over his head and fire Lindau, March's old friend and part-time subordinate on *Every Other Week*. March also acts on the principle (relevant to the mid-twentieth century) that a man should not lose his job because of his opinions. (Lindau is a Socialist, and Dryfoos, of course, is a reactionary businessman.) When Dryfoos flies into a rage at March, the latter walks out, to find that he has not just walked out of an office, but, like the crippled man of Howells' youth, has plunged through the thin, frail surface of organized life into the terrors below. Poor March does not even have the pleasure of feeling firmly righteous about his drastic action. As he stalks out past the astounded Fulkerson, March sees "something comic in his rueful bewilderment"; at the same time "his indignation kept him hot," but also "his heart ached with foreboding" (II, 137). When he gets home and appeals confidently to his wife's sympathy, she bursts into tears and reviles him. Acting out his anomic isolation, March stumbles out of his house and wanders the streets. Alienated from common sense by his lofty code and quixotic behavior, "he had not dreamt of this merely domestic, this petty, this sordid view of their potential calamity" (II, 141). Later the Marches make up, and Lindau resolves the squabble by voluntarily quitting. But Lindau does not, and cannot, solve the underlying problem. The satiric point has been made, not just in the static sense that romantic theories and stances are wrong, but in the more important dynamic sense that the man who tries to apply them may be destroyed.

Dryfoos tries not only to defend himself, as March does, but also to attack and mold reality, as Lapham did. Dryfoos fails and suffers, like the Paint King, but the world is much harsher in the later novel, and Dryfoos suffers much more than Lapham. He does not suffer in his pocketbook; he is not, except in passing, a satire on the hayseed millionaire who makes an ass of himself in the big city. (Howells had been something of a hayseed himself.) He is, rather, one of the first and best portraits of the man alienated by success from his world and from men, including his family. His bitter speech to his wife, quoted above, summarizes his feelings and his situation. His sense of doom ("it had to be") and bondage ("I feel like I was tied hand and foot") is expressed quite literally, but the speech is not a set piece; his self-analysis bursts under pressure through his frail, self-applied surface veneer of worldliness and cynicism. Howells always lets Dryfoos be himself.

Dryfoos belongs marginally to the family of Howells demons, the people who are driven by unknown forces to do evil. But unlike Bittridge in *The Kentons,* and other later Howells villains, Dryfoos is not a genial sadist or a deliberate builder of dominion over men and things. His activity makes him at first smug, but later unhappy and finally miserable. While March is living quietly according to his code of genteel honor, Dryfoos is living vigorously according to the code of the go-getter. This code is not really his; it is forced upon him when he is merely a backwoods Ohio farmer. It is a major sign of Dryfoos' basic decency and weakness (the two often go together in Howells)—or, in Freudian terms, it is a sign of his strong superego and a stronger id—that at first he violently resists the encroachment of the gas fields on his farm, and then, even more violently, accepts the wells, the money, the power, and all the harsh code that goes with them. This code demands vigorous enterprise conducted according to "business morality," which arises from a sense of superiority and invulnerability. Driven by this hubris, Dryfoos thoroughly destroys his farm and his old life; he becomes a dislocated will driving a dislocated source of power: his money, which represents not actual commitment but abstract potential.

In the Howells universe, all this spells deep trouble, and Dryfoos gets it. When he tries to seize and remake actuality in New York, he finds that everything goes wrong. When he forces himself on New York society, it recoils resiliently and he bounces off. The usual Howells clothes images operate again in this case. His daughters wear the most gorgeous fashions, but even to the most charitable eye, both daughters are untrained animals, the one a foolish puppy, and the other a panther. When Dryfoos, deprived of normal healthy occupation, focuses his energies on his son Conrad and tries to turn that dreamy youth into a driving businessman—into himself—the old man suffers his greatest setback. Apparently weak, but actually possessing his father's stubbornness, Conrad becomes all the more gentle and Christian as his father pushes him. Finally Conrad tries to intervene in the streetcar strike and is accidentally killed.

The old man is punished, and feels the punishment in all its severity, yet even here, Howells is the unrelenting satirist. The reader would like to see Dryfoos repent and change his whole character and manner of life, but he does nothing of the sort. His grief is not facile or "literary"; he is an existential portrait, and his grief is torn from him, as his former bewilderment was. He admits to March, "I ought to 'a' let him been a preacher! Oh, my son! my son!" and sobs with "a violence that made March afraid for him; but he controlled himself at last with a series of hoarse sounds like barks" (II, 268). This is the kind of creatural misery that is almost funny to the id of an unconcerned observer. As in the early sketch "Scene," the satirist of our expectations and proprieties paradoxically takes us to the limit of the grotesque in trying to show us the plain reality of life. Also, Dryfoos' action here reminds us of the Howells character's need to hold on to himself in a world whose surface is thin enough without one's kicking it. Right to the end, Dryfoos is himself. Before he bows to an outside code and takes a curative trip to Europe with his family, he sells *Every Other Week* to March and Fulkerson. He manages this deal—for a magazine that he always treated with contempt and that he now has reason to loathe—"with a hardness . . . which certainly left Mrs. March with a sense of his incomplete regeneration" (II, 327).

Dryfoos' son is an even stronger instrument of grim satire than the old man. Conrad is a parody of the Christ symbol. He has been taken for a genuine, if qualified, suggestion of Christ,[10] and certainly it is natural to look for some kind of a savior figure in this novel, someone who will lead us from the endless cramped confusion of the Howells world. Conrad is the character placed in that gap, and only if we study him with care will we see that he has just enough superiority to make him look Christ-like to the careless anxious eye, but not enough to keep him from being a satiric object. By using Conrad, Howells drives us back into this world to which we

[10] In *Howells and the Age of Realism,* Everett Carter thus describes Conrad: "Conrad, so full of humble love for his fellows, sacrificing himself for them, lost in grieving wonder at his 'Father's' forsaking, came close to a modern representation of Christ. . . . But Howells prevented the portrait from slipping into allegory by keeping Conrad human, ineffective, weak; a complex character; there was as much possibility of attributing his actions to the frustrations of impotency as to the satisfactions of altruism" (p. 222). Carter's interpretation resembles mine except for differences of emphasis so great that they become differences in kind. Carter does not seem to realize that Howells' strategies here are more than local in intention and effect.

are bound; he shows us that our need for a charismatic figure is abnormal, in the literal sense. Conrad by himself is also another of Howells' satires on the gap between one's picture of himself and the real world, between one's actual self and his picture of the world. As one of Howells' most strategic instruments, Conrad deserves careful attention, and such attention will show again that in the Howells anatomy-fiction meanings exist only in context, in patterned details.

Conrad is certainly selfless; he does die in trying to stop the streetcar strike, and in their grief the Marches pardonably see him as a Christ-like figure atoning for the sins of others. But Conrad's death occurs in the middle of a long novel, and we cannot ignore the context. While Howells is making the tragic picture of Conrad's life and death, he blurs that picture; and in the end Conrad is an ambiguous figure. His life is blameless and his aims noble, but he has the absurdity of the single-minded fanatic, who in satire is a humor character, not a hero. In Foxe's *Book of Martyrs,* Conrad would be one thing; in Howells he is another. We begin to get this blurred vision of Conrad as soon as we meet him. The point of view in this first meeting is that of the artist Beaton, a selfish ass but a sharp observer when he has his mind off himself.

> Leaning against the mantel there was a young man with a singularly gentle face, in which the look of goodness qualified and transfigured a certain simplicity. His large blue eyes were somewhat prominent; and his rather narrow face was drawn forward in a nose a little too long perhaps, if it had not been for the full chin deeply cut below the lip, and jutting firmly forward. (I, 180)

The point of view is Beaton's, but the style is the author's, and his apologetic method of description (which seems to imply "he's not as odd as he looks") is more damning than a direct attack, which might arouse sympathy. Conrad is more a Don Quixote than a Christ; he is good, but he is simple, and for the world he lives in, the simplicity is paramount. Like the

Don (one of Howells' favorite characters),[11] Conrad is an anachronism: "In a Catholic age and country, he would have been one of those monks who are sainted after death for the angelic purity of their lives, and whose names are invoked by believers in moments of trial, like San Luigi Gonzaga" (II, 40). But of course Conrad does not live in "a Catholic age and country." Environment, and the point of view proper to environment, make him ridiculous.

Like the lawyer, Atherton, in *A Modern Instance,* Conrad is subtly belittled. Howells usually shows us Conrad from the point of view of others, to whom he almost always looks odd. When we do see into Conrad's mind, we do so from the point of view of the author, and the superior viewpoint and the material combine to make Conrad look just a little foolish. Just before and after the reference to Gonzaga, for example, Howells presents Conrad's thoughts:

> As he now walked along thinking, with a lover's beatified smile on his face, of how Margaret Vance had spoken and looked, he dramatised scenes in which he approved himself to her by acts of goodness and unselfishness, and died to please her for the sake of others. He made her praise him for them, to his face, when he disclaimed their merit, and after his death, when he could not. (II, 40)

In his own mind Conrad, like many Howells characters, creates a romantic vision of himself, and to the outsider this vision looks like a sad burlesque of the notion of sacrifice. March expresses a typical common sense though hasty opinion of the romantic Conrad: "I never did like martyrs a great deal" (II, 36). The difference between March and Conrad is clinched in a little scene following Dryfoos' attack on March for hiring Lindau.

> ". . . Lindau has got hold of one of those partial truths that hurt worse than the whole truth, and—"

[11] See *My Literary Passions,* chap. iii.

> "Partial truth!" the young man interrupted. "Didn't the Saviour himself say 'How hardly shall they that have riches enter into the kingdom of God'?"
>
> "Why, bless my soul!" cried March. "Do *you* agree with Lindau?'
>
> "I agree with the Lord Jesus Christ," said the young man solemnly, and a strange light of fanaticism, of exaltation, came into his wide blue eyes. "And I believe he meant the kingdom of heaven upon this earth, as well as in the skies."
>
> March threw himself back in his chair and looked at him with a kind of stupefaction. . . . (II, 134)

March is conventional, flat, and uncharitable, but Conrad is eccentric; and in the world of satire, it is better and safer to be prudent and uncharitable than generous and eccentric. As the puzzled March later says to his equally baffled wife, "I suppose we must regard him as a kind of crank" (II, 145).

It is this ambiguous figure that dies during the streetcar strike. Howells carefully makes the episode satiric and its preliminaries nightmarish and absurd. Conrad's involvement with the strike results from a series of dream-like accidents starting far back and linked by a ring that, oddly and appropriately, belongs to Beaton, Conrad's alter ego in the novel. Beaton casually gives the ring to Christine Dryfoos to tease her into thinking he loves her. After old Dryfoos angrily forbids the girl to see Beaton again, she hurls it in her father's face along with Beaton's other gifts. Dryfoos absentmindedly picks up the ring and puts it on. At this point the tone of the chapter changes abruptly, and we enter the logical-illogical world of dreams. Dryfoos is a rangy, leathery old man, and Beaton is rather small and neat; but Beaton's ring fits Dryfoos. And, what is more important, Dryfoos is a prudish hayseed, contemptuous of art and loudly scornful of metropolitan elegance; in a determinedly realistic novel, he would never wear a swell's intaglio ring, but he casually picks up this one and puts it on. Certainly the scene is "unrealistic" and rather clumsy, but it is necessary on a level that has nothing to do with the small details of everyday personal and social life. Dryfoos *must* put on that ring because he is doomed, as an inhabitant of the Howells world, finally to act out his powerful hidden Oedipal relationship with his daughter, and to play his part in the series of nightmare events that now inexorably grip the major characters.

Dryfoos next rages into the magazine office and (to the surprise of no one, reader or character) encounters Conrad. He picks a quarrel with his son and strikes him, wounding him with the ring. (Thus this rather Wagnerian ring, like the procession around the magazine, binds the characters together in a circle of evil-doing that gets no one anywhere.) Conrad goes out, wanders aimlessly, and (again to no one's surprise) encounters Margaret Vance, a lovely, wealthy do-gooder, whose innocent romanticism has the most evil effects. She says to Conrad, "Can't something be done to stop it? Don't you think that if some one went among them, and tried to make them see how perfectly hopeless it was to resist the companies and drive off the new men, he might do some good?" (II, 230). After some five hundred pages of this novel, we have learned that men are in the grip of great capricious forces and had better not meddle with them; but Margaret Vance, shut off from reality by wealth, does not know that, and Conrad, who is a little crazy, will not know it. Besides, he is dreamily infatuated with Miss Vance, as we have seen. He feels that he is the appointed instrument, especially after he hears her penultimate words: "You are good and you are just!"; he ignores her last words: "But no one can do anything. It's useless!" (II, 231). Filled with extravagant ecstacy and with pity for his father, Conrad goes off. He talks to his father under his breath as he wanders along. At one point, he forgets where and why he is walking.

In an "exalted mood," in which "all events had a dreamlike simultaneity" (II, 232), he arrives at a battle between police and strikers and finds himself standing next to a man (Lindau; again, to no one's surprise) who is yelling sarcasms at the police. He is shot just before he begins to protest the clubbing of Lindau. The last thing Conrad sees is the face of the policeman, which is the face of the Howells world at its grimmest: "It was not bad, not cruel; it was like the face of a statue, fixed, perdurable—a mere image of irresponsible and involuntary authority" (II, 233). It is a frightening scene, one of Howells' most effective snapshots of evil and man destroyed by evil; but it is not a scene of martyrdom.

The martyr effect is squelched in several ways. Conrad does not go to the strike; he stumbles on it. (A Christ-symbol or martyr need not necessarily seek his fate from childhood on, but in the vicinity of his fate, he should act consciously fated.) Conrad never does anything "to save those mistaken men from themselves" (II, 232); Lindau does all the protesting. Authority does not attack Conrad; it attacks Lindau. The shot comes from "that turmoil beside the car" (II, 233)—that is, from no certain source, but symbolically from the center of confused life itself. Finally, the last image, that of the policeman's face, gives us an impression of chance and of general, undirected evil. A martyrdom demands deliberation (in the planning if not in the act) and some meaning (for the future, at least). In this scene we find only the suggestion that there is no meaning. Conrad is a chance victim, a Kafkaesque scapegoat (not a Christ-figure who is also a scapegoat). He is not a martyr; there is nothing to be a martyr to. Lindau, who really comes closer to fulfilling the requirements than Conrad does, is no martyr either.

The satire on our "literary" ideas about martyrdom continues after Conrad's death, as we see its effects. A martyr hardly exists unless he is commemorated. In the Howells world, however, people often exist only in terms of others' thoughts (recall Don Ippolito in *A Foregone Conclusion*). When the other characters think of Conrad, they think principally of themselves and their relationships to his memory, not of Conrad himself; and they think to no end. The Marches bury Conrad under their typically lengthy, uncertain analysis.

March, for example, points out to Margaret Vance that Conrad's life could not have been happy. "Perhaps he was of use in dying. Who knows?" (II, 245), March suggests. He is trying to be kindly, but he only succeeds in dissolving Conrad in his own weariness and uncertainty, and suggesting the ultimate isolation and mystery in which we live. Margaret Vance and Dryfoos are deeply shaken by Conrad's death, it is true; they both feel responsible and try to do something meaningful. Margaret Vance enters an Episcopal sisterhood; Dryfoos, in his fumbling way, tries to make amends to the dead (by having Beaton do a memorial portrait) and to the living (by letting March and Fulkerson buy *Every Other Week* at a fair price). But in context these reparations are full of irony. Miss Vance's action can change nothing, and Howells strongly underscores her helplessness by giving the last lines of the novel to the Marches' brooding over the matter. Dryfoos never gets the portrait because, good intentions or no, he is still Dryfoos, and he antagonizes Beaton so quickly that the sulky artist refuses to paint the picture. As for the magazine, March notes that Dryfoos gets much more for it by selling it to Fulkerson and him than by offering it on the open market. Even in sadness and retreat, Dryfoos is Dryfoos. "The man hasn't been changed by his son's death," says March; "it stunned, it benumbed him; but it couldn't change him. It was an event, like any other, and it had to happen as much as his being born" (II, 319). So Conrad's death has no meaning and no effects; it just happens. The theory of martyrdom—which is another attempt to codify life—is swept away in the flux of mysterious reality. When Mrs. March protests that March is fatalistic about Dryfoos, March can only say, "*I* don't know what it all means, Isabel, though I believe it means good" (II, 319).

This failure on the part of what seems to be the author's spokesman leads to another major satiric point of the novel—the knocking down of the literary conventions, and the reader's expectations, about protagonists. The Marches are the central figures in the action and in the evaluation of the action (in an anatomy both aspects are important). We expect them to be worthy actors and shrewd evaluators, but they are neither. The remorseless author shows them up and leaves the reader more at sea than ever. This pulling the rug from under the central characters is not new in Howells; it is at the bottom of his work in fiction, and shows how thoroughly the satiric impulse pervades him. In Howells' early novels, he separated actor and evaluator, keeping the latter role for himself. With *A Hazard of New Fortunes,* he returns to the observed protagonist-observer, the outgrowth of the hapless "contributor" of "A Romance of Real Life" and "Scene" twenty years earlier. The Marches themselves appear in many Howells books, and are often gently satirized; here the satire is deep.[12]

In the world of *Their Wedding Journey,* silliness does no harm. In *A Hazard of New Fortunes,* the Marches' silliness damns them and reminds us that men cannot control this terrible world. March likes to think of himself as a fine person, and his wife sees herself as the loyal helpmeet. But at the beginning of the novel, March cannot make up his mind to give up his insurance office and go to New York with Fulkerson, and his wife cannot help him. Howells resolves the situation in a typically abrupt and arbitrary way: with no warning, March is fired. The subsequent episode of apartment-hunting in New York ends not because March makes a firm and logical decision, but because he wearies of the search and rents an apartment he dislikes. In the most important crisis of March's life, the fight with Dryfoos about Lindau, Howells, as we have seen, chooses and shapes his material to make March and Mrs. March very different from the ideal. The end of the episode deserves further attention, because

[12] For a detailed summary, from another point of view, of Howells' use of the Marches, see Clara M. Kirk, "Reality and Actuality in the March Family Narratives of W. D. Howells," *Publications of the Modern Language Association,* LXXIV (1959), 137–52.

Howells develops it with care. After the Marches are reconciled to losing their position, they plan their future in one of those absurd reveries that Howells often uses as a satiric device.

> . . . They had nothing solid but their two thousand to count upon. But they built a future in which they easily lived on that and on what March earned with his pen. He became a free lance, and fought in whatever cause he thought just; he had no ties, no chains. They went back to Boston with the heroic will to do what was most distasteful; they would have returned to their own house if they had not rented it again; but, any rate, Mrs. March helped out by taking boarders, or perhaps only letting rooms to lodgers. They had some hard struggles, but they succeeded. (II, 145–46)

Here dramatics are mixed with genteel pretensions and with blind wilful indifference ("he had no ties, no chains") to the fact of human existence in bondage. A little later, when Fulkerson is sure that he can settle the quarrel, the Marches "felt themselves slipping down from the moral height which they had gained" (II, 147); but then March refuses the terms of the settlement, and Mrs. March "with a sigh . . . felt herself set beside him on that cold peak of principle again" (II, 147 f.). This oscillation destroys the Marches' dramatic, romantic stand, and makes them an involuntary burlesque. March is aware of the absurdity of his position, but still cannot control it. After Lindau quits the magazine voluntarily and Mrs. March points out that March can now go on as Dryfoos' employee, he says, "Yes, . . . I wish it didn't make me feel so sneaking" (II, 152). And after Conrad's death, when March is trying to make the unheeding Dryfoos realize that Lindau is also dead, he feels "the ghastly comedy of it" (II, 267), but cannot calm the old man.

By satirizing the Marches, Howells undercuts both the general idea that there is a system of solutions for "the ghastly comedy," and the specific opinions that the Marches offer. We can accept comments that explicate dramatic episodes, but we cannot take at face value the judgments that Lindau is a crank, that the poor are happy in their slums, that a society bud like Margaret Vance is worth any price, and so on.

Having destroyed the possibility of solutions and the authority of solvers, Howells leaves us alone with the problem of the world itself. In no other Howells book is this problem thrust so rudely in the reader's face. In *Annie Kilburn,* several years before *A Hazard of New Fortunes,* the world becomes seriously problematic (not casually or humorously so, as in the early books), but provincial Hatboro cannot stand for the whole world. New York City can and does stand for the world. Its nature, and man's relation to it, are central. That is one reason for the long and often-condemned house-hunting section in Book I. From the snug Eden of Boston, the Marches are thrown into the mystery of New York; and their effort to find a dwelling—that is, to find a viewpoint from which to survey the mystery—tells us something about the mystery and man's relation to it. Half-comic at first, their search grows boring, and finally suggests disturbingly that man cannot establish firm relations with reality and that reality is not firm anyway. Going endlessly up and down rich avenues and filthy alleys, in and out of lush flats and shabby tenements, the Marches and the reader learn more than they want to know, more than they can stand, about the grotesque disproportion between the prosperous, elaborately contrived surface of "civilization" and the unpleasant or horrible reality underneath. (In the apartment that March eventually rents, the "Jamescracks," as March calls the gewgaws that fill it, symbolize the city's strident, crowded pretense.) March's sudden, unintentional renting of Mrs. Green's apartment reveals the impossibility of making orderly decisions in New York (the world). The Marches' quiet, well-arranged life in their sedate Boston house is carefully established as a norm against which the New York life looks even worse than it does by itself. As the confused action of the novel continues, the Marches try to organize the New York world, but it still eludes them; and at the end they are simply carrying on as best they can. March feels a deep "sense of the striving and the suffering," and cannot "release himself from a sense of complicity with it" (II, 74); but feeling close to chaos does not organize that chaos, it simply makes it more frightening. In the usual Howells fashion, events burst upon the Marches; the frail surface is shattered again and again, until the Marches can have no confidence in it. The shooting of Conrad is a typical experience: sudden, shattering, unreasonable, and pointless. At other times, after one of the Marches' more complacent or unrealistic remarks about life, a living example bursts the calm like a god's warning to a blundering classical hero. A drunken whore fleeing from the police stumbles across the Marches' path just after March says that no price is too great to pay for a noble beauty like Margaret Vance; and a shabby immigrant foraging in the gutter appears in order to flaunt the Marches' sentimental fallacies about the poor. As a result the world becomes imminent, tense; it acquires a brittle, dangerous quality, and the characters must act, if they act at all, with exaggerated caution. Thus Howells satirizes and destroys our carelessly optimistic vision of the world, and leaves us with nothing certain in its place.

VII

> *. . . A demoniac presence, at the end of the lurid perspective, . . . implacable, immovable, ridiculous like all the rest, monstrous, illogical, and no more to be reasoned away than to be entreated.*

The later Howells novels reveal no qualitative change in Howells' satire, but rather a quantitative change. The world grows darker; the evil characters show more influence and energy; the good characters are generally more passive and guarded, and suffer more for their actions (when they are stupidly optimistic enough to act). I have already discussed *The Shadow of a Dream* (1890) and *The Kentons* (1902) as symbolic presentations of alienation. These books are also not mere "realism" or recordings, but satires on the simple-minded optimism not so much of Americans in particular as of human beings in general. A book like *The Kentons* may at first seem to be in the vein of local-color satire leading to Lewis, but it is more a precursor of Anderson and Faulkner; the object of the satire is the reader's false idea of the human condition, which it is the business of the novel to correct.

Similar novels of this later era are *The World of Chance* (1893), *The Landlord at Lion's Head* (1897), and *The Son of Royal Langbrith* (1904). *A Traveler from Altruria* (1894) is overtly utopian and uses an unreliable first-person narrator, but in many ways it resembles the other late novels. In these books Howells creates contrasts between theory and actuality, ideals and behavior, and from these contrasts grow the absurdity and grotesqueness that are the targets of satire. Theoretical explanations or optimistic generalities are mocked by dramatic scenes; dramatic scenes are made more portentous by the characters' feeble efforts at analysis. The use of observers and narrators focuses our attention on the radical problems of perception and interpretation, and the handling of such characters creates the typical Howells sense of puzzled concern. Thematically, too, the later books are much the same. Howells develops his usual themes of bafflement and helplessness and waste, treated in a satiric way that makes them seem sordid and small. There is a new stress on isolation. Characters and groups of characters wander about in symbolic deserts, collide, and wander apart. The city becomes not just the disturbing chaos of *A Hazard of New Fortunes,* but the lonely wilderness of modern American literature, of *McTeague, Maggie,* and *Sister Carrie.*

In these late novels, some characters again try to apply

codes to life; they are batted down more firmly than ever. In *The World of Chance,* a youthful, provincial novelist brings to New York both his first manuscript and his romantic ideas of art, and, as the experienced reader of Howells might expect, is severely chastised for his romanticism. Most of the central good characters in these novels are just cautious observers, however; even the youthful novelist eventually finds himself settling into the role of bewildered onlooker in a zany family of anarchists. Dr. Anther and Mrs. Langbrith, the middle-aged lovers in *The Son of Royal Langbrith,* spend most of their time together brooding over the miseries of their position (he cannot expose her dead husband's evil and she cannot destroy her son's blind belief in his father). When the pair do try to act, they are brutally pushed back and defeated. Westover, the central observer of *The Landlord at Lion's Head,* makes no attempt to block the growth of Jeff Durgin, the ruthless mountain-bred entrepreneur. Westover, in fact, cannot even hesitantly criticize Durgin's behavior without being told in return that his gentleman's code has nothing to do with real life. Westover does have one triumph: he gets married, to Durgin's castoff girl, in an ending that reveals Howells' conscious solicitude for his feminine audience. By the time of *The Leatherwood God* (1916), the good Howells characters are reduced to a small helpless chorus that is pushed around by a ferocious impostor and the bamboozled majority of the community. The most sensible character, a tough-minded old lawyer, cannot keep his beautiful and intelligent daughter from complete infatuation with the highly sexed swindler. To use Northrop Frye's term for the atmosphere of the strongest possible satire on the nature of things, this is "unrelieved bondage," [13] although Howells' vocabulary of symbolism is so limited that the texture of his "strongest possible satire" is pretty mild when compared to Swift's or Kafka's.

[13] *Anatomy of Criticism,* p. 238.

A Traveler from Altruria is, as I have said, very much like most of these later books in most respects; but in a few striking ways, it is different. It is not only that Howells uses the devices of the symposium, the unreliable first-person narrator, the Utopia, and the Noble Savage visiting corrupt civilization; it is not only that Howells says some very bitter things about the level of society that supported him. In this book Howells suddenly pulls himself together and says once and for all, and as strongly as he can, what he has to say. If *A Hazard of New Fortunes* is Howells' broadest work, *A Traveler from Altruria* is his deepest. It is his only modern novel, his only thoroughly symbolistic one.

Like the other Howells works, *A Traveler from Altruria* is shaped by satire; it brings out deviations from a norm of behavior and attitudes and makes those deviations look ridiculous or repellently grotesque, in the hope that the reader will reject them and pursue the norm. But *A Traveler from Altruria* goes beyond these subjects of satire. It is essentially an attack on attitudes toward opinions and on ways of thought and perception resulting from those attitudes. The snobbery and arrogance of plutocrats are nothing new, and not Howells' target anyway. He is really concerned with the stance, the outlook, of such people, for that is what determines the snobbery and the arrogance. In this sense *A Traveler from Altruria* is a modern existential work, probing beneath the transitory to the permanent, and showing ironically what it is to exist as a man.

A Traveler from Altruria (subtitled "Romance") is also like many modern works—and like some of Melville's and Hawthorne's in its combination of subtlety and intricacy with frankness of technique. Unlike the well-known major Howells fictions (*A Hazard of New Fortunes* and *A Modern Instance*, for example), *A Traveler from Altruria* does not pretend to be a plotted novel, a realistic picture, or a panorama. It is openly an artifact, without any attempts at artiness or showing off. Howells arbitrarily chooses characters and events for his own purposes, and does not try very hard to account realistically for them. Characters who are evidently allegorical are brought together for symposia that move efficiently to their conclusions and leave us ready for the next item on Howells' agenda. When representatives of different classes or outlooks meet, they waste little time on amenities but get down quickly to the matter at hand. All this is done so innocently that Howells gets away with it. Chapter Nine, for example, opens, "The next time the members of our little group came together, the manufacturer began at once upon the banker, 'I should think that our friend, the professor, here, would hardly like that notion of yours, that business, as business, has nothing to do with the education of a gentleman'" (p. 210). At the crisis of a discussion of blackballed union men, when one character is arguing that such men are expelled from society, he is instantly able to point out the window and say, "Like that fellow!," the "fellow" being "a vile and loathsome-looking tramp" (p. 176), in the narrator's phrase. This novel, then, carries to frank extremes the satirist's method of shuffling his material for effects already well developed in *A Hazard of New Fortunes*.

Howells uses this artificial method to attack many deviations. He reminds us of American ideals—esteem for labor, equal opportunity, respect for women, reverence for the free human soul, the free farmer—and shows us American actuality: labor is dishonored and bullied; women have no political rights; there is no such thing as equality; the small farmers are an angry rural proletariat; the farmer is crushed by mortgages and ends his life in the poorhouse; the Western utopia does not exist.

But all this is secondary to Howells' major purpose, first, to reveal the qualities in people that cause them to dishonor their ideas and to deny the dishonor, and second, to show that nothing can be done about these qualities. Perception is everything in Howells (I shall have more to say about this later), and the sin of the people in *A Traveler from Altruria* is that they cannot and will not see what they are doing. They are not really bad (except for one minor figure). Howells' representative businessmen and professional men are candid, articulate, courteous. With none of the pious mouthings or public-be-damned arrogance of the Vanderbilt era, Howells' banker reveals the unpleasant and often ridiculous secrets of American business life and shows how empty are American ideals. The representative broker even seems to approve of the socialists, who "don't stir up the strikers" and "are the only fellows among them [the workers] who propose to vote their ideas into laws" (p. 226).

"Trivial," not "evil," is the key word here. These characters, and most of the others, are very different from the monsters conjured up by Marxists or Byronic romantics (like Frank Norris). They are worse than bad, though; they are trivial. Especially in the romantic view, the great villains and evil men are sympathetic and perhaps even forgivable because they know the good, even if they do reject it. (The romantic interpretation of Milton's Satan is the familiar example.) Approaching existence not from the angle of youthful Byronism but from the much-despised angle of "teacup realism," Howells can see that evil in reality arises from weakness, timidity, silliness, evasiveness. Evil here is banal. Like Hannah Arendt's Eichmann, the satirized Howells character is not mean or cruel, but indifferent, denying or incapable of feeling and perception. He is hard working and often tired; he wants to succeed and be liked in the only world he knows, the only world he can imagine. He measures success in terms of what that world offers, and if he attacks that world, he will be attacking his own meaning. His psychic defenses are both sturdy and clever, and he cannot repent because he never knows that he has done anything to repent. The world created and dominated by the potential Eichmann is thus very genial, and totally dismal, like the world of the narrator in *Stops of Various Quills*, published the following year. The Howells man foreshadows Freud's adjusted neurotic and

Riesman's other-directed man. Most of all, it is a satirist's view, for it is both horrible and amusing.

Howells' businessmen may do wrong, but they are handled with understanding and some sympathy. They are victims of necessity in the grim Howells world. "Hot, worried, and anxious" (p. 2), they stumble off the resort-bound trains on Saturday night; and their one day of leisure hardly gives them time for rest, much less self-improvement. The responsibility for right perceptions and analysis rests on those who have the time to do more than emulate the Red Queen and run fast to stay in the same place. They are the clergy, the intellectuals, the women, and the artists. Howells satirizes them all. There is not much to say about the first group. It is dismissed almost contemptuously. During the symposia on the hotel veranda, the minister can do little more than comment sadly from time to time, while the businessmen listen with well-concealed boredom. Howells' virtual silence on the clergy is more damning than a long indictment.

The one intellectual, a professor of economics, is one of Howells' demonic characters. In the symposia he stands for that class of Americans that has the responsibility for intellectual truth. The professor not only fails in this duty; he aggressively devotes himself to falsehood and malice. He bears the weight of the moral satire that one expects will fall on the businessman. In the tradition of simple allegorical satire, Howells gives the professor a calculatedly ironic name, "Lumen," and a narrowly humorous character, limited to falsehood, sarcasm, and viciousness. The professor's first speech is a sarcastic thrust at Twelvemough, the romantic novelist and narrator: "What point in our polity can be obscured to the author of 'Glove and Gauntlet' and 'Airs and Graces'?" (p. 46)—a stroke no less nasty because apt. In his last appearance, the professor "beamed malignantly upon him [Homos] through his spectacles while he spoke" (p. 315). Wearing his "cold grin" (p. 210), he speaks frankly (as the businessmen do) but harshly and tritely (as they do not). He settles the fate of the elderly poor in Darwinian terms: "It is the only way to encourage independence and individuality. . . . Of course, it has its dark side. But anything else would be sentimental and unbusinesslike, and in fact, un-American" (p. 198). In former Howells novels, the human impulse to codify and to lean on the prestige of codes merely got people into personal trouble; here the impulse is used aggressively and sadistically to keep other people in trouble.

This professor often lays down the law about matters outside his competence and knowledge, yet he has nothing to say about his own field. During a long discussion of the value of college education to businessmen, the latter are objective and shrewd; but the professor, the only educator in the group, says not a word. During the Altrurian's long speech about his home (Chapters XI and XII), Lumen interrupts several times to tell Homos the sources that he stole his material from; but the Altrurian courteously undercuts the professor by admitting resemblances to the books of More, Bacon, and Morris. The professor can be identified with William Graham Sumner or other apologists for contemporary conditions, but the noting of such sources is unnecessary. With his name "Lumen," the professor, like the hero of *The Dunciad,* stands for darkness and ignorance; and his dominance truly means the triumph of chaos. The Howells universe is chaos to begin with, and not to grapple with that chaos, but to serve it, is to insure its eternal dominance.

The American woman—that is, the white Anglo-Saxon Protestant upper-middle-class society-woman, to make a distinction that Howells was not always aware of—is satirized in the person of a Mrs. Makely, wife of a typically genial and tired New York businessman. There is nothing new in Howells' characterization of Mrs. Makely. The praiseworthy Howells woman (or *jeune fille,* usually) almost vanishes from his novels after the mid-eighties. Given the succession of harebrains, snobs, and cats who fill his later novels, it is interesting that women should have been his major audience and perhaps natural that this audience should have shrunk with the years. Mrs. Makely is false, arrogant, and trivial; she is always making what women in the Howells world make—new social situations and modifications to existing ones—and the results are generally unpleasant and disruptive. There is a touch of the Howells demonic in her. She visits Mrs. Camp, a dignified, old farm woman, and gives the affair a bad taste by her gushing and patronizing. The Altrurian, who is made to be a little dense about women, continually finds himself interrupted and jarred by Mrs. Makely. His statements about Altruria she genially contradicts with remarks like, *"I know human nature,* Mr. Homos!" (p. 117), although Mr. Twelvemough, the narrator, points out that "as a cultivated American woman, she was necessarily quite ignorant of her own country, geographically, politically, and historically" (p. 135). She asks Homos to speak for charity, a task that he accepts in a simple way; but by pricing the seats high enough to eliminate the local people, she twists the affair into a demonstration of her own superiority and meddlesomeness. (The author arranges a small triumph over her by making the "natives" perfectly willing to pay heavily to hear about Altruria.)

In the earlier Howells world, Mrs. Makely's qualities are funny or even charming; in *Their Wedding Journey,* in fact, the amused author gives Mrs. March a similar bland ignorance of American life (p. 86). But we are no longer in that world of light satire. This is a world of darkness and crisis. The faults in the custodians of national morals and culture are no longer funny but dangerous. It is significant that the banker, one of Howells' most thoughtful characters, finds Mrs. Makely in bad taste, that the lower classes treat her with quiet contempt, and that her peers generally try to ignore her.

Triviality in women is less serious than triviality in artists, as Howells shows in his use of Twelvemough. This author embodies Howells' opinion of the romancers who in the 1890's stole away the audiences of Howells and James and delivered the country into the hands of Trilby, the Gibson Girl, and Little Lord Fauntleroy. But intense though Howells' feelings are on that topic, the main point about Twelvemough is much more serious. If the great majority of men are bound to their tasks, the clergy helpless, the intellectuals corrupt, and the women frivolous, then the only class left to see reality is the artists. In the person of Twelvemough, as small a man as his name implies (Howells is punning here on the bookman's duodecimo, or 12mo), Howells disposes of the artists, and that is the end of the last hope.

Twelvemough is "literary" in the bad Howellsian sense. He is not just an impersonal manufacturer of trivial romances with names like *Glove and Gauntlet* and *Airs and Graces;* he himself is trivial, frivolous, and flabby. He knows the limitations imposed upon him by his occupation, but instead of fighting them, he laughingly accepts them and settles down comfortably as a well-paid lap dog. When Homos asks him about the leisure habits of workmen, he tolerantly answers,

> "Well, . . . that opens up rather a large field, which lies somewhat outside of the province of my own activities. You know, I am a writer of romantic fiction, and my time is so fully occupied in manipulating the destinies of the good old-fashioned hero and heroine, and trying always to make them end in a happy marriage, that I have hardly had a chance to look much into the lives of agriculturists or artisans; and to tell you the truth I don't know what they do with their leisure." (p. 44)

Running away from life, Twelvemough yields the artist's privilege and task to cultivate the faculty of honest perception. There is no greater crime in Howells.

The satirist capitalizes on Twelvemough's failings by letting him tell the story. In his perception of the novel's world, the reader is chained to a narrator who is incapable of correct perceptions and resists or ridicules them when they are forced upon him. This use of the unreliable first-person narrator is

Howells' most telling blow (and suggests that he was a shrewder workman than most critics suspect). As if the world itself were not bad enough, we are made to see that world through the eyes of its representative. Indeed, because of Twelvemough's commitment to falsehood, the book almost never gets written. While working on a romance, he is asked to meet and help the Altrurian at the summer hotel. "But I had swung fairly into my story," he laments; "its people were about me all the time; I dwelt amid its events and places, and I did not see how I could welcome any guest among them, or abandon them for him" (p. 1). After tearing himself away from the fascinations of romance, Twelvemough finds Homos interesting, but is still so steeped in his own idiocies that he projects them onto Homos and implies again and again that Homos is also a romantic artist and that Altruria is his work of fiction. For Homos, who is often called a liar, this is the worst insult of all. For the reader, it is a cruel denial of the universal hope that man can do better, that he is not in bondage to his narrow known world, that there is some way out other than through spinning dreams.

In the body of Twelvemough's narration, as well as in his opinions and statements, he reveals the full horrors of the "literary" mind. He is self-centered, smug, irresponsible—an extreme distortion of the "I" in *Venetian Life* and *Suburban Sketches,* the contributor of "Scene" and "A Romance of Real Life," and Basil March in some parts of the March books. Twelvemough is best pleased with scenery and events when they arrange themselves artistically, that is, according to his literary ideas. Mrs. Camp's drab, tightly shut parlor appeals to Twelvemough "as a place where it would be very characteristic to have a rustic funeral take place," and he is "pleased to have Mrs. Makely drop into a sort of mortuary manner" (p. 155) as she asks about Mrs. Camp's health. Even though Mrs. Makely sometimes jars him, he gets along well enough with her, for she is something of an artist too, and she is a known quantity. As the book goes on, we see a great deal of her and correspondingly not so much of Homos; in fact the latter disappears for long periods (or the narrator avoids him), and then reappears only because he has been causing scandal by helping the maids or chatting with the bootblack. Twelvemough compares his task of shepherding the Altrurian to a prewar Southerner's task of sponsoring an abolitionist among slaveowners. "When the end came, I must be attainted with him" (p. 121), sighs the status-conscious romancer. And at the end Twelvemough is relieved. "His acquaintance had become more and more difficult, and I was not sorry to part with him. That taste of his for low company was incurable, and I was glad that I was not to be responsible any longer for whatever strange thing he might do next" (pp. 317–18).

Howells' strategy of narration dooms the reader to difficulty in getting at the point of the book, and then rubs in the satiric lesson in an experiential way; the reader not only hears about the evils of imperception, he suffers them. But Howells does more than this. He isolates the world of the novel from the world of Utopia (Altruria) and shows us that Twelvemough is right: only his world is real. The mountain resort and its surroundings form a complete social structure and an enclosing universe, and that universe is our prison. *A Traveler from Altruria* is finally an anti-Utopia, a satirist's Utopia. Howells, through Homos, describes Altruria at length, not in order to lead us toward practical action, but to emphasize our distance from the hope of practical action. Like Tantalus, the reader and the crowd of beaten-down New Englanders hunger for the marvellous world described by Homos; but when he is through talking, they turn around to find reality. They find, for example, Mrs. Makely gushing offensively over Homos; the professor sneering at him; the minister denying the possibility of the kingdom of God; the crowd dispersing; and life going back to its usual aimlessness. Man asks for bread and is given a stone and no hope for anything better; then he must submit to hearing ecstatic descriptions of bread. Besides being unattainable, Altruria and the Altrurian are not real. Altruria, it becomes clear, exists to remind us that we are imprisoned, and Homos exists to make us capable of realizing our situation. "There are moments," says Twelvemough, for once perceptive, "when he seems so entirely subjective with me, that I feel as if he were not more definite or tangible than a bad conscience" (p. 158). Homos is a kind of artist, then, a Howellsian artist. What he does is just as crucial, and in the end just as useless, as what Howells had been trying for twenty-five years to do in his own work.

The novel ends, then, on an implied note of total pessimism, just as it begins on one, though we cannot realize that at the time. Beginnings and endings are always significant in Howells. At the ends of novels like *A Hazard of New Fortunes, The Shadow of a Dream,* and *The Kentons,* the major characters may be buffeted and puzzled, but they do hold the center of the stage, they do carry on. In *A Traveler from Altruria,* however, the nice, perceptive people never hold anything; they have no power, never had any, never will have any. Socialism may be a subject in the novel, but it is not part of the world of the novel, which is ruled by power. The businessmen who run this world can allow Homos to speak to the throng of restless workers and farmers because these weaklings have no chance of putting Altrurian ideas into action. Twelvemough himself, though no more than a toady, speaks the language of contempt and indifference that goes with absolute power exercised in a closed world. At the beginning, you will recall, he is irritated at being taken from his petty work by his obligations to Homos. At the end, as I have noted, he is glad to get rid of the Altrurian, and remarks with contemptuous indifference, "I think he remained very popular with the classes he most affected. . . . As for the more cultivated people who had met him, they continued of two minds upon both points [that Altruria exists and that Homos is an Altrurian]" (p. 318). Altruria vanishes and leaves us in the grip of casual cattiness. This is the ultimate irony and horror for Howells: to be imprisoned inside the mind of a romantic novelist. This is Howells' penal colony, a world of passive victimization, the last stage of satire.

CHAPTER III

THREATS AND SALVATIONS: THE HOWELLS DEMON AND THE HOWELLS ARTIST

"He was the coolest and slickest devil!"
I don't know where he got it."

It is significant that Howells' satire on code-making and code-using reaches its peak in a story told by a real artist, a professional romancer. Twisting and degrading the gift of perception can go no farther. But these real and figurative artists, from Twelvemough to Mrs. Corey, are second in importance to the group of characters that I call "demons"—the people who not only twist reality but do so to dominate others. A Twelvemough is catty and indirectly harmful; a Howells demon is sadistic and deliberately, purposefully harmful. Such characters personify Howells' worst horror, his sense of evil as a powerful force bursting the calm surface and disrupting the frail structure of meaning created by harassed man. I have discussed his sense of the alien demonic in nature: the immanent force not only destructive but seemingly malignant, and growing more aggressive with each novel. The demonic character is a living concentration of this incomprehensible, frightening force. Some of these characters are quite obviously charged with what Howells could not name but which we now call libido, and all of them reveal Howells' instinctive but inarticulate recognition of this force, which he knew—and feared—because it worked in him too. Howells the prude is also Howells the creator, the father, the double, of the potent entrepreneur (Jeff Durgin), the stallion-like charismatic preacher (Dylks in *The Leatherwood God*), the sex-hungry young woman (Marcia Gaylord, Christine Dryfoos), the sadistic teaser (Bittridge, Breckon, Trannel in *The Kentons*).

The gradual growth and domination of these demons account for much of the darkening of the Howells world. These characters are traditionally "devilish"—intelligent, energetic, inscrutable, charming, ruthless, sadistic—but in the Howells world there is no God present to counter them, and their rising strength is paralleled exactly by rising darkness. These characters are a satirist's strategy for undermining blind faith in the power of goodness and the goodness of power; they undercut the nineteenth century's Byronic-Nietzschean adoration of the will as means and as end.

Some of the later demons are true villains, reducing the Howells novel to melodrama, but in the earliest books the demonic qualities are weak and hidden. Miles Arbuton, the snobbish Bostonian of *A Chance Acquaintance,* is the first in the line. To look at him reveals both the mildness of the early Howells and the continuity of his thinking. Arbuton is often arrogant, insolent, and abrupt, but when he is, he is sorry; he does not feel that his bad feelings are really him, for he sees himself as a gentleman. Of course he is heavily satirized both for his errors and his self-deceit, but nevertheless he is no open villain. At any rate, the subterranean forces that drive the Howells demon are seen in a favorable light in this first novel. The heroine continually wishes that Arbuton would act more "natural," and self-forgetfulness does improve him. When the passengers on the Saguenay steamer are invited to throw pebbles at a cliff, "suddenly Mr. Arbuton felt a blind, stupid, irresistible longing to try his chance. . . . As it struck against the cliff with a shock that seemed to have broken all the windows on the Back Bay, he exulted in a sense of freedom the havoc caused him." But "the next moment Mr. Arbuton hated them all" (p. 76) for seeing him outside his shell. Retreating into it, he spends the rest of the novel being pompous and unpleasant. The strong defense of the natural man is only momentary euphoria, not the mature Howells.

In most ways *The Lady of the Aroostook* is so much like *A Chance Acquaintance* that the changes in the handling of the demonic are highly significant. Again the arrogant Harvard Brahmin meets the simple, shrewd, small-town girl under unusual circumstances, and is smitten; but this time, in addition to providing a happy ending, Howells removes the strong unconscious forces from the hero, embodies them in a minor character, and makes them evil. The evil, as well as the character, is minor; the topic is not yet a major one in Howells' thinking. Staniford, the hero, is arrogant, but is polite at all times and puppyish when in love. The bad character, a Mr. Hicks, is no more than a pest. An alcoholic banished by his despairing father, Hicks slinks endlessly about the ship under Staniford's cold eye, finally gets some liquor, and makes an embarrassing scene. At its climax he swings wildly at Staniford, falls overboard, and is rescued by the disgusted Brahmin. On the surface all this is trivial romantic melodrama of the sort that Howells attacked in his criticism. But Hicks *is* significant, although the author does not seem to know why. After the squabble, Howells enters the narrative, attacks Hicks as "vulgar," and then continues:

> Yet his doom lifted him above his low condition, and made him tragic; his despair gave him the dignity of a mysterious expiation, and set him apart with all those who suffer beyond human help. Without deceiving himself as to the quality of the man, Staniford felt awed by the darkness of his fate. (pp. 201–2)

There is nothing in the novel—no event, description, or speech—to justify the portentous tone of this analysis. But if we know Howells' career, we can see that Hicks embodies the first clumsy stirrings of Howells' mature feelings about the demonic and the demonic man. Howells *says* that Hicks is possessed by awful forces beyond the ken of man, but only with Bartley Hubbard is Howells able (at least in part) to *show* this possession; and the full embodiment of the demon was to come much later than that.

Hicks is merely a pest. Bartley Hubbard, created only two years later, is the first of the great destructive Howells characters. Whether they are smashing things or human relationships, what these men really destroy is meaning. Sometimes they only cast doubt on the structure of meaning that the civilized characters have built and try to live in; sometimes the demons harass and damage that structure. In any case they open before the feet of men the hell of loss of meaning, the bottomless confusion under the carefully maintained Howells surface. Bartley Hubbard is not one of the energetic amoralists who stalk grimly among the meek in the later Howells novels. He is generally passive and easygoing; his bursts of energy lack reason and control, and collapse at a touch. Several times he walks out on his wife, once to get drunk and once to go west, but each time he is soon eager to get back to Marcia, despite her jealousy, which is the outlet of a libido stronger than his own. He deserts her for good only because his pocket is picked in Cleveland and he cannot afford a return ticket. Later, he works up a plan to divorce Marcia without her knowledge; but his petty machinations are crushed by her ferocious old father, who, even in old age, exudes "demonic vigor" (p. 409) and who never forgets or relents. After this unequal encounter, Bartley retreats to a western mining town and builds a small career in yellow journalism; but Whited Sepulchre, as the name suggests, does not lack demonic energy of its own, and Bartley is soon shot by an irritated citizen, thus ending the career that begins in Whited Sepulchre's ironically named analogue, Equity. Bartley is thus not a strong or successful character, and one can find many reasons for treating him sympathetically or at least judging him no worse than many of his peers. But he is a demonic character, nevertheless; he commits evil simply by existing as a person indifferent to civilization and outside of it. The Howells world is never so secure that such a person can be ignored. Given the strong influence of chance and the frailty of the world's structure, a Bartley Hubbard is going to cause trouble sooner or later, and no one can guarantee that the trouble will be small. In addition the social fabric tends not only toward weakness but toward self-destruction; like the citizens of Twain's Hadleyburg, the people of Equity and Boston are in enough trouble without a villain, and helplessly collaborate with him when he appears. It is for these reasons that Bartley suddenly becomes a leper in Equity, that the ethical Boston journalists eventually cut him dead, and that the anonymous irritated Arizona citizen is a public benefactor. "The natural man," as Atherton calls Bartley (and Marcia, too) is no longer the ideal, as he was in *A Chance Acquaintance,* but a "wild beast" (p. 472) and a shunned catalyst.

If Bartley Hubbard can be seen as the externalization of man's horrid potentialities, Rogers, the financier and Silas Lapham's former partner, is an externalization of actualities. He is a walking conscience, or, perhaps more accurately, a familiar who has been misused and has turned on his master. The demonic character in *The Rise of Silas Lapham* is Lapham himself, for he supplies the energy that causes all the trouble; Rogers is only the spring that Lapham pushes too far and that recoils against him, passionlessly and inexorably. (Rogers is a small, mild-looking man.) At the same time, this spring partakes of the sinister qualities of the alien universe. Howells is careful, perhaps overcareful, to make this point. Rogers is repeatedly presented as an innocuous surface covering unknown capacities for evil—all of this seen by Lapham, since Rogers is part of Lapham. During several crises, Rogers plays the tempter, and not just to Lapham. Early in the novel, Rogers gets Mrs. Lapham on his side and makes her persuade Lapham to resume business relations with his former partner; later, Rogers focuses her marital suspicions by sending her an anonymous letter appropriately cryptic and portentous: "Ask your husband about his lady copying clerk. A Friend and Well-wisher" (p. 362). Rogers thus looms up as more than a personal demon; he embodies, first, the most shameful and natural impulses—greed, jealousy—that rise through the surface of the civilized mind, and, second, the shabby mechanism—self-deceit, trickery, half-honesty—with which the corrupted man conceals and uses his corruption. Perhaps it is suggestive that Rogers' first name is Milton; the basic triangle of Lapham, his wife, and Rogers recalls the Miltonic triangle of Adam, Eve, and the tempter. (The movement from innocence to knowledge is the same in both cases, but the physical movement in Howells is the opposite of the Miltonic movement from Eden to the world.)

Rogers' demonic qualities are revealed most clearly in his final long scene with Lapham. He has invited Lapham to discuss the sale of worthless properties with some "English parties." Lapham at first refuses to consider the matter, but Rogers silkily points out that talking commits him to nothing. At the meeting Lapham finds that his refusals are treated as bluff and his harsh charges against Rogers as "genuine American humor." "It appeared to him as if the very devil was in it," (p. 348), Lapham thinks, a little too appropriately. He discovers that these bland Englishmen stand ready to sell out their employers; he finds that he is going to be wooed with the most terrible of temptations: liquor. Leaving in haste and worry, he misses the final glimpse of the cloven hoof. One of the Englishmen says, " 'We hoped for an answer—'oped for a hanswer,' he corrected himself, 'at once' " (p. 351). These people are not only unscrupulous and perhaps not even English; they are sinister, baffling. This final sudden intrusion of mystery makes Lapham's visit into something almost allegorical: the temptation of a sore-beset knight in the cave of the evil magician. That the device is used by a realistic satirist does not alter but increases the nightmare qualities of the scene.

In line with the growing passivity and meekness of the

central Howells characters, the later demons are not extensions of the mind, but independent figures close to alien nature and distant from ordinary humanity. Gerrish, the dry-goods tycoon in *Annie Kilburn* (1889), is an early representative of this class and a portent of later things. Gerrish is cold, aggressive, and sadistic; his store is a hell—"The women were afraid of him, and hated him with bitterness, which exploded at crises in excesses of hysterical impudence" (p. 79). He is Howells' classic embodiment of the Protestant mercantile spirit, denying Christianity on weekdays and in his church on Sundays. But Gerrish is a limited figure. He is a self-made man, and awkwardly conscious of it; his low origins show through and are seen and mocked by the central characters. His aggressiveness is largely nervous bluster, and the local aristocratic drunk is able to tease and handle him without difficulty. The treatment of this lawyer, Ralph Putney, shows that the demonic element still has some favorable qualities for Howells. It is liquor that ruins Putney's career and makes him hit and cripple his child, but it is also liquor that gives Putney access to the truth and allows him to be frank in a world drowning in humbug.

In Beaton, the young painter in *A Hazard of New Fortunes,* Howells objectifies another demonic quality—egotism—and combines it with a natural human weakness to make a fairly mild mixture. Like Bartley Hubbard, Beaton is important for his similarity to good people, but is more troubling than Bartley because more important. Bartley is only a small-time journalist. As a highly gifted artist, Beaton ought to use his gifts of perception well, but he cannot use them even to help himself. He is presented, interminably, as a victim of his own weakness. He meddles with others only to drop them; he makes three girls (representing three different types) love him because he is bored and unwilling to work. Rather than follow through with any one idea, he sculpts, draws, etches, paints, and writes, as the wind blows him. He is so absurdly perverse, in fact, that the sly Fulkerson makes him do things by begging him not to. Beaton rejects his aged, small-town parents, and then punishes himself for it. He is complex, but he seems to take up more space than he deserves, unless we realize that, like Hicks, he stands for something very close to Howells, something feared and not quite understood. He is a tempting double, all the more fascinating for his perversity and mystery. Late in the novel, Howells goes to the limits of his techniques of analysis, and probes at Beaton in an awkward, pre-Freudian manner:

> Then the consciousness of her [Christine Dryfoos'] money entered. . . . Beaton did not put it to himself in those words, and in fact, his cogitations were not in words at all. It was the play of cognition, of sensations, formlessly tending to the effect which can only be very clumsily interpreted in language. (I, 292)

Howells often uses uncertainty as a technique, but seldom in this anxious manner. The abandonment of his usual smooth style reveals that Beaton is very close to him and to the core of mystery.

There are other demons in the novel, all of them self-defeating like Beaton and thus not "hard" examples of the type. Christine Dryfoos, like Hannah Morrison in *A Modern Instance,* is pure demonic energy, pure libido; she is often and justly compared to a wildcat. After Beaton ignores her for the last time, he nonchalantly offers to shake hands as he leaves; in a "frenzy" of yearning and loss, "she flashed at him, and with both hands made a feline pass at the face he bent toward her" (II, 325). Fortunately, she lacks mind, the essential partner of energy in the Howells devil. Her father is equally energetic and somewhat more intelligent; he has the small cunning of a provincial businessman and moves in a much wider world than Christine, so he is in a position to do much damage. He does that, but he does it largely to himself. As I have already noted in more detail, he destroys his old life, puts his wife and daughters into social limbo, and destroys his only son's will and then, indirectly, his life. Dryfoos is dangerous, but we must sympathize with him, for with all his faults he is one of us, not one of the real demons.

The demonic characters of the early 1890's are also more victimized than victimizing. Northwick, the miserable embezzler in *The Quality of Mercy* (1892), and the characters in *A Traveler from Altruria* are so much the prisoners of their own views that they are like machines wound up and put into motion. What we fear from their example is not them, but the universe. Professor Lumen, the sarcastic economist, does line up with the really bad characters; he has malice and the force to make it felt. The narrator, Twelvemough, lacks the intelligence and strength to be a villain; he is an accomplice. In *The Shadow of a Dream,* as in *A Traveler from Altruria,* the characters are victims, but one of them introduces an ominous theme: the dominating power of the dead. Faulkner, a friend of Basil March, dies early in the book, but throughout, he is the major force, "a demoniac presence," March thinks, "implacable, immovable, ridiculous like all the rest [of the characters], monstrous, illogical, and no more to be reasoned away than to be entreated" (*SD,* p. 146). This excited string of adjectives is a major intensification of the Howells theme of bondage.

In the novels of the later 1890's, the demons take over the world. Jeff Durgin, the major character of *The Landlord at Lion's Head* (the novel does not have a protagonist) is, as it were, the son of Bartley Hubbard; he has the strengths, greatly increased, and lacks the weaknesses. He has energy, charisma, malice, social smoothness, humor, intelligence, and flawless powers of perception; he never loses control and he never forgets. He is entirely frank, and he is a mystery. This remarkable creation is handled with elaborate care by Howells. He discards the Marches, with all their limitations, and adopts as the observing center a bachelor painter, a man of trained perceptions, few illusions, and no inhibiting ties. But despite Westover's talents and opportunities, he cannot comprehend Durgin. During a walking trip through the backwaters of the northern Appalachians, Westover meets Jeff, then a small boy living on a miserable farm with his strong mother and consumptive father and brother. On this occasion Durgin first greets Westover rudely, and when he leaves, bombards him with green apples. Durgin, then, is naturally bad. He is himself; the admonishments of his mother have no more effect on his character than the physical examples of his father and brother have on his sturdy body. As the farm is slowly transformed into a summer resort and Westover watches, Durgin grows up and goes to Harvard (an essential confrontation with the world, though he wants to stay home and run the hotel).

The encounter of Jeff with Boston gives Howells a chance, as in *A Modern Instance,* to undermine moral authority and account for the demon's contempt for it, while keeping the demon's inherent badness well in mind. Durgin becomes involved with a fast Boston society girl and her alcoholic, clubman brother. Howells goes to great trouble to show that the involvement is not Durgin's fault. He "compromises" her by being alone with her in her house at dawn, but what really happens is that he is dragged into the house by her drunken brother, who passes out and leaves them "alone" in a technical sense. Later, Jeff kisses the girl brazenly, because she brazenly dares him to. When Westover tries to chide Durgin for his social errors, the latter is amused and bluntly derides his ideals. The reader is left in a moral dilemma, unable to condemn Durgin or absolve him. But nature backs Durgin: his well-insured hotel burns down just when he needs the money to build a new one, and no one can doubt that the fire is accidental. Durgin does lose his country girl to Westover, but he doesn't care, because he is incapable of love and has found a rich wife anyway. At the end, Durgin is biding his time up in the hills. He knows his own strength and ruthlessness, and he knows us, the nice and not-so-nice city people, and holds us in contempt. By leaving Durgin's real achievements to the future, Howells creates a sense of overhanging doom, more terrible in effect than a Dreiserian recital of actual accomplishments, and by making Durgin unhuman, indifferent to people and standards, Howells cuts off the last possibility that the doom can be evaded or displaced.

The Kentons, the next novel after *The Landlord at Lion's Head,* complements it. Jeff Durgin is the big-time combination of natural energy and indifference; the several villains in *The Kentons* are small-time combinations of energy and open malice. The terror in *The Landlord at Lion's Head* is all in the future; in *The Kentons* it is all around. Jeff Durgin has some clear reasons, even some socially recognized reasons, for his attitudes and actions; the villains in *The Kentons* have no justification in conditions or psychology for their behavior. The world of *The Kentons,* then, is the modern world of gratuitous cruelty, of Kafka and Camus. It is also the modern world of sexuality, or, more accurately, the Freudian world of libido, the energy that appears in many guises. The novel has four loci of this force: the reporter Bittridge, the major demon; Trannel, the Cook's tourist who torments Boyne Kenton in Holland, a lesser demon; Breckon, the young minister who is infected with malice but not defeated by it; and Ellen Kenton, the bewildered girl half-crushed by lust and jealousy, the feminine manifestations of demonism. These characters seem to have little in common unless we realize that they all embody the demonic or libidinal force issuing now in sadism, now in ill-timed wit, now in stifled yearning. *The Kentons* is thus Howells' major focus of demonism in man, as *A Hazard of New Fortunes* is his major anatomy of demonism in nature.

Bittridge is carefully equipped with the marks of the major Howells devil. He erupts "suddenly" (*K,* p. 8) into the world from an unknown village; he has no human ties, except for a mother dim to the point of being nonexistent except in what he coaches her to do; he calls Ellen Kenton "an angel" (p.

50); he holds Judge Kenton fixed "with a helpless fascination" (p. 62); even the tough Mrs. Kenton feels "something fascinating" (p. 82) in him. But in a sense he is a small-time fiend; he cannot remain serious, even when his career depends upon it. And because he has no motive for malice—no wealth to grasp or snubs to avenge, like Jeff Durgin, or nagging wife to attack, like Bartley Hubbard—Bittridge's acts are unfocused, gratuitous, arising solely from his psychological needs, which are invisible to us and apparently unknown to him. Bittridge is a modern, post-Freudian character, and if Howells had been more aware of what he had in Bittridge, this villain, who pops in and out of the story a few times and then disappears, might have been one of the milestones of modern fiction.

But Howells is interested in other matters. Developing the idea of the continuity of demonism, he shows that it is everywhere, everywhere different and everywhere the same, and thus satirizes our, and the Kentons', silly hope that we can escape from it. No sooner is Bittridge exorcised (by Kenton's older son, with a horsewhip) than Breckon appears to take his place. This teasing young minister, however, is carefully designed as a foil to Bittridge, as an example of the normal man sick with demonism but capable of surmounting it with the help of the great Howells virtue, perception. After teasing Ellen Kenton to tears, Breckon realizes that he has suffered "one of those accessions of temperament, one of those crises of natural man. He had allowed his levity to get the better of his sympathy" (p. 131). He purges and prostrates himself, is slowly forgiven by the understandably suspicious Kentons, and finally marries Ellen (after several hundred pages of complications irrelevant to him).

The other demon, Trannel, provides a counterpoint to both Bittridge and Breckon. As a mere "Cook's tourist," he has no ties or identifying marks at all. In a sense he plays the cruelest trick of all. He does not arouse sexual energies in a grown woman, or tease an aroused woman. He stirs up desires in an adolescent boy who does not know that such desires exist and has no idea of what is being done to him. Trannel plays upon Boyne Kenton's ill-concealed yearnings for the young queen of Holland, and finally persuades him that the queen, passing in her state carriage, has beckoned to him and wants him to help her. (Deliberately created false perception is, we must always remember, one of the unforgivable Howells sins.) Trannel never mentions to Boyne the word "love," which Boyne would consider silly. Boyne runs out to the carriage, is collared by the police, who naturally take him for an assassin, and is dragged off to the police station. Only the accidental appearance and tearful intercession of his sister Ellen save him from the nightmare he is in. In the meantime Trannel, who had appeared from nowhere, has of course disappeared for good.

Both Boyne and Ellen are willing victims; they are also infected with the demonic virus. In Boyne's case the cause is adolescence, and at the end of the novel we are assured that he will become a self-possessed man like his brother, who is sickened by his ferocious whipping of Bittridge. Ellen's case is more serious. Like Christine Dryfoos and Marcia Gaylord, she is possessed. This novel being quite firmly an anatomy, Ellen is much more analytical than Marcia or Christine. "Oh, it's like a drunkard!!" she moans. "I suppose they know it's killing them, but they can't give it up! Don't you think it's very strange, momma? I don't see why I should be so. It seems as if I had no character at all, and I despise myself so! . . . Sometimes I think the best thing for me would be to go into an asylum" (p. 34). And she agrees sadly when Boyne, in one of his fits of intelligence, says of feelings about persons, "Sometimes it seems like a kind of possession, doesn't it?" But she adds, "It seems more like that when we like them" (p. 254). The good characters, then, perceive that for them the demonic force is foreign and dangerous, whereas for the others, the haters, the force is congenial.

In Royal Langbrith, Howells develops the ultimate combination of energy, malice, coldness, and invulnerability, a combination that leaves his wife in a lifelong stupor, turns his son into a wilfully imperceptive fantasist, and drives his friend and partner to opium. In the idealized but revealing relief made for Royal's son, James, the dead entrepreneur's face "wore not the old-fashioned Websterian frown of the ante-bellum Americans . . . but had almost an eager smile, full of business promptness, and yet with refined intelligence, a sagacity instantly self-helpful, but ultimately not unkindly" (*SRL*, p. 197). (That the relief is actually based on James only reinforces the theme of domination by the past.) The reality behind the pleasant smile is explained by Royal's cranky older brother in an eruption that breaks the surface of the story and shatters James's world view. "He was the coolest and slickest devil! I don't know where he got it. He had the trick of making other folks do his dirty work—and he was full of that, I can tell you—and keeping such a hold of 'em that they never had the chance to squirm out of the blame" (p. 327). Royal's malice is for the long haul, unlike Bittridge's random cruelty; and Royal's cool planning, unlike Durgin's, is wholly shaped by the urge to hate and destroy. (With the help of his inventive partner Hawberk, Royal's mills did so well that he had no need to swindle Hawberk out of his share, much less drive him to drug addiction.) Rather than marry for prestige, Royal chose his wife from the ranks of his "female operatives," because he needed a woman who was stupid, helpless, malleable, and grateful even for his cruelty. The novel is so dominated by this real, unreal figure that it is close to being a ghost story, an ironic reversal of James's "The Jolly Corner," which was written within the same decade, and which also records the horrors of constant pressure from disembodied malevolence. In the James story, however, the hero seeks out and faces his enemy, and survives the ultimate moment to gain the prize of love. The young Langbrith evades the truth until it is forced on him, and Royal

Langbrith's contemporaries are never able to defeat him or his memory.

The last demonic character is Dylks, in *The Leatherwood God* (1916). He has all the demonic characteristics, stripped of superfluities, placed in the elementary setting of a frontier village, and treated in the simple manner appropriate to the artist's old age. Like so many of the other demons, Dylks erupts out of nowhere, "a stranger that nobody seen before, and nobody suspicioned was there until they hearn him" (p. 10). He leaps to his feet in a village church and snorts "Salvation!" and then " 'Hooff!'—like there was a scared horse got loose right in there among the people" (p. 9). Dylks goes on to fulfil these images of devil and stallion. He claims godhead, accumulates a large fanatical following, and turns the village into chaos. He is not the only Howells devil with religous powers (turned inside out, of course), but he is the only one to work directly as a perverted prophet. With effortlessly perfect insights into people, he gets cruel pleasure from seducing the minds of the men and the bodies of the women, and inevitably he is called a devil by the few rational characters in this near-allegory. As a "scared horse" he foreshadows Lawrence's St. Mawr: enigmatic, portentous, powerfully sexual.

Later in the story, however, we are shown the limits of demonism for the seventy-nine-year-old author, and we realize why Dylks was described as "scared." He is not independent; he is only a mechanism, part of a process. After he has been defeated by the local cynics and bully-boys (not by the perceptive rationalists, who are helpless), Dylks admits, "You think I had to lie to them, to deceive them, to bewitch them. I didn't have to do anything of the kind. They did the lying and deceiving and bewitching themselves, and when they done it, they and all the rest of the believers, they had me fast, faster than I had them" (p. 173). And many years later, Squire Braile, the shrewdest man in town, realizes that what kept Dylks "from playing the *very* devil" (p. 229) was fear. Any human embodiment of the demonic forces in nature has definite limits, we are told in effect. A devil-man is restricted by the smallness of human nature. But the Squire also notes that Dylks's flock kept right on believing after his exposure and after his death. The final and ominous point, then, is that by working through a combination of men, the demonic force can transcend the limits of the individual and pass beyond all limits. The ultimate villain is not man, but men, not the devil, but his accomplices. The catalyst-devil in the Howells novel need only open the tap and let the energy pour out of men; or, alternatively, he need do no more than seduce some one in a key position (a Twelvemough or a Lapham) and then let matters take their course toward chaos and destruction. In events great and small, in psychologies of man and society, and in art, the twentieth century has supported Howells' insight that the demonic can erupt from the most unexpected and innocent social situations, and that the most appalling destructiveness lies fallow in the most ordinary men. What Howells realized but could not afford to emphasize, Hitler was able to grasp ardently and offer to a generation of Eichmanns. In the theatrical phrase, Howells threw away his point, which was to interest the next generation of novelists and become an obsession later. Although no one can say now that Howells was not aware of evil or that he did not objectify it in his art, he can be criticized for lacking serendipity, the ability to know when one is on to a good thing.

II

. . . to look at life with the same wholesomely fantastic vision.

Most of Howells' characters belong to the two classes I have discussed: the self-destructive "artists" who try to codify and manage the inscrutable world, and the demons who badger and destroy the helpless members of the first group. There is a third group, who manage neither themselves nor others, but instead, try to understand the world and man, mind their own business, and occasionally help others. In the Howells world, they are the real heroes—or rather heroines, for almost all of them are women, not passionate ones (like Marcia Gaylord) but cool, self-possessed creatures. Some are more perfect than others; some stray from the type occasionally and then must suffer as the acting, codifying Howells characters do. There is no point in going over all the characters of this sort; there is at least one in each Howells novel. Like most of the non-demonic Howells types, these perceptive characters occur at their best in Howells' middle period. There is not much room for uninvolved observers in the world of the later Howells novel.

The true Howells artist tempers whimsy with enough human concern to avoid the pitfall of coldness (which Howells equated with sadism) and with enough objectivity to avoid the other pitfall of reckless involvement, which leads at least to trouble and often to defeat. The earliest Howells characters—the "I" of *Venetian Life* and *Suburban Sketches,* the "contributor" in *Suburban Sketches,* the Marches in *Their Wedding Journey*—are all playful to the point of tedium (and are sometimes chastised for their whimsy). These early examples are not perfect examples of any type, for Howells' methods and attitudes are still in flux. As I have shown, the Howells who creates the contributor has begun to satirize the mind that mechanically stuffs every perception into a "literary" pigeonhole, for such behavior leads at best to ludicrous errors of judgment and at worst to isolation from man. The Marches of *Their Wedding Journey,* however, are almost as literary as the contributor; every sight or meal or conversation is an occasion for a joke or literary reference or recited poem.[1] But the Marches' near-total

[1] See John K. Reeves, *op. cit.,* for a full discussion of these matters from another point of view.

alienation from the American scene makes their manner irrelevant. In fact, the whole book is irrelevant; it is a dead end. A critic observing Howells after *Their Wedding Journey* might well have wondered if Howells really had anything to say.

Howells' answer is *A Chance Acquaintance* and its heroine, Kitty Ellison. She is important in Howells' general approach to perception, but here I want to look at her from a narrower angle. She is carefully groomed and then used as an ideal character—a human being both alien and involved, satiric and sympathetic, analytic and self-analytic, capable after a crisis of noting, "I seemed to be like two persons sitting there, one in agony, and one just coolly watching it" (p. 272). As an orphan, she is something of an outsider (like Bartley Hubbard later), but she is lovingly brought up by her uncle in a large genial family, so that she is neither bitter and indifferent (Bartley comes from an orphanage) nor spoiled (Bartley had large, unearned gifts from an anonymous benefactor). Her uncle and cousin "educated her in those extreme ideas, tempered by humor, which formed the character of himself and his family," but "laughed at her when she needed ridiculing" (p. 5). Although the whole family worked for the Underground Railroad, they all found "droll points" in it, laughed at "grotesque mental or physical traits" in the runaway slaves, and had "irreverent" names for "the humorless abolition lecturers" (pp. 5–6). Kitty learned "to look at life with the same wholesomely fantastic vision" (p. 6). This phrase "wholesomely fantastic vision" is a key to Howells' development and his lifelong method. "Vision" stresses the idea of perception by a penetrating and imaginative mind; "fantastic" suggests the driving energy of whimsy applied to the perception; and "wholesomely" reveals Howells' method of controlling the energy of whimsy by referring to the Howells norm of decorum and moral seriousness (to be distinguished from the solemn priggishness of an Arbuton).

The combination of the wholesome norm and the fantastic vision is satire. Kitty Ellison is a satirist, and of the right sort. She perceives and ridicules, but she does so without cruelty; the "malice" in the following passage is only the satisfaction of the satirical temperament.

> . . . She helped to give some grotesque interpretations to the various scenes of the melodrama, while Mr. Arbuton stood beside her . . . ; and a spice of malice in her heart told her that he viewed this drolling, and especially her part in it, with grave misgiving. (p. 82)

She tells the dubious Brahmin that she would like to be a painter, "for it would give you a right to be a vagrant, and you could wander through the world, seeing everything that was lovely and funny, and nobody could blame you . . ." (p. 145). Like "wholesomely fantastic vision," these remarks suggest Howells' idea of the proper artist: the unattached sympathetic perceiver, capable of seeing both the truly romantic ("lovely") and the grotesque ("funny") sides of life. The curious phrase "and nobody could blame you" suggests that like Twain, Howells felt uncertain and faintly guilty about the role of the artist in the Gilded Age, and needed both a disguise and an apology. Arbuton, the representative here of the Boston intelligentsia, sees the artist as a serious, moralistic technician and severely puts the timid, provincial Kitty in her place. Here, then, we have the three parties that make the Howells artistic world: the genteel official artist; the vast, sluggish public whom he must uplift but not upset; and the ambiguous true artist, perceptive and evasive.

The next important proper artist in Howells does not appear until *The Rise of Silas Lapham* (1885). In *A Foregone Conclusion* and *The Lady of the Aroostook,* Florida Vervain and Lydia Blood carry on the line but are not symbols. The former effortlessly sees through the male characters Don Ippolito and Ferris, who err constantly because their perceptions are wrong and their conclusions ridiculous; she even understands her babbling mother. Although she occasionally blazes up in understandable fits of exasperation, she treats her men with the tolerance and caution of a gentle adult surrounded by children. She belongs to the line of Howells heroines, but she is so subordinate that she is not important. Lydia Blood, who coolly embarks on the "Aroostook" with a shipload of men, is a more vigorous character. Her simplicity and directness of vision would qualify her as a symbolic Howells heroine if, like Florida Vervain, she were not lacking in the keenness and reflectiveness that make Kitty Ellison a model of the type.

Penelope Lapham, Silas' older daughter, does fulfil all the requirements. Not only is she highly and properly aware of reality, she can make others see reality. She is a teacher, though she does not teach what the staid Bostonians have in mind. We can see her ability if we look at Tom Corey's changing pictures of her. When this son of a model Brahmin first sees Penelope, his perception is colored unconsciously by the contemporary "literary" ideal of feminine perfection. During this first meeting, he pays the most attention to Penelope's luscious younger sister; he looks at Penelope only because she makes one of her droll remarks, and he then "saw that she was shorter than her sister, and had a dark complexion" (*RSL*, p. 72). When Mrs. Lapham cites one of Penelope's jokes, Tom ventures, "She seems to have a good deal of humour" (p. 78). But Tom changes under Penelope's tutelage. Within a few days he is telling his unimpressed mother that Penelope has a "droll way of looking at things; or a droll medium through which things present themselves" (p. 139). Tom is improving; his alternative explanation of Penelope's nature strikes right to the core of whimsical perception. Finally, Howells presents the girl from his own point of view, to allow us to check Tom's perceptions for accuracy. He has Tom perch on the veranda rail at Lapham's summer cottage while Penelope talks.

> Her talk was very unliterary, and its effect seemed hardly conscious. She was far from epigram in her funning. She told of this trifle and that; she sketched the characters and looks of people who had interested her, and nothing seemed to have escaped her notice; she mimicked a little, but not much; she suggested, and then the affair represented itself as if without her agency. She did not laugh; when Corey stopped she made a soft cluck in her throat, as if she liked his being amused, and went on again. (p. 187)

A glance back at Kitty Ellison will show the family resemblance. The emphasis in both characters lies on deep but rapid perception, whimsical but sympathetic satire, and a determined avoidance of rigid forms. The artist courts his audience as Penelope courts Tom (the student of American sexual relationships may find it interesting that Tom does not court her), but holds himself aloof from the fawning of a Twelvemough. Tom is soon converted to Penelope's vision, and the advantages of this position are soon revealed, after Lapham makes a drunken fool of himself at the Corey's table. At first, Tom is disgusted, as the Brahmin code dictates he should be; but then his new outlook allows him to see the affair from Lapham's point of view. Later, he is able to court Penelope vigorously and then marry her against the quiet opposition of his family.

Like Penelope, the later Howells girls are generally passive mentors, of final importance to their men but of little importance in the world. This is the Howells age of bondage, when not even men, much less artists, can make headway against the world or against determined asininity. In *Indian Summer* Mrs. Bowen, like James's May Bartram in "The Beast in the Jungle," can do no more than wait patiently, with an occasional nudge, while the hero bumbles around in his private world of delusion. Colville eventually snaps out of his dream of himself as a young man capable of giving happiness to a young girl, and marries Mrs. Bowen; but a similar situation in *A Hazard of New Fortunes*, an altogether darker novel, has no such happy resolution. Beaton, the self-centered artist, flirts teasingly with Alma Leighton, also an artist, throughout the whole book; she yearns for him, at first hopefully and then bitterly. Perceptive and proud (Beaton is merely proud), she sees his unshakable triviality, but cannot plead with him and cannot abandon him. The situation endures almost to the end, in one of those painful and apparently insoluble situations that give Howells' "teacup realism" much of its cumulative effect. Near the end, Alma pulls herself together and freezes Beaton out of her life, but her triumph over him is wholly ironic.

The classic Howells girl in *A Hazard of New Fortunes* is Madison Woodburn, who with her father, a gentle caricature of the Southern Colonel, boards at the Leightons'. Howells gives her "eyes brimming with a shrewd mixture of fun and earnest" set in "an early nineteenth-century face, round, arch, a little coquettish, but extremely sensible and unspoiled-looking" (I, 151). She is, then, unmistakably a Howells girl (and a bit of an Austen girl), but obsolete (like Judge Kenton, another pre–Civil War type) in the uncontrollable chaos of the late nineteenth century. Significantly revealing the declining importance of her type in the Howells world, she has no active role in the novel. She is wholly a catalyst; she listens and watches, makes genial comments, steers conversations away from dangers and soothes her father's majestic dignity. Howells devotes some space to setting her against her father. With his fanatical devotion to "the broken Southern past" (II, 177), the colonel is absurdly irrelevant to the New York world; but because of that very fanaticism, he is like the other characters, each one lost in his private world and unable or unwilling to reach and influence the real world. But his daughter "took the world as she found it, and made the best of it" (II, 177). "The world" for her is Fulkerson, the go-getting publicist. He courts her, and she accepts him without any bothersome feelings of passion. "She trusted in Fulkerson. . . . She was not a sentimentalist, and there was nothing fantastic in her expectations; she was a girl of good sense and right mind. . . . She did not idealise him, but in the highest effect she realised him; she did him justice" (II, 177). To realize the world, to do it justice—this, not the slavish accumulation of surface facts, is what Howells meant by "realism." Like Kitty Ellison and Penelope Lapham, Madison Woodburn *is* Howells: the artist, the only true judge of the world, is a woman, imprisoned in a passive, secondary position, while demonic men rip up surface and meaning.

The line of women artists really ends here. Even Madison Woodburn is not a strong figure. She is more talked about than talking. In *The Landlord at Lion's Head* and *The Son of Royal Langbrith,* there are similar characters: Cynthia Whitwell, the sweet mountain girl who rejects Jeff Durgin and marries the narrator, and Hope Hawberk, who gaily endures her father's opium addiction and marries James Langbrith. Both girls have the Howells gift of seeing through the defenses and bluster of man. Each lives in Howellsian decorum and guides her man toward it. (Cynthia fails utterly with Jeff Durgin, as one expects.) But neither character is exemplary, for neither girl is sufficiently self-conscious and discursive to be an artist.

CHAPTER IV

HOWELLS THE CRAFTSMAN OF PERCEPTION

. . . a kind of vision, magnificent at times, and at other times full of indignity and pain.

IT SHOULD BE CLEAR by now that perception is one of Howells' great concerns. In my opinion, it is more than that. It is his central concern, his theme, the key to his sense of existing. My task here is to approach directly this theme of perception, show its meaning for Howells, and examine the ways he handles it—and thus indirectly show that Howells is more of a thinker, a technician, and a modernist than most readers and critics have ever suspected.

The Howells novel is not only satire, but a drama of perception.[1] Given the Howells world, that is natural. If the world is alien, we must try to get back into it, or at least, for the sake of sanity, establish the nature of the world and our relationship to it. When Putney, the shrewd lawyer in *Annie Kilburn,* says that truth is "a constitutional thing, and you can't separate it from the personal consciousness" (p. 302), he is making a point that applies to any Howells situation, and indeed establishing one *raison d'être* of the Howells novel. As

[1] Working along parallel lines, William McMurray has brilliantly developed this idea in his article "Point of View in Howells' *The Landlord at Lion's Head.*" Mr. McMurray has summed up the whole matter very well: "In his fiction, early and late, Howells saw reality as . . . mixed: rather than something fixed, single, and pure, reality, he found, was complex, multiple, and pragmatically made by men in their continuing experience, in their growing perception of the world and of themselves" (p. 213). In *The Landlord at Lion's Head,* the mountain of the title symbolizes reality and must be comprehended by Westover in his art if he is to grasp reality; since perception is relative, no "perception of all of Jeff Durgin is humanly possible" (p. 209). My approach to perception somewhat resembles McMurray's, but I emphasize Howells' artistic methods of stimulating and controlling perception, and his anxieties about perception and reality.

we have seen, failure and errors in perception create the satiric actions of many of his novels. In the later ones, errors do not make so much difference to the characters, for they are in trouble with the hostile world whether they perceive correctly or not. But even though Howells' satire is aimed directly at the reader's mistaken notions about life, Howells still labors to establish the relationship between perceiving man and perceived world. This investigation justifies my calling the Howells novel an "anatomy."

"Significance" is another key term related to perception. In Howells' world of relativism, significance must be created. This need is of central importance in Howells' art. Here as elsewhere Howells is the heir of Melville, whose persona says, "And some certain significance lurks in all things, else all things are little worth" (*Moby-Dick,* Chap. XCIX). Like Melville, Howells agrees all the time with the second half of the statement; but also like Melville, Howells cannot sustain a belief that the "certain significance" is always pleasant or recognizable, or there at all. In the first part of his career, Howells deals with the problem of creating significance; he seeks ways of placing an observer so that he may realize the world. At best, the observer then experiences that momentary fusion with the world that critics, following Joyce, now call "epiphany" but for which Howells had no word; more often, the observer undergoes a "negative epiphany," the sudden and total recognition of man's alienation from the world. Later in Howells' career, the problem becomes one of showing the pressure and hostility behind the apparently bland surface of reality; in this case the significance already exists, but must be surprised and separated from its shield, the enigmatic surface of things, while at the same time Howells makes us experience that bland surface.

Howells' emphasis on significance is inescapable. His early works abound in terms like "glamour," "fantasy," "pathos," "novelty," and "charm," which refer to moods created by, or creating, perception. Being in a holiday mood, for example, causes "glamour . . . to be cast upon familiar objects" (*SS*, p. 127). In Montreal the youthful Marches cultivate the "charm of strangeness" (*TWJ*, p. 247) and so zealously pursue "the fantastic" and "the pathetic" that *Their Wedding Journey* becomes Howells' *Mardi,* a voyage in search of perception and meaning. In his mature years, Howells goes beyond the linear action and the vocabulary of the picturesque, and designs his plots (ragged as they are) around significance. In the isolated New England world of Equity, everything depends on "impressions" (a common word in *A Modern Instance*), self-delusions, changes in interpretation, and so on. When the citizens of Equity suddenly turn on their favorite, Bartley Hubbard, and cast him out, nothing has changed in the town's perception of Bartley; but the significance of that perception has changed utterly. The situation in *A Traveler from Altruria* is similar. The sadness of the novel arises, not from mere differences of opinion about corporations, strikers, and other issues of the day, but from the staring fact that such differences arise from radical differences of perception and are irreconcilable. Working in a lighter way, the same fact of existence creates the mixups and conflicts in *The Rise of Silas Lapham, Indian Summer,* and the other partially optimistic novels. Perception and its significance in these novels work smoothly both as elements in the traditional machinery of comedy and as implicitly serious themes.

For Howells, perception has many uses. It creates the world by constantly recreating it. Like Whitman and other American symbolists, Howells does not impose form or views on the world, but seeks for new stances "in which the world takes on new shapes." [2] Like Poe's Usher and Faulkner's Compsons,

[2] Charles Feidelson, *Symbolism and American Literature* (Chicago, 1953), p. 27. These efforts of Howells to relate himself to his own world and to find meaning in it place him in the major American literary tradition that sought to evade the aesthetic implications of Hartley's association psychology and Scotch common-sense philosophy. (See William Charvat, *The Origins of American Critical Thought, 1810–1835* [Philadelphia, 1936], and Terence Martin, *The Instructed Vision: Scottish*

Howells characters often create their own mad worlds, and even the most thoughtful Howells character makes enough errors so that his world is essentially a private one. In the later Howels novels, like *A Hazard of New Fortunes,* where the real world cannot be reached or grasped even by the greatest efforts, the characters' worlds are automatically private, and only a slight tendency toward solipsism sends characters like Dryfoos and Colonel Woodburn off into worlds that are not just separate but unreachable.

That perception creates truth follows almost automatically. In *The Landlord at Lion's Head,* there is an incident that reveals this truth all the better for not being of crucial importance. Mrs. Vostrand, a social-climbing widow, rejects Jeff Durgin's suit of her daughter when Jeff is poor, but when he gets up in the world she is ready to accept him—so ready, in fact, that she totally misinterprets the facts about Jeff. After the artist Westover, who stands closest to reality in the novel, writes her the truth about Jeff—his arrogance, contempt, amorality—Mrs. Vostrand at once cables: *"Kind letter received. Married today,"* and then writes about "your generous

---

Common Sense Philosophy and the Origins of American Fiction [Bloomington, Indiana, 1961].) The cultural lag here makes it seem as if the writers of the "American renaissance" had never lived. Like Bryant and Irving, Howells had to overcome the belief that America was (perhaps fortunately) doomed to produce second-rate art because American life, young and sprawling, lacked the postulated density of historical and natural associations. (Recall that the classic statement of this position, in James's *Hawthorne,* appeared in 1879, almost thirty years after *Moby-Dick* and *The Scarlet Letter,* and sixty years after "Rip Van Winkle.") Howells' solution to the problem in his early books (see above, pp. 32, 57.) closely resembles Irving's and Bryant's: "Irving discovered that the American past actually did possess vitality if he adapted his treatment of it to the temper of his own mind and reassured himself and his readers, during his early years, with the knowledge that he did not take it very seriously. Bryant discovered that he could make serious use of external nature if he adapted his treatment of it to the stream of associations he found in his own mind and could normally anticipate in the minds of his readers. . . . Neither stirred any considerable depths in their personal reference." Leon Howard, *Literature and the American Tradition* (Garden City, New York, 1960), p. 87. The solution that I am discussing in this chapter belongs to Howells' maturity.

and *satisfactory* answer" (p. 437). Like the citizens of Equity, Mrs. Vostrand has all the facts plainly before her but perceives only what she wants to perceive, and out of that makes her own truth. Mrs. Makely and Twelvemough in *A Traveler from Altruria* are similarly dishonest and out of touch with the truth. In fact, the honest Howells character is rare. There is a handful of honest girls—Penelope Lapham and the rest. But we must agree with the commenting author that Dr. Anther in *The Son of Royal Langbrith* was "a character of rare strength," because he knew himself and "he could accept the logic of his self-knowledge" (p. 301). The rest of Howells' characters are driven by the demonic in its innumerable manifestations.

When the Howells figure does allow perception to work freely against his preconceptions and opinions, the result is less likely to be insight than confusion and error leading to opinions and thence to action. Thus perception creates the Howells novel. Thus, also, it creates the form (or lack of Jamesian "form") of the Howells novel. When action depends on perception, then action must wait on perception; and although Howells fudges his realism a good deal, he is still committed to presenting a world that takes its own time about offering chances for significant perception. This accounts in large part for the sluggishness of his novels. The ways in which he cheats in order to make life yield an above-average number of chances for perception reveal his purposiveness and his skill, and the limitations of his skill.

To deal with Howells' methods for creating perception, we need a calculus rather than a static descriptive geometry. From the smallest contact to the greatest epiphany, perception occurs for Howells only through change in the perceiver or the thing perceived, and the perception itself is only a momentary condition. The perceiver remains, and may be permanently changed by his perception, but the perception dies. This sense of the momentary oppresses Howells. It gives rise to some of his devices for fixing reality, and it yields the parade of observers who stroll through the Howells canon and try anxiously for a perception and then for the next perception, like a child grasping at snowflakes and hoping always to keep the next one.

Movement is Howells' principal device for causing perception, and thus for reaching the world and its significance. Either the world moves before the observer, or he moves before the world. The world's characteristic movement is the sudden upthrust of frightening reality through the bland surface of the world—or, in temporal terms, through the uneventful continuity of the world in time. (In order to create this effect, Howells must first have the uneventful flow, and that is another reason for the dullness and repetitiousness of long stretches of his novels.) I have already noted exploding events of this sort: the frightening apparition of the tramp in *A Traveller from Altruria,* the whore's scurrying across the path of the Marches in *A Hazard of New Fortunes,* the infectious children suddenly surrounding the innocent holiday-makers in "A Day's Pleasure," the repeated raids on the Kentons by the grinning demon Bittridge. In *The American Novel and its Tradition,* Richard Chase notes the startling way in which a tramp erupts from the bushes to shake the complacency of a typical Howells family in *The Vacation of the Kelwyns* (1920).[3] The aggressive thrusts by reality are most common in Howells' late works, where man is passive and the world dominant; but they appear also in early works, the most notable being "Scene," the contributor's encounter with death on a lovely autumn day.

The necessary movement can occur during the perception, or before it, in which case the observer and the world will both be stationary. The favorite stationary viewpoint in Howells is the overhead one—a window, a balcony (a whole chapter in *Venetian Life* is devoted to the effects obtained

[3] New York, 1957, p. 181. *The Vacation of the Kelwyns* was actually written in 1910 (Cady, II, 255).

from a balcony on the Grand Canal), the deck of a ship in harbor. In the energetic world of the later Howells novel, this kind of viewpoint is less important than it is in the earlier ones. Kitty Ellison's first insight into the dual character of Arbuton—his essential coldness and his exterior courtesy—occurs while she is looking out of a window at a Quebec scene and "turning substance into shadow—unless, indeed, flesh and blood is the illusion" (*ACA,* p. 98). Suddenly, she realizes that Arbuton, who has just smiled up at her, is the man whose haughtiness she has been analyzing at leisure and with penetration, thanks to her secure vantage point.

The moving observer is the classical Howells type. Movement, especially travel, provides perfect conditions for perception on both sides of the situation; it makes the world novel and the observer receptive and alert. The emphasis here is on movement as the basis for perception rather than as a mere shift of scene. When movement is of the latter kind, part of the machinery of the plot, it is presented indirectly, in summary, for there is no reason to present it dramatically. Whenever we have a Howells character shown in movement, we can be reasonably sure that he is there more to see than to get somewhere. One point of Howells' diction suggests this focus. His novels are full of pedestrian movement, but his characters rarely walk, they stroll. Beginning with the chapter entitled "A Day-Break Ramble" in *Venetian Life,* there is an endless stream of Howells perceivers, alone or in pairs (seldom in larger groups), who stroll, step, lounge, loaf, wander, wonder, and ramble through Charlesbridge or New York or any city far enough from Boston or New York to be considered exotic. Rochester, for the Marches of *Their Wedding Journey,* is such a place. "All strange cities are enchanted," says Basil (p. 105), and every factor combines to realize his idea—the two strolling observers, feeding and shaping their perceptions through comment; the nighttime desertedness of the streets; the way in which a lighted window frames and arrests a moment of flirtation. Almost any random opening of this book produces a similar passage; for example, "The rest of the evening they spent in wandering through the village, charmed with its bizarre mixture of quaintness and commonplaceness" (pp. 159–60), a sentence that could come from almost any one of the Howells novels before 1890. Even in the grimmer late Howells world, the apprehensive observer has occasionally to explore a new town or a significant setting. *A Hazard of New Fortunes* is the last novel in which there is a large amount of unalloyed perception-seeking by strollers, and it is the novel that finally places men in a world where much is to be endured and little new is to be learned. (The Kentons do not want to leave Ohio at all; the young novelist, Ray, of *The World of Chance* is certainly eager for experience, but the dampening influences of the hovering author and of Ray's cynical cicerone, Kane, largely offset the naïve youth's enthusiasm.)

For Howells the most rewarding and the most thoroughly explored method of provoking perception is travel by train. Of course this was a natural and seminal field; "the cars" were the new and thrilling way of travel in Howells' youth and were still the dominant form at his death. Only in the 1930's did writers appear for whom other forms of transportation were more pregnant with symbolism and romance. And the interiors of Pullman cars, a focus of American status-seeking and display in the Brown Decades, were natural stages for Howells' satires. (He wrote a series of farces called *The Sleeping Car, The Parlor Car,* and others.) But the major function of the railroad car in Howells is to locate and stimulate the perceiver by setting him far from his normal world and close to his present world, framing this present reality in a window, separating him from this picture with a glass or a screen, and changing the picture at such a rate that evaluation is easy and boredom impossible. Train travel for Howells, then, is more a catalyst and tool than a general intoxicant, as in Wolfe, or a symbol of power, as in *USA.*

For Howells train rides are always alienating. In his earliest works, the characters rejoice in their isolation. Even the "helplessness in any circumstances" of the sleeping Pullman passenger "begets a sense of irresponsibility, almost of security" (*TWJ*, p. 18) and puts him in a "fantastic mood" (p. 19), the most desired state. (Howells uses "fantastic" quite literally and precisely). The chapter in *Their Wedding Journey* called "A Day's Railroading" is Howells' classic exploration of the possibilities of train travel for the "true artist." Starting up the Mohawk valley in a coach, the Marches feel "much complacency" (p. 83) despite the terrible heat and dust; as natural fantasists or artists, they can ignore any difficulty if they are given the right condition for perception. "They cast an absurd poetry on the landscape" (p. 86), which is just alien raw material for them, as it is for Howells, who takes over for several pages of imaginary gallivanting through the scenery that the Marches are looking at. But even though the Marches "cast" their "poetry," even though they are creative artists, the word "absurd" adds a note of ambivalence; the alienated observer is becoming a satiric problem for Howells, not the implicitly accepted norm. Under the special circumstances of travel, the "vacancy and tiresomeness" (p. 89) of their fellow passengers becomes a spectacle to laugh at and to shape into a series of artful descriptions, not a condition in which the Marches are involved.

In the later Howells novels, this kind of alienation from man disappears, to be replaced by the condition of bondage, and the alienation from the world becomes a theme. In *A Modern Instance,* a journey by train (to Indiana for the divorce trial) takes the characters into another world, where a long-unseen character pops up suddenly, and conventional viewpoints dissolve into conscious puzzlement. Even the unimaginative, self-centered Marcia is moved to comment, "I feel like some one that has been called to a death-bed" (p. 480). A similar weirdness permeates the trips in *The Shadow of a Dream,* especially March's nightmarish journey from

Boston to Nevil's Midwestern home (a town that resembles Columbus, Ohio) with Hermia, after the latter has learned the content of her husband's fatal dream. In *The Quality of Mercy,* Northwick, a swindling businessman, has two miserable train rides—once when he flees from Boston to Canada, and again when he is brought back in handcuffs. Both trips are nightmare suspensions in misery. During the second one, Northwick dies, alienated from his family, his friends, his world, from his various selves, and, at last, even from the detective who sits unaware beside him.

The contrast between the Marches' condescending view of their fellow passengers and the mature Howells treatment is shown in *The World of Chance,* in the train episodes involving Ray, the young writer, who is at first lost in the romantic world of his novel, *A Modern Romeo.* On the way to New York from his provincial town, Ray not only notes the miserable state of the passengers, but becomes involved with them. After helping an exhausted young woman with her grumpy children, he lends her money when she loses her purse, and thus becomes involved with the strange Hughes family, whose misfortunes instruct him in the messy reality of life and the bondage of men. At the end he goes back to the provinces for a visit. It is while drowsing in a Pullman berth that he broods over the meaning of his New York experiences and realizes that what looks like chance was really Providence. This conclusion contradicts the preceding 374 pages, is undercut satirically in the following pages, and is presented from the author's point of view anyway; but these comments have nothing to do with the use of the train ride as catalyst, enabling Ray to break through confusion to meaning.

Toward the end of the century came a new form of railroading, the elevated train, which Howells exploited principally in *A Hazard of New Fortunes.* For his purposes, the el was ideal. It combined his two favorite ingredients for perception—movement, and a superior and isolated, but fairly close, viewpoint. March feels that the "Elevated roads" give him "such glimpses of material aspects in the city as some violent invasion of others' lives might afford in human nature" (II, 73), and points out significantly that "it was better than the theatre, of which it reminded him, to see those people through their windows. . . . What suggestion! what drama! what infinite interest!" (I, 95). A novel method rejuvenates in March his voyeurism of twenty years earlier; movement and the sharp separation given by two panes of glass justify the voyeurism, of which March feels ashamed when close personal contact is involved.

Despite Howells' emphasis on trains, he does use other forms of transportation for their effects on perception. Canal boats and river boats played a major role in the shaping of his own mind. As his biographer notes (Cady, I, 243 f.), a frontier bugaboo, the collapse of a canal's bottom and sides, gave Howells an important image, which I find crucial to his development and to his mature mind. In Chapter XXIII of *A Boy's Town,* the middle-aged Howells recalled in detail the effects of a boyhood canal-boat trip on his perception and his sense of alienation. His fiction depends almost entirely on strolls and trains, but in *Suburban Sketches,* "A Day's Pleasure" involves a day-boat trip; and in *Their Wedding Journey,* the Marches sail up the Hudson on the Albany night-boat. The "pretty prospect" (*SS,* p. 140) observed during the former excursion stimulates only whimsy, but the other trip provides several examples of important perception created by travel. "There is no other travel like river travel" (*TWJ,* p. 62), Howells announces in his best didactic manner. He then provides the Marches with an abundance of material, both human and inhuman, afloat and ashore, and concludes typically,

> So the play of which they were both actors and spectators went on about them. Like all passages of life, it seemed now a grotesque mystery, with a bluntly enforced moral, now a farce of the broadest, now a latent tragedy folded in the disguises of comedy. All the elements, indeed, of either were

> at work there, and this was but one brief scene of the immense complex drama which was to proceed so variously in such different times and places, and to have its *dénouement* only in eternity. The contrasts were sharp: each group had its travesty in some other; the talk of one seemed the rude burlesque, the bitter satire of the next. . . .
>
> What a stale effect! what hackneyed characters! Let us be glad the night drops her curtain upon the cheap spectacle and shuts these with the other actors from our view. (pp. 70–71)

The sequence suggests the power of small incidents to trigger deep feelings and revelations of central concepts in Howells. Here are two of his strongest qualities: his impulse toward satire, and his sense of formlessness. What follows this revelation, the retreat behind conventional rhetoric, is equally significant. Self-exposure and commitment, for Howells, are not entirely voluntary and are more than a little dangerous. Later in *Their Wedding Journey,* after a collison with a smaller vessel, Basil March sits on the forward deck, observes the dawn, and thinks of the man scalded in the accident. He wonders at the "abstraction" of his feelings (p. 78), tries to imagine being bereft of Isabel, and realizes that a man in love cannot grasp any state outside his own. The setting thus gives him a perspective on his own condition, and allows him an insight, about a mind-filling state, that is otherwise unavailable to the man in such a state. The unusual perspective, then, allows March to experience and analyze simultaneously—a feat of the first order, but one essential for the romantic author.

These changes in men and their perspectives play a much more important part than changes in nature; but the latter are of some importance, especially in the early works. "A Day-Break Ramble," in *Venetian Life,* is a lengthy experiment in the effects of early rising. At 4:30 A.M. Howells notes "a breezy freshness and clearness in my perception altogether delightful" (p. 19), but finds his sense of size so distorted that he feels himself colossal and a dog elephant-like. He is stimulated to all kinds of penetrating ideas, which he forgets at once, this being only a casual essay. In the early novels, there is a good deal of sunset-and-moonlight nature-rapture, conventional for its time, but sometimes shading into the real Howells method. One scene in *Their Wedding Journey,* during the boat trip up the Hudson, is especially significant. Very late at night, the Marches are awakened by crashes and yells; they realize that an accident has occurred and rush into the saloon where the women are all in dishabille. "The place with which she [Isabel March] had felt so familiar a little while before was now utterly estranged. . . . A mist of sleep involved the whole, and it was such a topsy-turvy world that it would have seemed only another dreamland, but that it was marked for reality by one signal fact" (pp. 72–73), which is that the two prostitutes on board are still shunned, despite the universal uproar. The odd time, along with the sudden confusion, has changed everything except the prejudices that are too deep for perception. A palpable condition of perception—here "the mist of sleep"—and the interpenetration of dreams and reality, are significant elements in Howells throughout his career.

As a device, weather also receives careful treatment in *Their Wedding Journey,* though later it is seldom used in this way. That aged romantic resource, the storm, enters briefly in Chapter I, and is examined for its effects on perception. Observing through their window, the Marches find "something splendidly theatrical about it all" and consider a passing horse car, swept with hail, to be "an effective and a very naturalistic bit of pantomime contrived for their admiration" (p. 4). The product of the unusual conditions here is mere whimsy, casually discarded; the device of the storm is too theatrical and unusual, too stimulating, to be really useful in the Howells world.

A more successful device is extreme, prolonged heat, which the Marches experience during a day in New York. "Great, brooding warmth" (p. 83) makes the later trip along the Mohawk charming, but that kind of heat is not unusual. What the Marches live through in New York is heat that puts men over the threshold from reality into the Howells hell, where men endure the constant suffocating pressure of an implacable force and are recompensed only with the insights that their condition gives them. Some significant Howells words appear here. The chapter is entitled "A Midsummer-Day's Dream"; the Marches' "spirits are low, for the terrible spell of the great heat brooded upon them" (p. 40); the noise of their train "struck through and through the car like a demoniac yell" (p. 41); their experience in walking the streets is "a kind of vision, magnificent at times, and at other times full of indignity and pain" (p. 45). Howells reinforces this sense of a nightmare hell with numerous images of endlessness. As the Marches walk down an avenue, the uniform brownstone blocks "oppressed them like a procession of houses trying to pass a given point and never getting by" (p. 47); "the spiritless air seemed to have a quality of blackness in it, as if filled with the gloom of low-hovering wings" (p. 49). The spectacle of the crowds—to anticipate Wolfe and his "manswarm"—"possessed the beholder with singular fascination, and in its effect of universal lunacy, it might well have seemed the last phase of a world presently to be destroyed. They who were in it but not of it, as they fancied,—though there was no reason for this,—looked on it amazed" (p. 50). The use of heat as device is evident. The early Howells method, half essay and half fiction, leaves little to the analyst, and is, moreover, so guarded (a lifelong Howells quality) that the passage risks little and accomplishes little. In the context of *Their Wedding Journey,* the words, images, and comments mean little; Howells is practising his scales, not writing a Kafka novel, and the clause "though there was no reason for this" expresses a no doubt sincere desire to quash impressions of tragic seriousness. But in the light of what we know about the Howells world, especially the later Howells world of bondage and patient suffering, this casual sequel in *Their Wedding Journey* is immensely significant. The chapter suggests what biographical study of Howells also shows: that he had a pre-existing tendency toward his later vision and needed only the proper circumstances to make it dominant.

Qualities of mood, either in the world or in man, are used by Howells in much the same way as these qualities of movement and weather. For Howells, novelty is one of the most important moods, one that is taken for granted much of the time, when it is generated by movement or unusual conditions; but sometimes Howells makes his characters conscious of novelty, and then the means of art becomes theme. Even his "contributor," the butt of satire in *Suburban Sketches,* is allowed to perceive novelty and its effects. In "A Romance of Real Life," the contributor wastes hours hunting through Charlesbridge with Jonathan Tinker, the mysterious sailor, but "could not feel that an expedition which set familiar objects in such novel lights was altogether a failure" (*SS,* p. 176). He feels close to Tinker, almost a shipmate. "The estrangement of all things which takes place, within doors and without, about midnight may have helped to cast this doubt upon his identity;—he seemed to be visiting now for the first time the streets and neighborhoods nearest his own . . ." (pp. 176–77). As a "possibly worthless vagabond," he "got a new and instructive effect" (p. 177) in the expressions of the neighbors he talked to. Thus unusual time and circumstances can create a novel mood that alienates and enlightens at the same time. The Marches, more mature observers, quite consciously create the same effect that the contributor stumbles upon; in Quebec, for example, they intend "to give the rest of the afternoon to that sort of aimless wandering to and fro about the streets which seizes a foreign city unawares, and best develops its charm of strangeness"

(*TWJ*, p. 247). "Novelty" here becomes "strangeness," a stronger word, suggesting the late Howells sense of alienation.

This cultivation of novelty is at the core of the long house-hunting episode that opens *A Hazard of New Fortunes*. When the Marches go into the dining car on their way to look for a house in New York, they are able, thanks to their unusual mission, "to escape for an hour into the carefree mood of their earlier travels, when they were so easily taken out of themselves" (I, 45); and in this mood their children, "by a fantastic operation of absence, seemed almost non-existent" (I, 46). Here novelty serves to overcome age and anxiety and produce the key "fantastic" mood. In New York, novelty continues to operate on the Marches. At first, the novelty of seeing that incredible artifact, the New York apartment, overrides their aversion for it; "they could not deny that the interest was unfailing, and that they got a great deal of fun out of it all" (I, 71). Later, as they become partly acclimated to New York (as the plodding reader must, too), "their house-hunting no longer had novelty, but it still had interest" (I, 79). In this in-between mood, they know as much as some inhabitants but still can see as strangers, and their perceptions are therefore daily richer. They rapidly lose, for example, a good deal of their old simple-minded love of the picturesque, which they now realize must be seen sympathetically, not from "a purely aesthetic view" (I, 80). This is not to say that their education in the human condition is more than hardly begun, but the surface ice of customary perception has been broken, and for Howells such a break is always the important moment. Given this start, the Marches will proceed to reconstruct and enrich their whole vision of things.

A special form of novelty is the holiday feeling, the sense of being released from the everyday structure and strictures of society and allowed to float as an uncommitted observer. Again the use of mood parallels the long span of Howells' feelings about life, from enjoyment of alienation from man, through worries about the consequences of such alienation, to a sense of permanent bondage to men (and the subsequent impossibility of taking holidays). The earliest Howells observers, the *I*'s of *Venetian Life* and *Suburban Sketches,* are on permanent holiday from their surroundings (Venice and Charlesbridge), and all their perceptions arise from that peculiar angle of vision. (Both the perceptions and the angle are satirized, as I have shown.) In "A Day's Pleasure," one of those crucial links between essay and anatomy-fiction in *Suburban Sketches,* the holiday mood is, as one could predict, a matter for open consideration in a contrived *exemplum.* While waiting for the boat, the leader of the excursionists kills time by strolling uptown from the pier.

> A holiday is never like any other day to the man who takes it, and a festive halo seemed to enwrap the excursionist as he pushed on through the busy streets. . . . When he stepped into a crockery store . . . a sense of pleasure-taking did not fail him. . . . Even when he reached the establishment where his own business days were passed some glamour seemed to be cast upon familiar objects. To the disenchanted eye all things were as they were on all other dullish days of summer. . . . Yet to the gaze of the pleasure-taker all was subtly changed. (p. 127)

The repetitiousness of the passage (which I have cut by half) reveals the pedagogic earnestness with which Howells makes and sustains his radical points that perception creates meaning and that perception cannot exist without the catalyst of the unusual perspective (here the "festive halo" of the holiday mood). (The reader will also note the capricious use of commas, a minor point, and the post-neoclassic abstraction of "establishment where his own business days were passed," a major point of Howells' style, which I will discuss below.)

The same lessons arise, somewhat more subtly, from the travel novels of the 1870's. Howells' travelers, honeymooners, or exiles in Venice are all on permanent holiday; their perceptions of each other, as well as of nature, are allowed free play, so that the blame for their errors and other obtuse clinging to faulty codes can be put squarely on them. This laboratory technique is no longer used in the big novels of the 1880's and later. Bartley Hubbard may be a stranger to Equity, the Laphams, Eskimos to the Coreys, and New York an astonishing exhibit to the Marches, but within *A Modern Instance, The Rise of Silas Lapham,* and *A Hazard of New Fortunes,* the characters are permanently entangled with each other and with their worlds. The only holidays come during the train rides that assume such symbolic qualities in the later novels, or, for a time, during changes of scene. The house-hunting episode in *A Hazard of New Fortunes* is such a change. But though New York City is novel and interesting to the Marches and puts them in receptive moods, they are not on holiday there. No matter how much Howells overuses the device of house-hunting, his choice of it is ingenious. Because the Marches are looking for a place to stay, they are pressing continually toward involvement with the city; and because they are hurried and having trouble, their search is charged with anxiety, the feeling appropriate for the late Howells figure but absolutely improper for a holiday-maker. One could also argue, like the Dreiserians, that the wearying length and jerkiness of the episode works to destroy any sense of the holiday mood; but it would be necessary to point out that confusion and stumbling are qualities of the Howells holiday from the beginning, the difference being that in *Their Wedding Journey* such contretemps are comic, whereas in *A Hazard of New Fortunes* they are not.

In addition to moods arising wholly or in part from the outside, Howells uses some that originate entirely within men. When raw stimuli interact with such moods, the result is perceptions, often analogous to the Joycean epiphany because they catch men suddenly, undefended by their code-armor. Because Howells was no Joyce, either in aims or talents, examples of this sort are not usually emphasized in his work. For example, in the first chapter of *A Hazard of New Fortunes,* Fulkerson tries to persuade March to edit a projected magazine in New York. Softened but not convinced, March leaves his office building, and in his indeterminate mood "absently lifted his eyes to it."

> It was suddenly strange after so many years' familiarity and so was the well-known street in its Saturday-evening solitude. He asked himself, with prophetic homesickness, if it were an omen of what was to be. But he only said musingly, "A fortnightly. You know that didn't work in England. *The Fortnightly* is published once a month now." (I, 10)

The little incident is significant, enough so to serve as basis for an illustration in the first edition; for it marks the end of March's old world (or Eden) and the beginning of his exile in reality. But Howells, the satiric realist, will not satisfy our eagerness for a treatment equal to the portentousness of the scene; he will not allow his remorselessly ordinary character to react like a Stephen Dedalus.

Other mood devices are similar in nature and in use. A mental state is picked up, often just after it has begun as a change from another state, and applied to raw material, the result being a thrust of insight. In "A Romance of Real Life," the contributor has a pronounced feeling of anticlimax when he learns that the man he has been helping is not a sailor home from a long voyage, but an ex-convict, just out of Charlestown prison; however, the unusual perspective afforded by this change of mood allows the contributor to realize that "the episode which had appeared so perfect in its pathetic phase did not seem less finished as a farce. . . . The more he pondered upon his acquaintanceship with Jonathan Tinker, the more fascinating the erring mariner became, in his complex truth and falsehood, his delicately blending shades of artifice and *naïveté*" (SS, p. 186). In Howells' later fictions, on the other hand, the characters who realize the truth and are dejected by it, then see the truth even more grimly and are even more dejected, and so on. The more that Westover, the perceptive center of *The Landlord at Lion's Head,* sees the truth about Jeff Durgin, the more clearly Westover realizes—in the literal sense of that word—the helplessness of decency and decorum before Jeff's amused ruthlessness. The same tightening spiral of mood and perception exists in *The Son of Royal Langbrith.* The character who leads us out of the maze of that novel is the only one who can force her own mood on reality and make it bow to her: Hope Hawberk, who cheerfully ignores Royal Langbrith's destruction of her father and his own wife and marries Royal's son. In contrast, a weak Howells character, Angus Beaton, the morose young painter in *A Hazard of New Fortunes,* becomes so glum about his girl's contempt for him that "the affair . . . estranged the aspect of his familiar studio" (II, 187). At the opposite pole of feeling, Conrad Dryfoos is put in such an "exalted mood" by his talk with Miss Vance that for him "all events had a dream-like simultaneity" (II, 232), and he walks fearlessly to his death. In both cases mood creates the special perspective that generates action and further moods—in Beaton's case, *accidia,* and in Conrad's case, involvement and death.

Other Howells devices for manipulating perspective come under the heading of "machinery"—the use of coincidence, the crowding together of unlikely people in peculiar situations, the shifting of moral bases, and the author's personal contributions (comments, generalities, uncertainties). Much of this machinery is involved in the question of the use of perception in satire, a question that I take up below, and much of it needs little discussion. In a sense the whole Howells world is one everlasting shift of perspective—not a slow definite movement, as in Mann and Marquand, but a series of Brownian movements. The Howells world, like the Victorian interior, is often crowded and "busy." Stupefyingly jammed with "Jamescracks"—vases, "dragon candlesticks," rugs and skins, portieres, "tidies," "Arab scarfs," clocks, "China pugs," and "red Japanese bird-kites" (I, 159–60), to name a few—the apartment of Mrs. Grosvenor Green figures the Howells world; and when the Marches reluctantly move into it, near the beginning of *A Hazard of New Fortunes,* they signal the awkward and irrevocable involvement of Howells' perceptive people in chaos. Given such a structure, the Howells world inevitably produces sudden symbolic meetings and epiphanies and as inevitably whirls on to something else. *The World of Chance,* written shortly after *A Hazard of New Fortunes,* focuses entirely on this Brownian aspect of the Howells universe. The "hero" need only exist passively in New York to be jostled into one unusual perspective after another, ably interpreted by his guide and mentor, Kane, the obliging and faintly sinister cynic who foreshadows Twain's Satan in *The Mysterious Stranger.*

II

. . . a fantastic vision at the best.

Having created and studied perception on one level, Howells rises above it to the level of the author's perspective on his own characters, and uses perception satirically. He perceives and evaluates perceptions—their flaws and achievements, their modification by preconceptions and weakness—in order to produce the kind of satire that I discussed in Chapter II. In this respect the Howells novel is the adventure not only of the perceiving central character (if there is one), but also of the author perceiving the character. It is what Robert Langbaum calls the "lyrical drama," the action whose basic purpose is to help the narrator (who can be the author) find and celebrate his stance in the world.[4] Howells' supreme

[4] *The Poetry of Experience* (New York, 1957), pp. 207–9.

satiric thrust is to define this stance as indefinable (so that "celebrate" is hardly the word). All that we can be sure of is his panic, his sense of being on the surface of an alien and aggressive reality. Howells' lyrical refrain is "I don't know," hardly the cry of a satisfying and popular author. The Howells perspective, even if undefinable, is, at any rate, a negative one, sometimes strong, more often weak and vague. Howells' ways of creating this kind of perspective can be divided into implicit and explicit; though the latter are the most characteristic of this author of anatomies, the former are of interest first.

When the perceptions by themselves are charged with negative qualities, we have the ironic method, rising at its peaks to negative epiphanies, implied sudden realizations of disunion with the world. This is not Howells' usual method, but he uses it more often than one might think. Most of his earliest semi-fictions in *Suburban Sketches* are loaded with authorial comment and abstractions, but he does "freeze" some scenes, such as the mourning Irishwomen and obscene boys in "A Pedestrian Tour" (p. 65), and a crowd of slum-dwellers who gape fixedly at the observer's train in "A Day's Pleasure" (p. 118). In these scenes opposites are fused and the ordinary flux of reality is arrested, the sum being mysteriously portentous. This fusion of freezing and contrasting is studied much more carefully in "Scene," one of the crucial early Howells exercises. Here the author does direct and evaluate; we are not left to form our own conclusions about the contributor, "that literary soul," and his "romantic story for the suicide" patched up "after the pitiful fashion of this fiction-ridden age" (*SS,* p. 191). But although there is still some nudging at the end, when the girl's corpse is brought back on a wagon surrounded by gaping neighbors and capering children, the essential point of the sketch—the basic terror of life—is allowed to make itself:

> In the bottom of the cart lay something long and straight and terrible, covered with a red shawl that drooped over the

> end of the wagon; and on this thing were piled the baskets in which the grocers had delivered their orders for sugar and flour, and coffee and tea. As the cart jolted through their lines, the boys could no longer be restrained; they broke out with wild yells, and danced madly about it, while the red shawl hanging from the rigid feet nodded to their frantic mirth; and the sun dropped its light through the maples and shone bright upon the flooded flats. (p. 194)

Twenty years later, Howells extended the principle of "Scene" and found his supreme negative epiphany, near the end of *A Hazard of New Fortunes*. This is Conrad Dryfoos' perception (already mentioned) of a policeman during the streetcar strike. As Conrad advances to help the old anarchist Lindau, who is about to be clubbed, "something seemed to strike him in the breast" (II, 233). Conrad tries to speak, but his is paralyzed. All he can do is look at the policeman in a moment of pure perception. "The policeman stood there; he saw his face: it was not bad, not cruel; it was like the face of a statue, fixed, perdurable, a mere image of irresponsible and involuntary authority" (II, 233). Then Conrad falls dead. The passage is richly meaningful; it is the goal of almost six hundred pages of rambling and confusion. With nicely calculated irony, Howells gives this insight into the meaning of things to a man who cannot speak, who is in the act of dying. (Cf. Eliot's "I could not/ Speak, and my eyes failed . . . ,/ Looking into the heart of light, the silence.") The rendering of the perception itself benefits from the use of the flat, tired, competent style of so much Howells "realism." "The policeman stood there"—simple existence, simply rendered, gathers weight and becomes terrifying. The continuing into explanation—"like the face of a statue"—is relevant and typically Howells, but unnecessary for creating the startling effect of quiddity. The phrases "the face of a statue" and "a mere image," however, do suggest the inhumanity of the policeman; he is a demon disguised as a man, and the more he just stands there, the more he unqualifiedly *is*. Yet the Howells demon, we should recall, is partly human; he may be "irresponsible," but his condition is "involuntary," and he shares in the bondage of men.

When, a few years after *A Hazard of New Fortunes,* Howells speaks in his own voice in his poems, he is as cold and flat in his presenting of nightmares and reveries as he is in the policeman scene. Closely associated in time and mood with *Stops of Various Quills* (1895) is *A Traveler from Altruria* (1894), the only Howells fiction using the supremely ironic device of an unreliable and hostile narrator. With its symbolic use of point of view and its coldly economical use of exemplary scenes. *A Traveler From Altruria* is one large negative epiphany and is thus Howells' only "modern" novel. In most of the many other Howells novels, the flat negative epiphany is eliminated—for the reader if not for the characters—by the mass of authorial intrusion or by the analysis and self-consciousness of authorized observers (the Marches in particular); and any flaws in such observers are seldom allowed to escape without open examination. And even the most negative of epiphanies is acceptable to the reader as experiencer, or to the reader as observer of experiences. Anything in the Howells world is a discovery, and no matter if the discovery is unpleasant. When life is conceived of as a search, then what is found becomes secondary to the act of finding. Howells and the Howells observer, in fact, find masochistic pleasure in discovering the grimness of the human condition. A rosy world would give them less to talk about.

Again, the house-hunting episode in *A Hazard of New Fortunes* is a salient example. The more exasperating the Marches' search, and the more unpleasant New York, the more they analyze and comment, and the more they thrust forward to the next gloomy illumination. By the end of the novel, their old Eden in Boston is a dead issue, a bore. When Mrs. March revisits Boston, she is afraid of the severe New England faces, and longs for the "heterogeneous gaiety of New York"; her children find the streets "very queer and clean and empty" (II, 77). Even these children, who had loudly lamented the move to New York, are soon more than willing to stay there; Tom March, a boy of about sixteen, even begins to absorb some of Lindau's radical ideas, which open up radically new worlds of perception. New York may be a hell, but it is also a catalyst, and its advantages outweigh its disadvantages.

III

> *Who was he? what was he? why was he? the mind played forever around these questions in a maze of hopeless conjecture.*

The kinds of explicit manipulation used for satirizing perceptions may be conveniently divided into hidden and overt. The former involves juxtaposition of material and coincidence; the latter, the author's comments, generalities, and uncertainties, and his manipulation of style, especially that which produces the characteristic Howells tone of whimsy.

Howells uses juxtaposition to create either a limited effect in a certain area, or an afterimage that enters into the reader's perception for some time and fades slowly away. The satiric effects of these methods can be specific—the undercutting of some character and what he stands for—or general—the blurring (sometimes to the point of anarchy) of structures of meaning, and the hedging of commitments to such structures. To look for examples of these techniques is to read the Howells canon. His whole lifework (one could justifiably say the work of his life) is one long backing and filling and temporizing that fills dozens of volumes and gets him nowhere, but keeps him going despite his ills. (I am of course speaking here of Howells the man, not Howells the man of letters, or Howells the critic, or Howells the family man, or any of the many other Howellses.) Some chosen examples must suffice. *The Shadow of a Dream,* one of Howells' most mature works, offers many. In this novel, life, in its fullness of accident and pain, is juxtaposed against the Marches' naïve belief in the order and meaning of things. They discuss pain and find it useful; then Faulkner, March's old friend, suffers a frightful heart attack, lives in misery for a few hours, and dies in a sudden and revolting agony. When March, "for our own sanity," denies that "existence" is "a series of stupid, blundering accidents" (pp. 108–9), we have already seen Faulkner's death; and soon we are shown the death of the minister, Nevil, rubbed and pressed to jelly between a train and the wall of a tunnel. Following this scene, the most grisly in Howells, are several pages of further March ruminations, cast in a style that emphasizes his flight from reality: "My wife . . . does not permit it to be said, or even suggested, that our feelings are not at our bidding" (p. 218). The excessive vigor of her rejection prompts us to consider the theory more carefully than if she discussed it objectively.

The ridiculous discussion or reverie occurs often in Howells. In the example above, from *The Shadow of a Dream,* it is placed some distance away from the reality that undercuts it, but sometimes it is close. I have mentioned the little scene from *A Hazard of New Fortunes* in which the Marches, after the quarrel with Dryfoos, are cast from their high, noble plane by the self-deception of their inflated reveries. In *A Modern Instance,* Bartley Hubbard and Marcia Gaylord are similarly cut down in the opening chapters as rapidly as they are built up or can build themselves up. Bartley impresses Marcia by ridiculing books; "it gave her a still deeper sense of his intellectual command when he finally discriminated, and began to read out a poem with studied elocutionary effects" (p. 11). Her father is portrayed as absurdly blind to implications. When she was small, "he would not let her be forced" (p. 102), we are told; but only a few pages later, he is pleading with her not to brood about Bartley: "You *must*—

you *must* try to control yourself, Marcia. . . . You're disgraceful" (p. 111).

The finest bit of undercutting in Howells occurs near the end of *A Modern Instance,* when lawyer Atherton and his society wife Clara judge the barbaric Hubbards and are themselves judged. Recall that Bartley and Marcia have been satirized since the beginning of the novel, and that one by one their judges have been taken down: Squire Gaylord, the townspeople of Equity, Bartley's friend Halleck. The Athertons are the last resort of morality. As these wealthy Brahmins sit "late over their breakfast in the luxurious dining room . . . overlooking the Back Bay" (p. 468), Atherton holds forth at great length to his wife about Halleck and the Hubbards. After several of his long periods, his wife agrees anticlimactically.

> "Yes," answered Clara, deeply moved, even as a woman may be in a pretty breakfast-room, "and such a good soul as Ben always was naturally. Will you have some more tea?"
> "Yes, I will take another cup. But as for natural goodness—"
> "Wait! I will ring for some hot water."
> When the maid had appeared, disappeared, reappeared, and finally vanished, Atherton resumed. (p. 472)

The author's ironic thrust to undercut "deeply moved" is obvious; less plain is the function of the realistic details for creating satiric contrast. Here "realism" is not the legendary tedious recording of pointless details, but a literary instrument used with care to create a moral effect in a work of satire, and backed up by the handling of style (for example, the plodding repetition of "appeared, disappeared, reappeared, and finally vanished"). The Athertons' high moral tone is vitiated not by huge sins, or any conventional "sins" at all, but by the cumulative effect of the ritual necessities of gracious living.

As the episode continues, Howells adds the final undercutting thrust. (I quote Atherton's remarks at length, even though their meaning is not the central point here, in order to reveal their cumulative weight, an essential factor in the undercutting to follow.)

> . . . Atherton resumed. "The natural goodness doesn't count. The natural man is a wild beast, and his natural goodness is the amiability of a beast basking in the sun when his stomach is full. The Hubbards were full of natural goodness, I dare say, when they didn't happen to cross each other's wishes. No, it's the implanted goodness that saves,—the seed of righteousness treasured from generation to generation, and carefully watched and tended by disciplined fathers and mothers in the hearts where they have dropped it. The flower of this implanted goodness is what we call civilization, the condition of general uprightness that Halleck declared he owed no allegiance to. But he was better than his word."
>
> Atherton lifted, with his slim, delicate hand, the cup of translucent china, and drained off the fragrant Souchong, sweetened, and tempered with Jersey cream to perfection. (p. 472)

Atherton's ideas are there to be accepted in large part; they certainly summarize a major theme of the novel (the attack on permissiveness, part of the modern code). But at the same time, the neat summary is belittled by the carefully rendered details that follow it. Here again realism goes far beyond mere recording; for we have not only the choice of one action (drinking tea), but also the style—the carefully chosen adjectives, the dainty rhythm (created by the hesitancies and insertions, especially "sweetened") as prissy and priggish as the Athertons themselves: a code has been placed against the simple quiddity of existence, and the latter has won, as it must in Howells.

As one has grown to expect, Howells then goes on to make his point overtly. He has Clara and Atherton chide themselves for condemning others and forgetting their own luck. Then Howells makes even this essay-like explicitness functional; for no sooner have the Athertons confessed their sins than they go back to judging and condemning. "This whole thing is disorderly" (p. 474), grumbles Atherton accurately and old-maidishly. When Clara asks her husband if he is really going to write a tart letter to Halleck, the lawyer ends the novel with "a troubled sigh" and the words "Ah, I don't know! I don't know!" (p. 514). This state of mind parallels the reader's, and not just in *A Modern Instance*. After five hundred pages of Equity and Boston, we, as well as Atherton, no longer know what is right, who is to speak for the right, what the shape of the world is, or what we can do to find its shape. Each answer has been juxtaposed to what will demolish it.

Juxtaposition, then, produces the Howellsian anarchy and its accompanying sense of bondage. Successive events have little or nothing in common, or add up to nothing; but they do share the characteristic of meaninglessness, so that the Howells world has an upside down logic after all. In addition, the successive actions are habitual ones, either in terms of the individuals concerned, or in terms of the classes to which they belong. Even when successive events have nothing to do with each other, the characters experience them in habitual ways, and in Howells the emphasis is on the characters. The scenery or other changing background is raw material for perception (except in some early works, as I have pointed out). Howells suggests this quality of habitualness with considerable skill. Arrivals in railroad stations, tea parties in Brahmin drawing rooms, conversations between friends—even melodramas like Squire Gaylord's oration to the divorce court in *A Modern Instance*—these, or events like these, have happened before and, given the right circumstances, will happen again. In Howells' mature fiction, this effect is rendered indirectly, notably through flatness of style; but in the early sketches, the effect is created in the bluntest way, for example, the change from the use of the present tense to the continuous use of the past tense right in the middle of

Howells' first sketch story, "A Day's Pleasure." Sensitive characters like the painter Beaton are driven almost berserk when they realize in Howells' negative epiphanies that they are doomed to one form of habitual action, the circle of their selves. In a sense the advantage of the novel for Howells (who, we should remember, began as a poet) is that it allows the suggestion of habitual action. And even when he returned to poetry in the 1890's, he wrote little about particularly lyric epiphanies; the epiphanies in these poems come rather from his realization that specific occasions are examples of habitual conditions.

Juxtaposition also allows Howells the necessary luxury of "hedging" his statements. To read the Howells novel is to examine the financial transactions and conditions of a speculator who has so hedged his investments with short sales, puts and calls, straddles and straps and strips, that his real position is a mystery to the outsider and perhaps to himself. Howells has been called "lazy" by one critic.[5] The term is unfair, but there is some truth in it. Howells does not conceal his beliefs because he is frightened of what people might think or because he can't be bothered to take the trouble; his life contradicts both points.[6] He shifts from one viewpoint to another, one world to another, one narrator to another, because his artistic vision—or, more precisely, his denial of *a* vision—demands such shifts. To stand on one view means to postulate either a fixed, orderly world or a solid viewpoint, and in the Howells world, there is neither. The central Howells characters travel and move a great deal; even characters like the Kentons, who belong firmly to one world, are painstakingly moved around in order to shake up their views and our views of them. Most of Howells' rustic philosophers, for example, are forced at least once to leave

[5] Richard Chase, *op. cit.*, p. 177.

[6] See Cady, II, 69 ff., for a full discussion of Howells' courageous public stand during the hysteria over the Chicago Haymarket affair, and Cady, I, 201 ff. for Howells' lifelong habits of hard work.

their cocoons and go to town, where their ideas and standards evaporate, even without Howells' satiric assistance (which is of course freely given). Once in Boston, Kinney and Squire Gaylord (in *A Modern Instance*) and Whitwell (in *The Landlord at Lion's Head*) lose confidence in themselves and look pitiful to the eyes that admired them when they were in their northern village and woods. Even the Dryfoos clan, with their demonic energies, and the Kenton family, as close as Howells could get to ordered continuity of values, look clumsy and narrow in New York City, where their codes no longer match their perceptions.

Howellsian juxtaposition works backward; it modifies our view of what has gone before. The "afterimage" works forward; it sheds its gradually decreasing influence over later events. Its effects resemble those of juxtaposition, but are milder; for having one's present perceptions modified by memories of the past is not as shocking as having one's memories and beliefs shaken by immediate perceptions. Besides, the modifications by the afterimage occur in a mild and steady way, unlike the succession of shocks following the jerky juxtaposition of different events. The Howells mood ("glamour," "fantasy," "pathos," for example) produces the afterimage effect, usually mild and often pleasant, especially in the early works. Under appropriate circumstances, such a mood can linger on to influence future perceptions to the point where an unusual perspective is created. I have discussed a prominent example, the steamboat episode in *Their Wedding Journey,* in which an unusual situation creates an unusual mood at an unusual hour, and penetrating perceptions follow. This kind of glow is shed throughout Howells' early novels by special conditions—holidays, youth, honeymoons—and accounts largely for their popularity. In later novels the afterimage is not always so pleasant and can, in fact, become decidedly unpleasant. The "Bittridge effect" shadows the Kentons throughout their novel. Whenever his influence wears off, Bittridge reappears, or, in the second half of the book, similar characters appear, to keep the Kentons in a state of confusion and strain bordering on hysteria. In general, the Howells demon (like Bittridge) works economically, as a kind of battery that discharges its force into a circuit and then is disconnected until the tingling charge has died away and a new jolt is indicated. *The Son of Royal Langbrith* is stronger than that. The demon there never appears in person, but the consequences of his action and the bitter memories of him hang over the whole novel, just as his portrait dominates the library, where his son sits and draws factitious strength from his father's image. And instead of dying out, the aftereffects increase until they have destroyed Langbrith's former partner. Because Howells mercifully puts a gap between generations in this novel, the aftereffects stop with Langbrith's generation, and his son and his partner's daughter flourish.

The formlessness of the Howells novel is itself the most sweeping kind of implicit satirizing. Even if a given Howells novel can be assimilated in part to some traditional artistic form—such as the *Bildungsroman* (*The World of Chance*) or the Austen comedy of affectation (*Indian Summer*)—it will be only one part of the "immense complex drama" having "its *dénouement* only in eternity" (*TWJ*, p. 70). This situation makes formlessness inevitable, from the point of view of the novel, if not from the point of view of the anatomy-fiction. The only form is the form of learning: experiencing, evaluating, assimilating. Since learning is a process, and "form" in fiction refers to things and their relations, the term "form" is a misnomer when one is talking about Howells. There are, and there can be, no clear-cut beginnings or endings, and no necessary boundaries to perception or thought, especially since for Howells learning is difficult, and the learning process itself cannot have a clear shape or a predictable conclusion. Because Howells always uses the point of view of an adult (even when he is working close to children, as in *The Kentons* and *A Boy's Town*), his novels cannot have the firm beginnings of the classical *Bildungsroman.* Also, learning for Howells is often negative; the characters are busy learning what is not true, what they should not or cannot do. Thus the end of the Howellsian learning process takes us off in the opposite direction from the one that we expected at the beginning. One great advantage of this situation, however, is that Howells can keep everyone worrying away at reality until it yields up its meaning.

If Howells postulates formlessness, yet he allows form and thus some kind of organized movement through a corollary of formlessness—coincidence. In the Howells world, as in the world of modern physics, something is bound to happen if we put enough particles into enough motion for a sufficient time. The more crowded the particles are, and the more they range about, the more likely is some kind of collision. The stuffiness of the Howells world, which I have pointed out elsewhere, increases the chance of collisions. For all of Howells' geographical breadth and wide interests, his characters live in small or even cramped situations, especially in terms of social life. (Hence the sneer "teacup" realism from Frank Norris, whose claustrophobia is so evident in his choice of settings and themes.) Consider *A Hazard of New Fortunes,* Howells' longest novel, his attempt at a social panorama. In this novel the characters, especially the Marches, observe the great crowds and worry about the great issues, but the cast of the novel is surprisingly small—three families and a few individuals involved with them—and this group lives a narrow round of work, quiet family life, and social ritual.

The social life of this era encourages coincidence. The at-home, that sober predecessor of the cocktail party, formalizes coincidence and makes it possible for Howells, in novels like *Indian Summer,* to base entire actions on accidental meetings occurring day after day within a small group. The at-home combines a fixed container (a certain house at a certain time daily or weekly), with a fixed potential content (a social set) and a random actual content (the members of the set who come on a given day). "Crushes" and "spreads" and balls are used in similar ways; in fact, they form the necessary minimum structure of the Boston sections in *The Landlord at Lion's Head,* just as the rituals of summer-resort life give shape to the Lion's Head sections of the same book. In minor works such as *April Hopes* and *A Chance Acquaintance,* these social ceremonies, which extend even to sightseeing, provide almost all the structure, such as it is. During and from these affairs arise the misunderstandings, anxieties, and grudges that create the Howells actions and his pervasive theme of alienation.

Given the Howells world only, the coincidence is neutral; but Howells uses it ironically, and it is, therefore, a device of satire. So many of these accidental meetings lead to trouble, or at least to confusion, that coincidence becomes one of Howells' central devices for overturning our belief in an orderly world and for substituting the demonic world.[7] Like those Chaucer characters who must keep an eye out for Satan in the bushes, the Howells figure must move warily among threats of sudden confrontation. I have mentioned some of these sudden apparitions before. Such coincidences also serve to create the vital mood of novelty, the catalyst of perception.

Coincidences serve not only generally to create the Howells world, but specifically to attack certain points. Since most Howells novels contain coincidences used in this way, it is possible to mention only a few. In *A Modern Instance,* coincidences are used to undercut the characters and satirize them. Whenever Bartley Hubbard gets himself started toward a good life, coincidence intervenes and trips him up. On his way to Atherton's office to ask for advice about studying

[7] Recall that Eric Bentley finds coincidence essential to that basic dramatic form and *Weltanschauung,* melodrama (see above, p. 29). "That notorious device: outrageous coincidence," of which Bentley finds "some particularly gross examples in the supreme tragedies, . . . intensifies the effect of paranoia . . . enlists circumstances in the enemy's ranks . . . represents a projection of 'irrational' fear" (*The Life of the Drama,* pp. 202, 203).

law, Bartley meets his friend Ricker, an editor, who tells him that Witherby, the owner of *Events,* is looking for him. Bartley, "curious and impatient" (p. 219), drops in on Witherby for a moment, stays to be offered an editorship, accepts it, and starts down the road to his destruction. Bartley's interest in the law is decidedly a good sign, for even if the Howells lawyer is sometimes imperfect, the law itself represents stability and decency. Witherby's brand of journalism, however, springs from one of Howells' greatest horrors: the union of moral slackness and demonic energy. Ricker's accidental meeting with Bartley is therefore symbolic, almost allegorical; the good-natured newspaperman, who thinks he is doing Bartley a favor, is an unwitting emissary of the devil. Because the novel is an anatomy and the story, as the title shows, is an *exemplum* in a sermon, the hint of allegory is appropriate. Later, Bartley pulls himself together and resolves to abandon his slovenly behavior (such as gambling with his friend Halleck's money); "his good instincts awoke, and put forth their strength" (p. 388), Howells tells us, only to add at once the harsh, undercutting stroke, "such as it was." Having in fantasy mastered the law and entered Congress, Bartley strolls genially home, to find his wife in one of her demonic rages. By coincidence she has met Hannah Morrison, the red-haired teaser from Equity, the cause of Bartley's first troubles and now a prostitute, who denounces Bartley to Marcia as her seducer. The inevitable quarrel follows. Bartley leaves her in a cold rage and goes to Cleveland. Once there, he repents and decides to buy a return ticket, only to discover that his money is lost. From there, his life goes rapidly downhill to its sudden end in Arizona. This string of coincidences is acceptable for two reasons. In a satirical anatomy, we tolerate manipulations, designed to get us to the point, that are not acceptable in impersonal symbolic fiction. Also, given the Howells world and Bartley in it, his destruction is inevitable; and that being so, one day is as good as another, and the question of timing subordinated to other problems.

In the later Howells novels, these fated meetings suggest the bondage of men in the Howells universe. The affair of Jeff Durgin, the Harvard "jay" from the hills, and Bessie Lynde, the cynical post-debutante from Boston, is one case in point. Thanks to the tight interlocking of the social worlds of Harvard and Brahmin Boston in the 1890's, these two are thrown together at teas, crushes, and balls, although they would never meet under any other circumstances. Helplessly watching their affair is the painter, Westover, who, as a kind of privileged hanger-on, circulates at all the Brahmin parties. Durgin's contact with society ends with a horsewhipping at the hands of Bessie's brother, who searches deliberately for Jeff but finds him only by chance. Rising to the level of fate, coincidence later helps Durgin by arranging to have his old but well-insured hotel burn down while he is in Europe and in need of quick cash. These coincidences are as appropriate and inevitable as the ones in *A Modern Instance.*

Just as trains and train rides are important in the stimulation of the characters' perceptions, they play a large part in Howellsian coincidence and, therefore, in the stimulation of the reader's perceptions. Recall the gruesome death of Nevil (the lover in *The Shadow of a Dream*) just after he has agreed to seek reconciliation with the heroine. An unnamed parishioner, a messenger of fate who appeared briefly earlier in the novel, holds Nevil in conversation exactly long enough so that Nevil steps off March's train as it is leaving the station and entering a tunnel. Thus the hand of coincidence quite literally squashes a man who has just decided to live. In *Annie Kilburn,* Peck, the cantankerous minister who foreshadows Howells' interest in Christian Socialism, is mortally injured by a train just at the right time for his death to make Annie miserable and guilty.

Toward the end of *The Son of Royal Langbrith,* Howells ingeniously uses a railroad incident to cause young James Langbrith's inevitable discovery of his father's evil. John Langbrith, Royal's dyspeptic brother, is returning after a futile effort to ease his misery in travel. For several pages, Howells methodically describes John's movements, physical situation, and feelings—a small masterpiece of misery. A long paragraph tells of John's dismal snack at the New Haven lunchroom, and his hurry to get aboard the train. Then, "as he crowded through the narrow aisle on his way to take his seat again, he glanced into the smoking-room and met the eye of his nephew, who turned at the same moment from watching the shipping in the harbor through the windows and over the platforms of the cars receding on the sidings" (pp. 321–22). Neither man is much surprised, and the scene continues toward John's outburst to James about Royal's villainies. What is curious in the quotation, and appropriate to my discussion, is Howells' reduction of the meeting to the flat level of fact, on which the event is no more important or unusual than any other fact—John Langbrith's gray "holiday," his pie and beans and coffee, the ships and railroad cars seen by James. Here, as elsewhere in Howells, "teacup realism" effortlessly reduces all existence to Brownian movement and at the same time raises it to mystery and portentousness.

Besides manipulating formlessness and form, Howells proceeds more directly to evaluate perceptions. First of all, there are his observers, whom I have largely discussed elsewhere. Howells' constant use of observers blunts experience and vitiates the effects of his epiphanies. Especially when there are double narrators (such as the Marches, or one character-narrator and "I"), the raw material of reality is so thoroughly examined and dissected that little is left to strike the reader directly. (Compare Melville, who in *Moby-Dick* worked out a method that allowed experience its full impact and evaluation full play.) Under the Howells' treatment, life can be only a problem; and since that is what life is anyway in the Howells universe, his use of observers is an enrichment rather than an impoverishment.

More open and much more prominent in Howells are his

devices for direct manipulation: comment and generalization, indications of uncertainty, and whimsy. Aside from "teacup realism" and style, comments and generalizations are the most noticeable characteristics of the Howells novel. It is hardly possible to read for long in his major novels without encountering constructions like the following: "His habit was one that does not promote sympathy with one's fellow creatures" (*LA*, p. 90); "the loud obstinacy of a man whose women always have their way" (*RSL*, p. 259); "he behaved toward her with a lover's self-forgetfulness" (*ACA*, p. 185); "talking of their lives and their loves, as young men do" (*WC*, p. 1). This impression is not in error. Once the straight essay and half-essay of the early books gives way to fiction, Howells makes increasing use of comment. In *The Lady of the Aroostook,* there are over sixty comments and generalizations; in *The Rise of Silas Lapham,* about one hundred; in the novels after the nineties, fewer, but still a noticeable number.

These devices largely create the Howells anatomy. No other technique comes close to comment as a method of fixing incidents in formulas and people in classes. Comment makes drama difficult and satire pre-eminent; it distracts one's attention from the mysterious and dangerous world of nature and fixes it on the human reason, a dependable stronghold and a stable base for perception. The resulting situation is not unlike that of the forts in the Old West: security in a small area is virtually assured at the cost of surrendering knowledge and control of everything outside. Comment is also a motif that creates and sustains perspective, makes objects real, and connects them to the continuum of the observer's experience; such a connection is desirable and necessary because the observer is, as I have said, a point of stability in an ambiguous world. Comment for Howells asserts fact against symbol, essay against drama, the artist's problems against possible solutions.

These terms, "generalization" and "comment," should be

distinguished, even though both refer to authorial statements in the present tense. The generalization is brief; it arises in the course of the narrative and gives it a nudge but does not interrupt it—for example, "'I was not busy with my inventions, Madama,' answered Don Ippolito, who sat in the womanish attitude priests get from their drapery . . ." (*AFC*, p. 133). The relative clause develops Don Ippolito's character and at the same time turns him from an isolated portentous instance into an example taken from a class, from a potential artistic symbol into an actual scientific symbol. The generalization reminds us of the presence of the hovering narrator, but the momentum of the narrative itself continues almost undisturbed across the brief gap. On the general level, this small generalization has little effect in itself; but in combination with the many similar bits in the novel, it makes this long fiction an *exemplum*, an anatomy and not a novel. The generalization, then, is a calculated device. The Howells comment, on the other hand, parallels the digression of the classic English novelists; it brings the novel to a full stop while the author openly discusses a point. Howells being a smooth writer of exposition, these comments are often trim little essays; but this very neatness adds to the distraction. It is perhaps significant that Howells' use of comment declines after his novels of the early eighties. (*Their Wedding Journey* and the early works of fiction can be seen as long essays with a certain amount of fiction added.) In the major novels of the late eighties and nineties, direct comment virtually disappears, to be replaced by the Marches' discussions.

The Rise of Silas Lapham, a major and a transitional novel, is an interesting locus of comment and generalization. The distinction between generalization and comment can be easily seen in the opening paragraphs of Chapter XIII, in which Mrs. Bromfield Corey arranges the fatal dinner for the Lapham family. The chapter begins, "Having distinctly given up the project of asking the Laphams to dinner, Mrs. Corey was able to carry it out with the courage of sinners who have sacrificed to virtue by frankly acknowledging its superiority to their intended transgression" (p. 242). Here is the Howells satire on women, so great a prop of his career, and underneath is a more serious criticism of human self-deception; here, too, is the nudge toward *exemplum* from dramatic fiction. After this opening come a dozen lines of narrative, as Mrs. Corey and her daughters consider whom to invite. Then they all think "of one of the most comprehensive of those cousinships which form the admiration and terror of the adventurer in Boston society" (p. 243). After this comment, which perhaps unwittingly reveals Howells' ambivalent feelings toward his adopted culture, he adds two paragraphs developing, in the author's voice, the topic of the alien in Boston. The passage is interesting social history, and further reveals Howells' feelings as an "adventurer" among the Brahmins; but it leads us far from the narrative and has no clear function in terms of the plot, satiric themes, or general attitudes. When we are finally returned to the narrative, there is a sharp sense of dislocation; for the comment, after breaking the movement of the narrative, has built its own momentum. The fictional narrative is now an appendage to the comment, an illustration of a general rule.

In a sense, all of *The Rise of Silas Lapham* is an appendage to comments and generalizations. Since there are about a hundred of them, the reader is, so to speak, never out of range of one. Consequently he is never allowed to forget that the novel is a satiric anatomy of the human condition in general and certain American elements in particular. Since the fiction is inside the essay and we are invited to share in the essay, which the characters in the fiction know nothing about, we are given a superior point of view—a necessity for satire and a powerful inducement to it. This feeling of general superiority to the general inferior run of mankind carries over into every page of the book and helps cast the negative Howells feeling over the most dignified moments (the minister Sewell's blast at romantic novels and their evil effects, for example.) A few comments are used to create the grim mood of later Howells bondage. Referring to the Laphams' belief that their sorrow about Irene is unique, Howells says, "Each one of us must suffer long to himself before he can learn that he is but one in a great community of wretchedness which has been pitilessly repeating itself from the foundation of the world" (p. 336). But essay cannot work unopposed against narrative. The world of the Laphams and the Coreys is not as grim as Howells' remark; we are not yet within the world of bondage, though we are in sight of it.

The use of uncertainty—terms like "doubtless," "as if," "perhaps," "probably," "must have," "it might almost be said that"—is as characteristic of Howells as his use of comment and generalizations. Every time we come to a sentence like "It was evidently not the social aspect of the matter which was uppermost in her mind" (*LA*, p. 46), or "The young man smiled, as if amused by some of his impressions of the Lapham family" (*RSL*, p. 138), we are reminded again that life is mysterious and impenetrable, man inscrutable, and observation even of surfaces difficult. Each "perhaps" destroys the drama of the characters and tells us that the drama in the Howells novel is really the drama of the author, his open-ended search for reality and his record of failure in that search. Howells experiences the world of his books and struggles for keys to it; we share the experience, the struggle, and the failure. Occasionally, the uncertainty is applied directly to the whole world by being combined with a comment: "Women do not generalize in these matters; perhaps they cannot pity the faults of those they do not love" (*LA*, p. 212). Here, the narrating "I" peers speculatively at the world just as the "contributor" wonders about the drowned Irish girl in "Scene," or as the strolling Marches of *Their Wedding Journey* gaze at alien wonders framed in lighted windows.

Again, *The Rise of Silas Lapham* is an excellent example of technique in action. In this novel the author not only uses eleven different terms of uncertainty ("no doubt," "doubtless," "perhaps," "apparently," "probably," "as if," "seemed," "must have," "it is questionable if," "it might almost be said that," "and no proof that she meant more"), but on four occasions offers alternative reasons for a character's actions or thoughts. Some of the uncertainty is tactical. When Howells makes Tom Corey smile "as if amused by some of his impressions of the Lapham family" (p. 138), the intention is to continue the confusion about which Lapham daughter Tom loves. (Until Tom proposes to Penelope Lapham, there is no indication that he loves her, or that he loves Irene Lapham either, though the other characters, blinded by their romantic codes, assume that he admires the conventionally pretty Irene.) At other times, uncertainty adds to the satiric effect. When Tom Corey, after Lapham's financial collapse, says of Penelope, "She's acted nobly," the author adds, "Mrs. Corey, whose thoughts cannot always be reported, said she was sure of it, and that all she desired was her son's happiness" (p. 486). Throughout the novel, Mrs. Corey has been under mild attack as a supercilious hypocrite, and the dry reference to uncertainty combines with Mrs. Corey's remarks, both sarcastic and earnest, to clinch the point.

At other times in *The Rise of Silas Lapham,* the mature Howells' effect of bafflement arises from the use of uncertainty. There is bafflement for the characters:

> Lapham stole a troubled glance at his wife, and saw that there was no help in her. Whether she was daunted and confused in her own conscience by the outcome, so evil and disastrous, of the reparation to Rogers which she had forced her husband to make, or whether her own perceptions had been blunted and darkened by the appeals which Rogers had now used, it would be difficult to say. Probably there was a mixture of both causes in the effect which her husband felt in her. . . . (p. 463)

and for the hovering narrator:

> ". . . I don't think I shall feel strange amongst the Mexicans now" [said Penelope to Tom Corey as they left the Corey house for their honeymoon in Mexico].
>
> . . . I only meant that I should have you all to myself." There is no proof that she meant more, but it is certain that our manners and customs go for more in life than our qualities. The price that we pay for civilisation is the fine
> e. Perhaps we pay too
> ɔ persuade those who
> t this is so. They may
> isgiving, the recurring
> young people's depar-
> ed. (p. 509)

the best examples of the
k" technique, in which
against uncertainty and
: to decide where we or

sy, is the last Howells
referring here not to
particular use of humor
ion. Kitty Ellison, the
e, is again of central
ise of humor. Because
rceiver, her humorous
Kitty, an orphan, was
eme ideas, tempered by
himself and his family"
sked their lives for the
y ever got more amuse-
ed "lived in the family
physical trait" (p. 5);
bent, began even as a
sals, and to look at life
vision" (p. 6). Whimsy

here is not just a way of seeing, but a way of defending oneself against reality (the Howells continuum of shocks, human misery, and demonic energy) and against man's codifications of reality, which include even the worthy causes for which the Ellisons risk themselves. As events and qualities and "extreme ideas" come into reality, whimsy meets them head on and tames them.

In Howells' earliest work, whimsy is used more simply as one way among several of creating perspectives and hence, of creating satire. Whimsy is also a simple device for creating interest in Venice or Charlesbridge, and it is applied as mechanically to the narrator's disappointment at the flatness of Charlesbridge as it is to the delight in the novelty of Venice. In either case the dash of whimsy on everything soon becomes tiresome, as Howells evidently realized; for dishonesty and self-stultification through whimsy is a major sin of the "contributor," who is so severely handled by the narrating "I" in "A Romance of Real Life" and "Scene." The invention of the Marches allows Howells to indulge in whimsy without inhibition while at the same time allowing the "I" to attack them for it, and *Their Wedding Journey* is one long round of whimsy. The playfulness begins on page one with Howells' coy disclaimer of ability to write sustained narrative and romance, and continues on page two with the first appearance of the characters, as Isabel March chatters with Basil about her dread of being taken for a bride. On page four a hailstorm is seen as "splendidly theatrical," and every detail is cheered for its aesthetic contribution. The waiting room at the station confirms Isabel's belief that "*salles d'attente* everywhere are delightful" (p. 7). The book continues through train rides and boat rides and strolls and excursions, inexhaustible sources of fun.

But in *A Chance Acquaintance,* the world is beginning to replace the observer as aggressor, and whimsy is beginning to be the defense against the demonic, personified, even if only mildly, in Arbuton. When Arbuton snubs Kitty, she is deeply wounded; but is still able to say later, "I seemed to be like two persons sitting there, one in agony, and one just coolly watching it" (p. 272). In the mature Howells, then, whimsy is a stabilizer, maintaining the precarious tilted balance of man and nature that yields perspective. The imperceptive Howells characters, like Marcia Gaylord and Silas Lapham, merely suffer and survive; but the perceptive ones defend themselves with bitter whimsy. Ben Halleck, for example, loves Marcia, but hardly dares admit it to himself, cannot admit it openly as long as Marcia adores her boorish Bartley; and still cannot confess it after Marcia is divorced and Bartley is dead. Penelope Lapham must patiently endure her father's collapse, the rivalry of the Laphams and Coreys, and the two families' obsession that Tom Corey really loves Irene. In each case the grotesqueness, the Faulknerian "outrage" of the situation, is developed to the hilt and beyond; and in each case only a native playfulness of spirit, embittered by experience, is given the character to keep him going. Ben Halleck has the greater burden and the weaker power of whimsy, and he is destroyed.

In the novels around 1890, the Marches develop whimsy to a high point. Huddling together, they repel the confusion and madness of the outside world with their jests. March is the principal humorist, for Mrs. March has a Howells woman's resilient toughness, and serves anyway as the foil to her uncontrollably whimsical husband. The whimsy is involved in a pattern of advance and retreat, defeat and regrouping, outside and inside. The Marches sally forth, engage reality, are defeated or baffled, and then return to their refuge to talk it over. In *A Hazard of New Fortunes,* the house-hunting episode consists of a series of such cycles. Reality is the roaring streets and irrationally planned apartments of New York; the refuge is the Marches' hotel or a quiet restaurant. If necessary, the refuge is the Marches' own relationship, never a placid one, but proof against attack from outside. In any case the Marches put reality at a distance, and do so—must do so

—to protect themselves. When they sit together in Washington Square, they know it is time to go home when they see "the benches filled with lovers"; March opines that "the thought that at the same hour the same thing was going on all over the country, wherever two young fools could get together, was more than he could bear . . . and the fact that it must go on for ever, as long as the race lasted, made him tired" (II, 63). One should not make too much of this; but certainly, March is feeling the burden of time and lightening it with whimsy. Even the unpleasant view from the el train bows to whimsy; and though the Marches are not as simple-minded about picturesqueness as they once were, still they can note the Bowery in terms of the "gay ugliness—the shapeless, graceless, reckless picturesqueness," and March can find "certain audacities of the prevailing hideousness that always amused him" (II, 143). March can admit that he goes too far, and Isabel can chastise him:

> "Shall we go to the *Hole in the Ground* to-night?"
> "I am going to Boston."
> "It's much the same thing. How do you like that triviality? It's a little blasphemous, I'll allow."
> "It's very silly," she said. (I, 89)

Yet, this silliness must be allowed if the Marches are to keep in practice for serious onslaughts of reality. (In this example whimsy is also Howells' defense against the arrogance of Boston, as Oscar W. Firkins pointed out in his excellent early study of Howells' humor.) [8]

The Marches' temperamental and physical distance from the world emphasizes the gap between the Marches and alien reality. In *A Hazard of New Fortunes,* they talk over Dryfoos' bullying of March in the security of their house. In *The Shadow of a Dream,* they experience the strange and fright-

[8] *William Dean Howells: A Study* (Cambridge, Mass., 1924), p. 322.

ening Faulkner, his ambiguous relations to his wife and friends, and his oddly decayed seaside estate; then, taking refuge in their room, they discuss the situation in detail. Suddenly, they hear a knock at the door; it is Mrs. Faulkner announcing lunch. Dropping their analysis hastily, they resume their social faces and go out again into the Faulkner world.

In the later Howells world of bondage, whimsy grows tired along with the characters, and its limitations become visible. In travel books like *Their Silver Wedding Journey* (1900), the characters have trouble keeping up the facade of lively amusement and often slack off into apathy. Many of the poems in *Stops of Various Quills* reflect this exhaustion. "Twelve P.M." describes "the luxury" of putting aside "one's perfunctory smile" and becoming "wholly and solely one's sheer self again" after one of those jovial, heavy banquets of the late Victorian age. In *A Traveler from Altruria,* whimsy is not just a bore, but a danger and an accessory of evil. When the whimsical response to reality becomes automatic, it cuts a man off from reality; and when such a man stands between us and reality, then we are cut off from reality too. Twelvemough, the first-person narrator of *A Traveler from Altruria,* employs whimsy so often that he becomes whimsy; and he is fatuously proud of it because he is fatuously proud of himself. From his reporting of the comments and behavior of others, we get glimpses of the contempt that ordinary practical men feel for him; but in general we are held helplessly to his point of view and its screening powers. Whimsy helps to steady a weak temperament like Twelvemough's, but the price is too great. Twelvemough sees what he wants and needs to see, and swiftly discards, or does not see, what he does not need. Thus the cure ends by conquering the patient, and the reader is forced to share in the defeat.

These later books also show, however, that whimsy is still a useful defense in a world dominated by sniggering demons. *The Kentons* and *The Son of Royal Langbrith* both confront the decent man with the indecent, and teach the characters that the best defense is a good offense. In each novel the older people (Howells' contemporaries) cannot armor themselves in contemptuous wit, but the young can, and it is the young who save whatever is saved. Mr. and Mrs. Kenton are both virtually defenseless; Kenton in particular is vulnerable, for Mrs. Kenton has her housewifely energy and small concerns to help her keep going. When Bittridge laughs in Kenton's face, he can do nothing except mutter "Go away" (p. 87) and feel "stifling" (p. 89). His son Richard revenges him by cowhiding Bittridge, but Richard is also defenseless: after the revenge he becomes "deadly sick" (p. 95) and must lie down. Ellen Kenton, the older daughter, and Boyne, the young son, are also humorless and simple, and they are easily victimized by Bittridge and Trannel. In *The Kentons* the only armored character is Lottie, the younger daughter. Being female and adolescent, she attacks and retaliates not with wit, but with sauce and sarcasm. "That disgusting Bittridge has been here with his horrid wiggy old mother," she says (p. 91) in the letter to Richard that results in the cowhiding. And after Trannel gets Boyne in trouble with the Dutch police, she listens "in silent scorn" (p. 284) to the family's recriminations and finally bursts out in a disjointed tirade: "What else could you expect of a Cook's tourist? . . . That seems to be the Kenton way. Anybody can pull our noses, or get us arrested that wants to, and we never squeak" (p. 284).

The Son of Royal Langbrith is a less mythical and more complex treatment of the theme of demonism, and the characters are much more aware of their situations than the Kentons are. Laughter, Howells notes in a significant generalization, "is the prevailing American mood in the face of any mystery" (p. 109); but laughter has its limits for the older characters here. When Dr. Anther is ready to tell Judge Garley that Royal Langbirth "was the devil," the doctor abandons the Judge's "jocosity" (p. 110) and cannot even smile. Mrs. Langbrith is entirely devoid of humor herself and cannot even recognize it in others. She so dampens Anther that in his many talks with her he can never rise above a kind of sad irony. And these people do need some kind of defense, for their disembodied opponent, the "sardonic spirit" (p. 281) of Royal Langbrith, is as cruel as Bittridge in the flesh. Only one character can rise above puzzled helplessness or wry irony, and that is Hope Hawberk, the daughter of the man that Langbrith drove to opium. She is not just congenitally cheerful; she selects cheerfulness and humor as her existential stance. Some of this humor, and the ability to create it, she inherits from her father, who cannot tell about the green monsters of his dreams without making her laugh. (In his cheerful bitterness, he recalls Putney, the drunken lawyer of *Annie Kilburn* and other books, who dominates the horrors of his life—his alcoholism, his scandalous behavior, his crippling of his own son through drunken carelessness—by jesting about them.) "It's pretty awful," Hope tells Dr. Anther about her father's dreams. "She laughed in a queer way, and then the tears burst from her eyes" (p. 140). Whimsy is "queer" in Howells; it cannot always or entirely conceal the horrors and threats bursting through reality, and it is tainted with them. But the Howells world is in all ways impure and imperfect, and whimsy works as well as any other method for stimulating perception, the *sine qua non* of Howells' art. That Howells has a central artistic concern, and that he manipulates a number of artistic devices, does not in itself make Howells a great or even an important writer; but it does make him more of an object of legitimate critical interest than the autobiographical "realist" of traditional scholarly interpretations.

CHAPTER V

THE LIMITS OF NEGATIVITY: QUESTIONS OF FORM, STYLE, AND ACHIEVEMENT

"Ah, I don't know! I don't know!"

BEING largely technical, the preceding descriptions and analyses are merely preparatory and incomplete. Function is not virtue; a characteristic may be a fault. Having said what Howells does, I should now point out the effects of his actions and his inactions. Most evaluation of Howells has been concerned with the latter. The modern critic, in fact, often condemns Howells for not being someone else. I would note that Howells is necessarily limited, like any man, by not being other than himself; but I would condemn him not for this, but rather for not being more fully himself. The attacks on Howells have come from every direction. Howells' biographer, who is generally conservative in critical outlook and vocabulary, calls the last sections of *A Modern Instance* "an artistic failure—in fully and clearly presenting the final states of being at which the main characters arrive—linked with an intellectual failure to *think through* to their last conclusions the ideas for which the main body of the novel's drama stood" (Cady, I, 208). In *The American Novel and Its Tradition,* Richard Chase echoes Cady and then adds severe judgments from the point of view of the advanced wing of academic critics:

> The trouble with Howells in general is first of all that he never tried hard enough. There is a real laziness, as well as a prudishness, about his mind, and in his novels he is always making great refusals. He had a furtive, cunning intelligence which perhaps knew more about ordinary American life than any novelist has ever known. But he had little

> imagination, little power of making a fable, of launching an exciting action, little power even of establishing an atmosphere that could be sustained through a novel. He lacked, as James said, that "grasping imagination" which an American novelist would need if he were to deal fully with American life. What little imagination he had was incapable of grasping, as imagination, the facts his intelligence perceived or of imparting to his novels a coherent form. His stories are full of unbridged gaps, and he is seldom able to give that indispensable impression, as James always does even in his inferior work, of a coherent action that includes and relates all the elements of the fiction. There is no *voice* which we can recognize as Howells. (Chase, *op. cit.*, p. 177)

In each case the critic wants Howells to be something else; Chase, in fact, wants him to be Henry James. Now of course James was a greater artist in every way than Howells, but that judgment does not help us solve the problem of Howells. These critics are partly right, but they are misusing (or, in a sense, not using) their correct analyses; they are of a piece with the military critics who condemn General Grant for not being a dazzling tactician like General Lee, without realizing that tactics are dictated by strategic situations. As I hope I have shown, Howells does "fail" to write the ironic-dramatic-architectural "modern" novel, for which I use the critical shorthand of "Jamesian." "Failure" to "think through" the ideas of "the novel's drama" is likewise characteristic of a novelist who is concerned not directly with ideas and drama, but with our relation to them. The question of laziness depends on one's demands on art and the artist. Again I say that we must look at Howells (as historians now look at Grant) in his own terms and see what could be done to make him be more fully himself. If we approach him that way, we will find plenty of flaws—some technical, some philosophical—and no lack of qualities that will keep Howells from ever being admired.

Howells' most obvious technical flaw is a simple ignorance

of the methods that he needed, given his obsession with demonic forces and existential alienation. He does not command the symbolistic methods in which, as Charles Feidelson has shown, the classical American authors rooted their work. I am talking about Symbolism, not symbolism. Howells could create symbols, but he could not consistently raise them, and thus finally keep them, above the crucial threshold into the realm of portentousness and fascination. If Howells were a true and consistent "teacup" realist, this gap in his abilities would not matter. But as I have shown, such Howells characters as Bartley Hubbard, Jeff Durgin, and Bittridge are by no means flat, realistic portraits; and such typically Howellsian events as sudden intrusions, coincidences, and violent deaths are by no means mere reportage of everyday middle-class life in the late nineteenth century. Like Hemingway, Howells was concerned with the accurate rendering of his world, but he tried to do more. Many of his characters and episodes loom portentously; like many of Poe's, they are projections of his own mental situation. But his success with Symbolistic methods is sporadic, because he lacks skill and control (whether conscious or unconscious, does not matter). One can see that Bittridge is a threat to civilization, an embodied id spreading panic. The eyes of the Kenton family are riveted on him in fascination and terror, but our eyes are fixed on him with nothing stronger than interest and comprehension, because he is not made to intrude on *us*. For Howells, the anatomist and satirist, things may some times willy-nilly become symbols, but they are always cases. To use Freudian terms, the Symbolistic method demands the steady co-operation of id and ego, the one to supply the force and the other, the control and expression. When the ego ignores the id, the latter may sometimes fall in step with the former, or may burst through its control; but in general the result will be the kind of interesting demi-sociology that fills the wide gaps between the most powerful and significant scenes in most of

Howells' work. The reasons for his failures (and successes) as a Symbolist lie deep within the mystery of his personality; they are paralleled, but not caused, by the limitations of the culture of his time. When Howells grew to maturity, American Symbolism was drying up. He inherited Melville's crisis of belief and Hawthorne's crisis of artistry. Behind *A Modern Instance, The Shadow of a Dream,* and *The Kentons* lie *The Confidence Man,* with its protean devil in a baffling, ambiguous world, and Hawthorne's last manuscripts (*The Ancestral Footstep, Dr. Grimshawe's Secret*), the record of pathetic failures to turn abstractions into symbols.[1] Unfortunately for Howells' future reputation, he worked unrebelliously within the restricted tradition given to him, although he was perfectly capable of recognizing Symbolist talent when he saw it in Stephen Crane.

For Howells the satirist, a more serious defect was his ignorance of the now-commonplace methods for getting at half-conscious or preconscious feelings and thoughts. The modern novelist can use various forms of stream of consciousness; he can use Symbolism to show the conscious or unconscious projection of deep mental states upon the outside world. Howells knew something of both methods, especially the latter (the Marches frequently experience and examine projection); but he used them awkwardly and disjointedly, and never tried to master them. In his later years, he shared the enthusiasm of the age for psychic phenomena; he published several books of short stories on hauntings, return of souls, psychic influence, and similar topics. Among the important novels, *The Shadow of a Dream* (1890), *The Son of Royal Langbrith* (1904), and *The Leatherwood God* (1916) explore psychic influence by the living and the dead. But in handling these matters, Howells never got beyond the

[1] See Edward Hutchins Davidson, *Hawthorne's Last Phase* (New Haven, Conn., 1949); Edward H. Davidson (ed.), *Hawthorne's Doctor Grimshawe's Secret* (Cambridge, Mass., 1954); and Hyatt H. Waggoner, *Hawthorne: A Critical Study* (rev. ed.; Cambridge, Mass., 1963).

awkwardness of Beaton's self-analysis of his feelings for Christine Dryfoos, a passage that I have quoted but one that deserves further attention:

> . . . The man who had no control over himself liked logically enough to feel his control of some one else. The fact cannot otherwise be put in terms, and the attraction which Christine Dryfoos had for him, apart from this, escapes from all terms, as anything purely and merely passional must. . . . Then the consciousness of her money entered. It was evident that the old man had mentioned his millions in the way of a hint to him of what he might reasonably expect if he would turn and be his son-in-law. Beaton did not put it to himself in those words; and in fact his cogitations were not in words at all. It was the play of cognitions, of sensations; formally tending to the effect which can only be very clumsily interpreted in language. (*HNF*, II, 292)

Here comment is not helpful or functional, but embarrassing; it is an admission of defeat. After all, even a self-taught author like Melville was able to master the principles of *erlebte Rede* (for example, the masthead episodes in *White-Jacket* and *Moby-Dick*). When Howells says, ". . . The attraction . . . escapes from all terms, as anything purely and merely passional must," we can clearly see his interest in the irrational, his nervous fear of it, and his self-deceiving excuse that without knowing much about it, he knew all there was to know; and that without knowing much about the possibilities of language, he knew all there was to know about that. Although we can interest ourselves in the complexities of Howells' fears and inhibitions, and the reasons for them, we should attack Howells the artist for evading a central artistic question, for ignoring his own thesis that one's knowledge of the world is forever limited and uncertain. His awkwardness and limitations here cannot be ignored. The great modern novelists—especially the Continental ones, whom Howells so much admired—advanced the possibilities of the art form. Howells invented nothing and advanced nothing, and it is therefore natural that he has never played a part in the history of the novel. His technique is a defense, a private affair.

Another of Howells' major technical deficiencies, probably the most immediately noticeable one, is his lack of control, producing confusion and triviality. It is one thing to present a universe that is illogical and uncontrolled; it is another thing to present it in an illogical and uncontrolled way. Howells' use of comments and generalizations, for example, is essential, but not every comment and not every generalization in Howells is essential; and sometimes, the shift from narrative to comment is jarring. In *A Hazard of New Fortunes,* Fulkerson wants to ask Colonel Woodburn to mediate between March and Dryfoos after the quarrel over Lindau. The colonel's daughter speaks to him, and he looks up "through his glasses with the sort of ferocity elderly men sometimes have to put on in order to keep their glasses from falling off" (II, 161). One can argue that the generalization is "creatural realism," to use Erich Auerbach's phrase; and also that it has a satiric function, to show that irrelevant concerns and impressions intrude even at the most important moments, despite our sentimental beliefs in the unity of personality and effect. But really, this passage is an irritating intrusion. This moment is narrative, moving rapidly (for Howells) toward a major climax of the novel; it is not the time for comment. There is plenty of room for the point in the preceding 490 pages. Again, one can argue that in the Howells world, any moment is the proper moment for anything. I have already used this idea to explain and justify Howells' lavish use of coincidence. But we must distinguish between artistic confusion and literal confusion, between creating the illusion of chaos and creating chaos itself. Howells was not a Dadaist, although his sense of life foreshadows Dada and the modern *avant garde* interest in the absurd; and he was not a literalist in the Isherwood (*I Am a Camera*) manner (not that Isherwood was himself). In his best work (*A Traveler from Altruria, The Shadow of a Dream*), Howells may give the impression that he or his narrator is a camera recording existence, but he does so by choosing and arranging his material, including the "irrelevancies" and "interruptions" and coincidences. As I have said, the explosive interruptions and the sometimes outrageous coincidences in his novels are functional in terms of theme and plot, and the coincidences in particular are often aimed at the half-conscious desires and fears of the reader, who cannot believe that Nevil (in *The Shadow of a Dream*) will ever be able to live in content, and who finds it somehow appropriate that at the height of happiness he should be crushed by a train. As for smooth, professional handling of intricate techniques, Howells was capable of that and admired it. Recall the opening of *Venetian Life*, when he rejoices to see at once a play and the "working of the machinery" (p. 9) in the wings. A reading of Howells' plays, especially his farces, reveals that Howells not only admired artistic dexterity, but could practice it to such a degree that, even by Victorian standards, his plays are "well made." Among his novels, *A Traveller from Altruria* and *Indian Summer* are intricately organized mechanisms in which little attempt (in the former, no attempt) is made to hide devices from the reader.

We can and should attack Howells, then, for lapses from his own method, and for methods that do not work his own ends. Often, Howells seems to lose control on a large scale; but what actually happens is that in his constitutional dislike, or perhaps fear, of fixity and narrowness, he changes focus, point of view, tone, until his aims themselves are vitiated. This incessant, nervous, crabwise movement cripples and characterizes more than one of his major works. Consider *A Modern Instance*. Howells tries to make Bartley Hubbard unpleasant and repulsive, yet in some ways sympathetic and fascinating. He makes the villagers of Equity applaud Bartley's "smartness" and the newspapermen of Boston attack it;

perhaps we are to assume that small-town people are cloddish and city professionals noble, but the point is not clarified. Sometimes Bartley's point of view is used, with frequently intense ironic effect; at other times, when similar effects could be obtained, Howells writes from his own point of view, or the point of view of Equity, or that of a group, or that of a single character. The focus is now on Bartley, now on Marcia, now on Halleck, now on a group or a society; and it is difficult to see who or what the book is about. Is it about Bartley and Marcia as a pair? Or is it about Bartley alone, about a remorseless Byronic wanderer whose married life and early affairs are only intervals in an artificially truncated career? Or is it about society, Bartley and the others merely being handy plums plucked from what James might have called "the semi-fluid pudding" of the Howells novel? Some incidents, like the courting scenes and the crucial quarrel with Bird, unfold with economy and point; others—Bartley's visit to Kinney in the logging camp, Halleck's talks with Marcia and Atherton—go on and on, with little sense of time or even of aim. I am not quarreling with the idea of the anatomy-fiction, with its license to do anything necessary, or with Howells' conception of existence as Brownian movement. I am attacking the point that license to do anything gives coherence to an assemblage of doings chosen at random. Howells himself does not accept this idea completely. Form enters, clumsily, through the use of comment and generalization, which push a little here, haul a little there, and frequently get in the way, so that we are left with many of the disadvantages of license and few of its advantages (such as energy and immediacy). Thus Howells undercuts himself and his own statements about the world (his works of art), as well as others and their statements.

Howells' lack of control reflects his lack of "location," one of his basic flaws. As Robert Langbaum explains in *The Poetry of Experience,* the Cartesian artist seeks to understand the world from which he is separated, to reunite thought and feeling, and he does so in momentary experiences of insight ("epiphanies"). This "poetry of experience" depends on "located quality."

> What Dr. Johnson understood to be the *"local"* or located quality of Denham's "new scheme of poetry" is in fact the essential characteristic of a poetry of experience. For locating the statement of value makes it an occurrence, something which happens to someone at a particular time in a particular place. The problem in writing such a poetry, the problem which Denham and most of the meditative-descriptive poets of the neoclassic period failed to solve, is to keep the poem located—to keep the dramatic situation from turning into a rhetorical device and the landscape from turning into a metaphor for an abstract idea. It remained for the romanticists to solve this problem; and their solution suggests the technique for a poetry of experience, for whatever is new in the form of romantic poetry. (*Op. cit.,* p. 47)

To solve the problem, the material of the poem must be organized

> within a particular, even an extraordinary perspective, [which] keeps the landscape [for example, in Wordsworth] intact by giving evidence of its being looked upon. It locates the poem more firmly by specifically locating the speaker with reference to everything he sees and hears; and this establishes the concreteness not only of the landscape but of the speaker as well. . . . The particular perspective marks out the limits within which the poem has its existence. . . . The emphasis on particularity . . . is a guarantee that the poem is an authentic experience which gives birth to an idea rather than the illustration of a ready-made idea. (pp. 47, 48)

These remarks have peculiar relevance to Howells. A large part of his mind was by cultural pressure a neoclassic mind, a "meditative-descriptive" mind, and his failure was that which Langbaum ascribes to such poets. But Howells' existential problems were romantic, his artistic problem was Wordsworth's—to reach and explain an alien world—and his grave error was not to use Wordsworth's method as an organizing principle. Within small sections of the Howells novel, there is "location" and there are epiphanies; but the sections are seldom integrated and there are few unified effects because there is little firm location. Not that Howells lacked interest in the problem of location—his absorption in point of view lasted from the opening chapters of *Venetian Life* through the mature anatomies to the last novels. But very seldom does he *consistently* locate a novel, or even try to do so. My questions about *A Modern Instance* reveal the confusion that one feels when trying to locate Howells' novels for him. After his first books, Howells almost entirely abandons that simplest of locating devices, so obvious to moderns and so useful even to the "naïve" Twain: first-person point of view. The first person is always implied in the comments and generalizations; but that method is clumsy compared to such alternatives as withdrawing the authorial "I" and using a character as "I," or plunging the author completely into the book and keeping him there (as in Sterne). When Howells does employ the locating device of the narrating character, in *A Traveler from Altruria,* he has a brilliant success; but in his next novels, he goes back to his old devices. Limited omniscience, precisely controlled to suggest the limitations and ambiguities of perception, was beyond the powers of Howells, and not sympathetic to a mind that needed some form of the first person at all times. The Howells novel is a distorted and unsuccessful lyric, or rather, a succession of such lyrics, each one an awkward grab at a moment, in an epiphany. The Howells novel successfully evades being a forthright record of one man's collision with reality, or a symbolic record of a surrogate's collision with reality, and therefore is neither.

For Howells there is no alternative between location and chaos, between choice of methods and confusion of methods. His temperament cannot believe in location. His controlling image beckons him toward a surface apparently available as a solid reference point, but then betrays him with a fall into confusion. Like the image of confusion, the confusion of methods is basic. At times, Howells' art is moral; at other times, it is existential (in the literal sense). Mr. and Mrs. Atherton in *A Modern Instance* are moral touchstones; at the same time, they are just themselves, a genteel professional man and a spoiled but earnest rich girl; and the perspective from which we are invited to condemn the Hubbards turns out to be no perspective at all. The confusion appears on technical levels, too. Not only are essay elements and fiction mixed together, so that one is jerked back and forth between the two, but comments themselves back up now moral views and now existential ones, so that we are referred now to the idea that there are standards and now to the idea that there are no standards—only facts, events, and riddles. It is often hard to tell whether a mixture of *A* and *B* consists of *A* causing *B*, or *B* causing *A*, or *A* despite *B*, or *B* despite *A*, or just *A* and *B*. Too often, the lack of location results in the neoclassic quality that Langbaum refers to: the existential situation in a novel becomes simply a device, an *exemplum* varying in length from a few sentences to eight hundred pages, and any stasis in the novel is not an epiphany wrung from the flux of time, but the meaningless, dead stasis of intellectual abstractions. Use of titles like *A Modern Instance* shows that Howells had the *exemplum* approach well in mind, and no one who admits the validity of the anatomy as an art form can quarrel with that. But then we find that the "examples"—characters like Bartley Hubbard, Squire Gaylord, Dryfoos, Jeff Durgin—lose their typicality, acquire demonic energies, and step forth autonomous characters in their own right, dominating and living outside of the action, like the Hamlet and Falstaff of the Romantic critics.

The effects of non-location extend to those elements of form that have to do with reader satisfaction. Tension, anticipation, foreshadowing, the sense of resolution, are not lacking in Howells; in his plays and certain of his novels (*Indian Summer, The Shadow of a Dream,* for example), he shows himself professionably capable in such matters. But these works are of two sorts: the high-level hack job, and the firmly located work of art. In the most significant novels, the ones that meant the most to Howells and cost him the most, plot values vary from decidedly subordinate to almost nonexistent. Like certain *avant garde* works of the 1960's, the major Howells novel is a "happening," an event that has its own inscrutable value. The most one can say is that certain characters, and the reader, learn something by observing the happenings during a certain span of time. This could be said of a major modern novel like *The Ambassadors,* but the resemblance is shallow. James seizes the possibilities of point of view, locates his novel firmly, and makes it impossible for us to feel the novel except as Strether feels it. Howells uses comment to prod his materials, but without great effect, and we are left to find tensions and movements for ourselves. The death of Conrad Dryfoos, for example, could be a climax; but after a look at its context and treatment, one realizes that it is not the climax of anything, and that it occurs in a world where definitive climaxes do not happen. Its apparent result —Dryfoos' withdrawal from *Every Other Week*—might have happened at any time, and would have happened sooner or later, Howells is careful to inform us (*HNF,* II, 319–20). The central movement of the story is the Marches' growth from naïve dwellers in Eden to experienced people of the world. Howells offers plenty of material for that movement, and it would be a simple reader who did not see it; but Howells does not insist upon it. Confusingly and confusedly, he spreads before us his world and lets us make up our own menus.

The Howells novel, then, reduces everything certain to a problem, whereas the work of art traditionally reduces problems to some kind of certainty—a certainty of ignorance or ambiguity if not a certainty of knowledge. The strategies of art help set up and shake down problems for solution, just as the mathematician's formulas help to clarify his problems. For romantics, the "located" perspective is one of the great strategies; but for Howells, perspective is, like other devices, itself a problem. Howells thus finds himself in the quandary of having to use certain (that is, exact) expressions to say that nothing is certain and that in some cases nothing can be said. Even the greatest nihilists, and their audiences, have had the perhaps improper satisfaction of enjoying the methods and the triumphs of art while loudly saying nay. Howells does not even say nay; he says "maybe" or "I don't know," and then qualifies even that. In the end we can only be sure that a problem of some uncertain kind exists, and that we are not going to have the consolations of art.

Although this study is not biographical, I advance some factors in Howells' life and milieu that, if they did not directly cause his artistic qualities, were aids and parallels to them. One is overproduction. In writing more than one hundred volumes (fiction, travel, reminiscences, criticism, poetry, one-act plays, full-length plays), Howells left his mental gates open so continuously that he had little chance to build up pressure behind and in his work. James could produce an enormous canon of works "done" to his own high standards because his pressure was supplied by his devotion to art; when artistry was lacking, or working at a low level (as in his plays), he could be lifeless, too. This kind of frantic production was a defense for Howells, not (after his early years) a necessity imposed by physical need or the spur of ambition. He never lived in Grub Street, and by the 1890's, his earnings were substantial by any standards.[2] Given sufficient internal pressure, Howells was capable of strong artistry and irony, as in *A Traveler from Altruria* and that bitter

[2] See Cady, II, 192 ff., for a thorough and revealing discussion of Howells' financial position in this period, during which, Cady estimates, Howells' income was "probably the real equivalent of $100,000 a year in 1958" (p. 192).

short story of the Spanish-American War, "Editha." Howells' steady overproduction helped him to evade the natural point that for him, the novel was a lyric, the "lyric cry" of Stephen Dedalus. (He began, we should remember, as a poet and an admirer of poets.) His situation may be compared to that of the young modern novelist whose first novels are explosive discharges of adolescent pressures, but whose later works are slack because the novelist's pressures are being discharged piecemeal on other things—controversy, high jinks—after his first success. If the lyric novelist has nothing to say, he will (uncommonly) say nothing, or simulate and stimulate pressure and tend toward rhetoric and bombast. For the Jamesian maker-artist, this problem is not so important. Howells did not have it when he was turning out well-made plays, problem novels, belletristic essays, and criticism; but he did have it when he turned to serious fictional representations of his vision of life.

There is also the question of the audience. It helps locate the Howells novel as no other factor does. Indeed, the Howells novel can be said not to exist outside of the perspective given it by the audience. Like the earlier Victorian novelists, Howells had with his audience a rich rapport, one that he openly resented at times (and perhaps secretly did all the time), but which he wrote for and to. Among its other functions, comment in the Howells novel works to bypass the third party (the work of art) and to help the author speak directly to the audience. In this use of comment, what matters most is not the content of the comment but the intimacy of the gesture. (The content, too, can matter, if it is already known to the audience.) Howells tells us about old men's glasses; he pushes aside Silas Lapham and says of the crowd on the Nantasket boat, "To a straw-hatted population, such as ours is in summer, no sort of personal dignity is possible" (*RSL*, p. 111). Another time, he speaks unnecessarily of a church service ending "in that subordination of the spiritual to the artistic which marks the process and the close of so much public worship in our day" (*LA*, pp. 113–14). On each of these occasions and a thousand others, the reader will respond, "Just so," and hold the work and the author up with his praise. Or rather, the reader of the 1870's and 1880's did so. In the 1890's readers began to turn away toward the dreamland of Graustarkian romance; and from the turn of the century to the present, the more sophisticated audience has been irritated by, or at best, mildly interested in, "intrusions" (as we now call them) and amused by the faded images of the Brown Decades. *Daisy Miller,* a book of strong contemporary appeal, is still carried by its artistry; the Howells novel, its original audience dead, must find new grounds of appeal.

Another Howells difficulty related to the problem of the audience is the incongruity of his situation to his talents. In Howells a strain of the eighteenth-century neoclassic mind is combined with romanticism and caught in a nineteenth-century romantic situation. The "genteel tradition" of Boston was not entirely sympathetic to Howells, but because of the location, not because of the gentility. Like Mark Twain, he was, and to a large extent liked being, that which he attacked; and this ambivalence gives his work, not the clear-cut manic-depressive qualities of a Dostoevski, but a typical evasiveness. This genteel, belletristic tradition was not only part of Howells' time in the East, but part of his world as a boy and a young man in the Midwest. The tradition was firmly rooted in colonial and Federalist culture; it resisted the early romantics and attacked the Lake poets and Cockneys; it assimilated the romantic tradition without yielding to it.[3] This tradition

[3] See William Charvat, *The Origins of American Critical Thought, 1810–35* (Philadelphia, 1936) for a thorough discussion of the era that sired Howells. "In no other period in American history," Charvat points out, "has our culture been so completely and directly dominated by the professional classes. . . . The predominance of lawyers and ministers in the critical world explains in part two major characteristics of the criticism of the periods: its judicial and its moral tone" (p. 5). "Much of the best American criticism of our period concerned the English romantics. It was judicial, not appreciative criticism. The result was that the elements of English romanticism not acceptable to the American temperament were

moved west by mail (the Eastern journals and newspapers of the time) and in person (the editors, professional men, professors, and genteel consumers). In our emphasis in recent years on the folk tradition and underground culture of the frontier and post-frontier eras, in our interest in tall tales and raw humor, we have tended to forget or belittle the frontier's deep respect for culture and propriety. The Cincinnati women at whom Mrs. Trollope laughed may have been gauche by standards brought straight from London, but Mrs. Trollope forgot that in imitation, gaucherie does not imply insincerity. The Michigan frontier explored by Mrs. Kirkland in *A New Home* could be inordinately oafish, but that can easily be explained as an upside down tribute to what the oafs were secretly yearning for. Neoclassicism and romanticism, gentility and primitivism, were inextricably combined. The Grangerfords, the great symbolic clan of *Huckleberry Finn,* are corrupt not because they are primitive, but because they try to conceal their animality from the world and themselves under what they think is the style of eighteenth-century English country gentlemen, with the result that they are neither gentlemen nor true primitives, but savages. Emmeline Grangerford's paintings and poems are funny because they try to be wildly romantic and prissily correct at the same time.

Howells grew up in this world—a world in which Cincinnati was referred to both as the "Athens of the West" and "Porkopolis" (Cady, I, 14), in which newspaper editors like his father could discuss Swedenborg's mystic doctrines at one moment and write harsh political editorials the next (see Cady, I, 15, 16 ff.). As a young man, Howells frequented Columbus drawing rooms, where style and wit were as

---

winnowed out. Byron was banished before the period closed; Keats and Shelley were neglected; Wordsworth and Coleridge were accepted with reservations; Hazlitt was attacked; Scott was welcomed. In the American romantic period up to 1860, there was little of the influence of Shelley and Keats . . ." (p. 3).

important as the ability to write romantic poems (Howells' favorite was Heine). But Howells' mind was largely neo-classic; his sympathies were with the abstract as opposed to the figurative, direct statement as opposed to symbols, clear heavy comprehension of the actual world as opposed to vague escapism from that world. His literary career is, in a sense, the slow triumph of his unsparing Swiftian side over his early love for the "picturesque" and for "glamour." His love of generalizations and comments and examples and analyzing (rather than participating) observers reflects this underlying bias, as does his earliest and deepest literary passion, his love for Cervantes. With his debilitating timidities and neuroses, Howells would not have felt secure in Fielding's day; but otherwise, he would have been at home there. His era, however, was the late nineteenth century. Even the charismatic Mark Twain could not conquer the genteel romanticism of that age, or the qualities in himself that responded to it. Howells, who had enough trouble keeping himself sane and productive without fighting the whole world, could not take an unequivocal stance in his world, and his failure to do so is inevitably reflected in the confusion of his novels.

II

. . . organized lifelessness full of a strange semblance of life.

Underlying every question about Howells, every virtue, every flaw, is his style. It has had many admirers. In a chapter that remains after forty years the best discussion of Howell's style, Oscar W. Firkins reminds us that Mark Twain, a careful stylist himself, was deeply impressed by Howells' style. The modern reader, for whom Howells' subject matter no longer has immediate appeal, cannot help being struck by Howells' style. Like the general cast of his mind, it is closer to

Addison and Fielding than to his immediate predecessors. It has few of the characteristics and faults of the windy rhetoric standard in Howells' youth or the journalism of Howells' maturity. It is self-conscious; we are never allowed to forget the perceiver analyzing, organizing, and choosing, and aware of himself busy at these tasks. There are innumerable set pieces, especially in the early novels, with their travel-book qualities; and as I have said, these set pieces allow Howells to explore the possibilities of perception and its use.

But despite the set pieces and the "realism," this is not a style that seizes concrete things and actual events and devotes itself to them. The content usually seems remembered, brought in for a purpose, screened for relevance, and submitted to the style. The events do not happen *now;* the facts do not enter by their own power or for their own sake, as they can in great anatomy writers like Rabelais and Swift. The Howells style shows him to be withdrawn, watchful, alienated. He controls threatening reality by caging it in his deadening, anaesthetic style.

Firkins accurately identified one important basic quality of Howells' style forty years ago:

> The style of Mr. Howells . . . is no trick. . . . The style has a preexistence in the psychology, is in essence the ingress of that psychology into language. The peculiarity of the writing might be defined as a rare ease and quietness in the setting forth of delicately intricate relations. But this trait merely images, merely registers, the lasting condition of its author's mind. The impartial and almost universal curiosity of Mr. Howells made it natural that, in his perception of one object, he should become vividly conscious of all its kinsfolk and neighbors; and his eye for relation enabled him to traverse instantly and readily the manifold threads of connection which fastened it to the surrounding world. Since he was adept in all the leanings or inflections of a thing, his options in expression were numerous, and, in this spaciousness of choice, it was easy for him to solve the recurrent problem of style, to discover the

doubly apt phrase which at once fills up the measure of the thought and integrates the contours of the sentence. (Firkins, *op. cit.*, pp. 320–21)

The precision of Howells' style often adds dryness or even a note of contempt to his grasp of qualities and relations; he often writes as an anthropologist or sociologist rather than as a novelist (or "anatomist"). In *The Landlord at Lion's Head,* for example, we are told of the Vostrands' failure to get into Boston society: " . . . Towards the end of February, when good society in Boston goes southward to indulge a Lenten grief at Old Point Comfort, Genevieve had so many vacant afternoons and evenings at her disposal that she could not have truthfully pleaded a previous engagement to the invitations Jeff Durgin made her" (pp. 129–30). The comment on Boston society might be no more than casual irony were it not for the curious choice of "indulge" and the positioning of the dry clause as an aside in the sentence. "Indulge" offers a bitter glimpse into the pretense and empty bustle of the very class that had long claimed Mr. Howells as one of its chief ornaments. As a grammatical aside, the clause is a bursting of the flat narrative surface; for a moment, the demonic in Howells shows itself. This is the harsh sociology of Veblen (whom Howells praised) and Mills, not the objectivity of the modern academic sociologist. For the most part, however, the Howells style is bland, an instrument of concealment. Like the critic Firkins, we are diverted by the ingenuities of the style from what it is not doing and often from what it is doing; in this condition we may fail to realize that Howells often uses his verbal skills and his "eye for relation" to ease himself and us away from the disturbing quiddity of a thing to its abstract qualities and relationships.[4]

[4] In its abstractness, if not its neatness, the usual Howells sentence is curiously similar to the late-Melville sentence as Werner Berthoff describes it: "Melville's desire for thoroughness of treatment seems on the whole to increase as his books accumulate, and results eventually in the casual tortuousness and heaviness of much of his later prose. The sentence-

This smoothness is part of Howells from the beginning. In the essays and stories of *Suburban Sketches,* Howells maneuvers dexterously from one observation to the next; and we do not realize the full strength of his feelings, because he does not want us to know, or, more likely, because he cannot afford to find out. At some points in Howells' mature work, this gliding effect reinforces his contemptuous irony, and it is then that Howells' style has its most powerful moments. With apparently indifferent competence, he presents a situation, an action, or a character, and the impact emerges from the reader's sudden and belated recognition of significance and irony. I have discussed a few of the most impressive of these scenes: the undercutting and discrediting of lawyer Atherton and his wife Clara in *A Modern Instance;* the biting phrase "such as it was" following a deadpan discussion of Bartley Hubbard's "better nature." In reading the passage about the Athertons, one may at first be aware only of the author's diligence and competence at choosing and expressing the realistic details of American life and, in particular, the minutiae of breakfasting in a Back Bay mansion. Only after a delay does one realize that Howells has irrevocably cut the ground from under the embodiment of standards in the novel. Toward the middle of *A Hazard of New Fortunes,* there is a similar sequence, which will stand here for the author's

---

making in *The Confidence-Man* and *Billy Budd,* in particular, is of this nature. Increasingly he seems to build each new syntactical period out of the consciousness of a certain quantity of things to be got into it—details, contingencies, cross references, explanations, analogues—without which his statement might be judged incomplete. Its job is more and more to *contain,* less and less to *discover* and *display.* The element of free inquiry and exploration which gives his earlier writing much of its rare force and expansiveness tends to be replaced by static enumeration, in the process losing for pace and momentum what may have been gained for seriousness of consideration. . . . After *Pierre* [these sentences] . . . no longer act *primarily* to thrust upon us the feelings, sensations, material densities, excitements, and felt intimations of the encountered things of 'this world' " (*The Example of Melville* [Princeton, 1962], pp. 169–70). The point is that Howells, throughout his career, and Melville, after *Moby-Dick,* faced many of the same problems of epistemology and confidence.

practice throughout the book. Christine and Mela Dryfoos, the daughters of the gas-country millionaire, have been packed off unwillingly to Saratoga with their mentor, Mrs. Mandel. Christine yearns for Beaton, the conceited artist.

> . . . With Mela's help she wrote a letter, bantering Beaton on his stay in New York, and playfully boasting of Saratoga. It seemed to them both that it was a very bright letter and would be sure to bring him; they would have had no scruples about sending it but for the doubt they had whether they had got some of the words right. Mela offered to bet Christine anything she dared that they were right, and she said, Send it anyway; it was no difference if they *were* wrong. But Christine could not endure to think of that laugh of Beaton's and there remained only Mrs. Mandel as authority on spelling. Christine dreaded her authority on other points, but Mela said she knew she would not interfere, and she undertook to get round her. Mrs. Mandel pronounced the spelling bad, and the taste worse; she forbade them to send the letter; and Mela failed to get round her, though she threatened, if Mrs. Mandel would not tell her how to spell the wrong words, that she would send the letter as it was; then Mrs. Mandel said that if Mr. Beaton appeared in Saratoga she would instantly take them both home. When Mela reported this result, Christine accused her of having mismanaged the whole business; she quarrelled with her, and they called each other names. Christine declared that she would not stay in Saratoga, and if Mrs. Mandel did not go back to New York with her she should go alone. They returned the first week in September; but by that time Beaton had gone to see his people in Syracuse. (II, 85–86)

The sentences are cold, dull; there are no direct quotations; everything is recorded flatly by a thorough and indifferent reporter. Yet the passage confronts us ironically with a demonic world. Christine and Mela are ferocious in the depth and directness of their passions. Sounding, with its clumsy repetitions, loose co-ordination, and lavish use of semicolons, as if it had been written by the girls themselves, the passage makes the girls' savagery mysterious and frightening. The author has visited his idea of the hell in man and has returned too exhausted to use energy on anything except simple presentation; but his feelings of fear and revulsion are written into his manner, or more precisely, his lack of manner. It is in this sort of thing that "realism" antedates certain common aspects of modern art—the interchapters of *In Our Time,* for instance.

The passage from *A Hazard of New Fortunes* also illustrates one of the most notable qualities of Howells' style: parataxis. Mela does this, and Christine says that, and Mrs. Mandel replies thus. The writing is coherent; there is never any trouble in understanding Howells. No one has ever felt exasperation (admiring or not) in reading Howells, as many have felt in reading his friend James. But at the same time, one never feels in Howells the sense of connection that James and Melville try to express. For Howells, connection exists, if at all, on levels too deep to comprehend, as he tells us many times (usually through the Marches). Within the world of visual perception, he can record successive events flawlessly, but he cannot find any connection among them unless he selects and reorganizes them in the manner of non-fiction. This accounts in part for his characteristic emphasis on essay and his use of *exempla* rather than symbolic drama. Whenever connections exist in his work, they have been added between the perception and the statement of the perception. We are given, not *symbolic* single events, which would imply networks of connections, but *characteristic* events and states, which imply only vague, inconsequential relationships of things in the same class. His mind is Aristotelian—classifying and static, not modern, dynamic, and aware of process. Single events in his works are not differentiated from descriptions; when Mr. March escorts his wife to her Boston sleeper in *A Hazard of New Fortunes,* Howells has a chance to record the night scene along the elevated railroad and at the Central Depot (the predecessor of Grand Central Station).

> She now said that the night transit was more interesting than the day, and that the fleeting intimacy you formed with people in second and third floor interiors . . . had a domestic intensity mixed with a perfect repose that was the last effect of good society with all its security and exclusiveness. He said it was better than the theatre, of which it reminded him, to see those people through their windows. . . . What suggestion! what drama! what infinite interest! . . . The track that found and lost itself a thousand times in the flare and tremor of the innumerable lights; the moony sheen of the electrics mixing with the reddish points and blots of gas far and near; the architectural shapes of houses and churches and towers, rescued by the obscurity from all that was ignoble in them, and the coming and going of the trains marking the stations with vivider or fainter plumes of flame-shot steam—formed an incomparable perspective. They often talked afterward of the superb spectacle, which in a city full of painters nightly works its unrecorded miracles. . . . What forces, what fates, slept in those bulks which would soon be hurling themselves north and east and west through the night! Now they waited there like fabled monsters of Arab story ready for the magician's touch, tractable, reckless, will-less—organized lifelessness full of a strange semblance of life. (I, 95–96)

Here a reasonable sense of immediacy and particularity gives way without resistance to indirection and generality, and then to romantic journalese and the resounding, facile rhetoric of the Everett-Webster era. The style is mechanical; its complexities have not been won by thought or conflict. Unfortunately, there is a great deal of this style in Howells.

This emptiness appears in other ways. In *A Hazard of New Fortunes* (to draw again on this central Howells text), Mrs. Horn, a frigid society matron, contemplates the dislike of her niece, Margaret Vance, for the social principle of *quid pro quo*. I quote no more than part of the middle of the passage.

> That was part of Margaret's originality, which pleased her aunt in proportion to her own conventionality; she was really a timid person, and she liked the show of courage which Margaret's magnanimity often reflected upon her. She had through her a repute, with people who did not know her well, for intellectual and moral qualities; she was supposed to be literary and charitable; she almost had opinions and ideals, but really fell short of their possession. She thought that she set bounds to the girl's originality because she recognized them. (II, 4)

This is an extreme example, perhaps affected by haste or weariness, but it is not substantially different from the dominant Howells style. The monotonous sentence structure and the almost complete absence of connectives except for "and" and "but" reveal the unorganized nature of the Howells world. Even in cases where his sentences are rich in internal connectives, the sentences are not connected to each other by logic or rhetoric. At the end of each sentence of the quoted passage, there is a definite stop; then, after an interval of vacuum, comes the next sentence. (This is not at all like the Hemingway "and then" style, with its effects of strain and control.) Also, there are few participles to suggest continuing action. Here is another example, taken, not from a meditation, but from a sequence of action and comment.

> In the cares which Mrs. March shared with her husband that night [after the death of Conrad Dryfoos] she was supported partly by principle, but mainly by the potent excitement which bewildered Conrad's family and took all reality from what had happened. It was nearly midnight when the Marches left them and walked away toward the elevated station with Fulkerson. Everything had been done, by that time, that could be done; and Fulkerson was not without that satisfaction in the business-like despatch of all the details which attends each step in such an affair, and helps to make death tolerable even to the most sorely stricken. We are creatures of the moment; we live from one little space to another; and only one interest at a time fills

> these. Fulkerson was cheerful when they got into the street, almost gay; and Mrs. March experienced a rebound from her depression which she felt that she ought not to have experienced. But she condoned the offense a little in herself. . . . (II, 235)

And so on. Mrs. March's feelings are not presented or even discussed; instead, we are told, in an abstract way, how she kept herself going, and we are at the same time told that March feels the same way she does. The phenomena and conditions of life have thus been related in the way that boxes in an organization chart are related, but there is nothing viable or dynamic or even concrete in the passage. Each sentence is one of those neatly rounded periods praised by Firkins, followed by a pause. The comment and the generality help to force the already strongly abstract material further toward the dimension of typicality. Except for this push in the direction of the general, the style is passive; it does not reflect or reinforce any attempt to realize grief in general or the feelings of the Marches in particular. The style is, then, not "realistic," if we use that term with anything approaching strictness. The details of feeling, the concrete experience of grief, are avoided, because of Howells' fear of the demonic, and the tacit excuse is that the knowledge of such feelings can be taken for granted. In any case, the stiffness and numbness of the style effectively repress the reader's tendency toward strong reactions. The modern reader will go away from this passage—and the many others like it—bored and disappointed, without knowing exactly why. Upon a little reflection, he will realize that he has been cheated, has been dexterously made accessory to a fraud, an attempt to substitute the appearance of rendering existence for actually rendering existence.

Howells' lack of interest in process also reflects his fragmented, limp approach to reality. This lack of interest did not arise from ignorance. Howells was master of many journalistic trades—typesetting, political reporting, writing of sketches and humor, editing of newspapers and magazines. He knew how to find out what the literary market wanted and how to shape his material to fit the demand without vitiating the material. Acting as his own agent, he dickered in the marketplace and won high prices for his literary products and his personal services. He had a good eye for the kind of essay, story, or passage that could be reworked for anthologies; he knew how to tailor one-act plays for American amateur theater groups. He skillfully sold his personality in an era when the ability to give successful interviews and shine at public banquets was essential for the man of letters who wanted full recognition and the money that went with it. Like Twain and James, he was a successful literary tradesman. "Nobody knew the business of authorship better than Howells," says his biographer.[5]

But Twain glorified in his worldliness (not that he had full reason to do so); James was proud of it and paid it the negative compliment of attacking it in some of his best stories. Howells did not care either way. Selling his talents and his self was what he had to do. He did it as well as he could, and neither liked nor disliked the techniques involved. Newspapermen, publishers, and editors abound in his novels; but we hear little about the technical processes of their work, and what we do hear is often unfavorable. The magazine *Every Other Week* is the center of *A Hazard of New Fortunes;* its editor, Basil March, is the central character if anyone is; much of the story occurs at its office; and some attention is given to the magazine's problems. But that amounts to very little (a few pages all told) in relation to the immensity of the novel and its events; there is little passion or excitement in the discussion of the events and decisions that lead to the creation of the magazine's individuality. Other American authors with non-literary skills have been unable to resist putting in their

[5] Cady, II, 187. For a full discussion of Howells at the peak of his business abilities, see Cady, II, 187, 189 ff.

extraneous knowledge for its own sake, or have happily been able to make their knowledge the basis of symbolism and symbolic actions. But the process of getting out the magazine does not interest Howells. He is interested in the characters' responses to the situation that embodies the process. We do not see very clearly how Basil March edits *Every Other Week;* we never see him sitting at an actual desk, thinking actual thoughts about actual manuscripts, and going through actual professional routines. What we learn is what he feels in general about the conditions of his work and the effects arising from the interactions of people brought together by the magazine. In *The World of Chance,* the process of getting a novel published is reduced to pure luck; in *A Hazard of New Fortunes,* Beaton's method of designing the cover for *Every Other Week* is aimless doodling.

In *A Hazard of New Fortunes* and elsewhere, the man who is enthusiastic about his craft generally becomes the butt of satire. The great technician in this novel is Fulkerson, who knows and tells everything there is to know about advertising, publicity, literary syndicates, and manipulating people. Though he is decent enough to inspire love (some of it at the author's convenience) in Madison Woodburn, the symbol of good perception in the novel, Fulkerson inevitably becomes a figure of amusement; for his skills are irrelevant and his views absurdly inadequate when life resolves itself into simple questions of character, power, or the movements of chance. The shallow technician of journalism is satirized much earlier in Howells, beginning with the "contributor" of *Suburban Sketches* and continuing with clever reporters like Bartley Hubbard, Bittridge, and Pinney in *The Quality of Mercy.* In *A Modern Instance* and again in the opening pages of *The Rise of Silas Lapham,* we learn of Bartley's methods of ascertaining demands, seeking out valuable material, and working it up into a form acceptable to the yellow journalism of his day. Howells brands all of this skill and effort as pointless and selfish, and even cruel. His fear of the wrong kind of artist, the manipulator or romantic falsifier of life, underlies this dislike of the slick professional. Not for him the religion of professional technique, the world of Melville and Twain and Conrad, Hemingway and Faulkner, in which mastery of skills helps man to stand up to the demonic world or to create his own order and meaning from the flux of events and perceptions. For Howells there are no such defenses; he is thrown back on others.

Connected with Howells' lack of enthusiasm for technique is his lack of interest in the concrete and sensuous aspects of life. His style reveals a largely abstract world. What matters is relationships—man's feelings in the presence of the world, and the interactions of those feelings. It is all rather mathematical, a diagram rather than an anatomical drawing. In Howells' mature art, a scene may be laid in a parlor, but the parlor is not seen as an environment with densities and effects in space and time; the parlor is instrumental—a place for characters to encounter each other and for effects of experiences to be gathered. In *The Landlord at Lion's Head,* Jeff Durgin is made to acquire certain conclusions about the rich by meeting them in the mountains, at Harvard spreads, and in Boston drawing rooms. We do not sense Jeff's experiencing of these episodes, and indeed, Jeff, unlike the heroes (Julian Sorel, Frederic Henry) of the classic and modern *Bildungsroman,* does not truly experience his change from rustic to worldling. We are given a scene, and later, we learn that Jeff has drawn certain conclusions from the scene and has therefore changed somewhat in character. Linking abstraction and voluntarism, this method is the opposite of the Balzacian engulfment in milieu that characterizes authors as apparently different as Twain and James.[6] Howells' earliest work is often more concrete, but only because concreteness and the experience of concreteness are interesting problems for the young author.

[6] For the discussion of milieu (in Balzac and other nineteenth-century realists) that I have in mind, see Erich Auerbach, *op. cit.,* pp. 413–25.

Concreteness in Howells' mature works is instrumental (for satire) or pictorial. The drawing room of Mrs. Green's apartment in *A Hazard of New Fortunes* is presented with such great richness that the incautious reader might be reminded of Madame Vauquer's parlor in *Père Goriot* or one of James's English country houses. But the long description of that flat serves rather to make the alien environment grotesque (as well as to create the effect of density that I have discussed). The Marches' own house in Boston is not described in this way, or at all, because it is not to be satirized. It would never occur to Howells to create the Marches by building a dense Boston environment around them or by dwelling on their appearance. Like March on the steps of his Boston office (*HNF*, I, 10), Howells never notices things sharply unless or until they are strange to him. And when he or his characters do notice reality, it is not as milieu, but as picture, something outside the person and perhaps threatening him, not something penetrating and shaping him. *A Hazard of New Fortunes* abounds in word pictures of the New York streets, elevated railroads, and trainsheds. The characters do not *experience* New York, though. It is all that Howells can do to sense that there are connections between that pictured world and the characters.

With this limited paratactic style, this peculiar cramped fluency, Howells cannot celebrate reality, either by rejoicing in it or retreating from it. Howells' great contemporaries and successors may be critical or even contemptuous of politics or society or mankind, but there is always something for them to celebrate, and they shape their styles in order to do so. This shaping demands commitment, and commitment involves exposure and risk. The defensive Howells style exposes little and risks nothing; it does not seek to impose itself; and as one result, few people either care much for Howells or dislike him much. Almost every important modern author has been parodied, and the greater the author, the more uproarious the parody; but Howells is not parodied. This is not a question of subject matter or "life-style." James and Hemingway, in those respects so different, offer themselves equally to parody because in committing themselves totally to the celebration of the human consciousness, they shape styles that reflect their own needs totally and others' needs not at all. If every one shared the peculiar ecstasy of James or Hemingway, then it would be impossible to parody them. It is thus a backhanded admission of Howells' low-level universality that no one exaggerates his style; in fact, it would be bad manners to break down Howells' defenses by ridiculing them.

This cautious, abstract style not only lacks velocity; it lacks mass, or, to use Professor Lovejoy's term, plenitude. In the earlier major American authors, and in Howells' greatest contemporaries, enthusiasm and bulk go together, sometimes not with much discrimination, but in the greatest instances, in a state of fusion. Love of technique—in an occupation or merely in the art of observing—usually accompanies the other two factors. As a result, we have *Walden, Song of Myself, Moby-Dick, Huckleberry Finn, Life on the Mississippi*—all the central masterpieces of American literature. Even in James, a more cautious author, the sense of life's richness survives the worst misjudgments and disasters, and in *The Ambassadors* plenitude provides the text for James's most famous sermon (based on Howells' comment, not his actions). There is something involuntary about this sense of life's richness. It survives Melville's epistemological crisis, and gives *The Confidence-Man* a richness and variety that partly denies the grim theme of the novel; even the guarded last sentence ("Something further may follow of this masquerade.") suggests not just the baffling ambiguities of life, but also its inexhaustible flow and richness. Conversely, if it is difficult to lose this sense, an author may acquire it, and then he may be qualified to enter the major ranks. When Faulkner stops being the gloomy minor aesthete of *Mosquitoes* and *Soldier's Pay*, and accepts his own world, he becomes one of the major authors of the century; for the infinite richness of

Yoknapotawpha County makes it equal the world. While reading *Sartoris,* for example, one can experience Faulkner's grasping of incidental bits of his world (the crowded square at lunchtime, the farm where Bayard Sartoris drinks, the old houses), and his fusion of elements into the final, unmistakable Faulkner world in the long episode of Bayard's escape to the hills.

There is none of this in Howells. He does sense the richness of the world, but he senses it as problem or as threat, not as joy in itself. The opening pages of *Venetian Life,* which may be taken as the official opening of his career, reveal his early habit of reducing the world to a series of problems in perception and the rise of perception. In that significant little sketch "Scene," he shows that innocent joy in the surface of the world is soon destroyed by the demonic forces bursting through the surface. One may profitably compare "the contributor" at the end of "Scene" to Huckleberry Finn or Ishmael after one of their appalling adventures. The Howells character is shaken and helpless, but the other two, after facing evil squarely, shrug off their gloom and return to their buoyant pleasure in existing in a varied world. The later Howells exposes his characters to the teeming reality of the late nineteenth century, but never lets them risk fusion with it. The Marches stroll through the East Side, ride the el, and sit in Washington Square among the drunks and the lovers; but they are always aliens, observing and observed, neatly shut off from their surroundings by the Howells style, which (as Firkins showed) is supremely competent at revealing abstract relations, but which cannot or will not penetrate. "The Marches paid the charming prospect a willing duty, and rejoiced in it as generously as if it had been their own" (*HNF,* II, 71): the implication is that an ecstatic embrace of reality is not to be thought of, and that a polite, restrained approval is all one can expect.

Howells' abstraction and defensiveness are part of the growing abstraction and defensiveness of American culture in the late nineteenth century. In *Patriotic Gore* Edmund Wilson has taken as a theme of the post–Civil War period the use of professionalism as protection and solace by men educated in the prewar tradition of humanism and Roman ideals. The Gilded Age did not want educated men of this kind and, indeed, did not want professional men except as hired technicians who, in business lingo, could "get results." Oliver Wendell Holmes, Jr., Wilson's major example, triumphed as a man who got results, but sustained his self-respect and his reputation by mastering the law and tradition. Secure in his carapace of professional skill, but secure only as long as he remained in that carapace, Holmes endured through the late nineteenth and early twentieth centuries to become a father symbol in his old age.[7] Wilson's thesis can be extended to the three most important writers of the day, who were all professional men of letters and who each had a unique protective covering. Samuel Clemens created and wore the armor of professional humorist with the result that he became the mask, as far as the general public was concerned. In what by contrast would seem to be a mood closer to his own, he wrote books like *Joan of Arc* and *The Prince and the Pauper* that are really the product of another suit of Clemens armor, the defender of gentility. The products of the genuine Clemens were unpublishable, he felt. Using the carapace of art, James managed to protect himself (for example, from women, as Leon Edel shows)[8] and do work of lasting value. Howells also managed to protect himself. After the artistic climax of the 1840's and 1850's, it was no longer possible for American authors to risk the exposure of the Emersonian eyeball, open for the greatest union with nature (and hence the greatest knowledge), but also maximally vulnerable. Emerson, Thoreau, and the other

[7] Edmund Wilson, *Patriotic Gore: Studies in the Literature of the American Civil War* (New York, 1962), pp. 754 ff., 782, 789–96.

[8] *Henry James: The Middle Years: 1892–1895* (Philadelphia, 1962).

classical American authors do not deny the Bittridge in life, but feel confident to deal with it, and do not feel that Bittridge will attack them as he attacks Howells' innocent and bewildered Kentons. The Walden landscape, offering difficulties but concealing nothing, can be profitably compared to the Howells world, enigmatic and problematic or threatening. Hawthorne's cautious and ambiguous manner, reflecting a fundamental lack of confidence, links him to Howells.

Howells' smooth professional style—rising sometimes to brilliance, falling often to weary dullness, but generally successful—helped him to hold himself together; but he had no energies left over for art. For him language could be a refuge, but it could never be, as it was for Flaubert, a religion enabling him to master reality. Ironically, confidence and symbolic concreteness were to be restored by young men associated with Howells, either as students or enemies. The half-controlled vigor of youth replaced the balanced philosophical vigor of maturity. As inevitable results of this adaptation, which endures to the present, successful works have the flaws as well as the virtues of youth, and authors often run down when or if they grow up. Thomas Wolfe, James Jones, Norman Mailer, and Thomas Heggen (who killed himself) are recent examples. It is interesting that James Gould Cozzens, one of the few contemporaries we think of as mature (whatever his faults) has an outlook and a method that recall Howells in many respects. Cozzens is wary and suspicious; he locates ordered virtue in the small town and chaotic evil in the great cities; he uses protagonists like Basil March—competent, responsible, unoptimistic, careful; he presents actions that explode in an imperfect but functioning system and dislocate it. In Cozzens and contemporary neoconservatives, the tensions that are only latent in *The Kentons* have done their work and isolated the small town from the city, the standpatter from the progressive. If Howells had faced and used these tensions rather than avoiding them, and if he had not developed his style into the brilliant, evasive instrument described (in terms of its brilliance) by Firkins, he would not have found himself in the humiliating position of helping younger authors and being rejected by them.

Altogether, Howells simply lacked creative power—what Coleridge calls imagination or the esemplastic power, the ability to control and synthesize on a large scale. He was unable to force the world to obey him; he could not accept, or grapple with defeat, the demonic poser of life. It was all he could do to try to contain that force; but in art there is no alternative to conquest, and the demonic force conquered him. It shows through in his books as the destructiveness that drives his satire to undercut every standard. Sometimes it appears as a sneaking admiration for his demonic, destructive characters. After reading a number of Howells novels, one must be struck by how little real happiness there is in his world for his ordinary decent people. The only characters who enjoy themselves are the disagreeable or evil ones; in fact, as Howells' career goes on, his villains get more fun out of life and suffer less than his early cads. Bartley Hubbard bumbles, now into a good humor and now into trouble; but Bittridge and Jeff Durgin are always in control of themselves, and the more miserable their victims are, the more genial they. Jeff Durgin is Howells' only fully integrated personality, in the modern understanding of the term, and he is Howells' only thoroughly successful demon (Bittridge overreaches himself and is driven off).

As an author of the generation following Melville and Hawthorne, Howells was faced with the problem of recreating the dying tradition of American Symbolism (if the work of twenty or thirty years can be called a tradition). Potent and sensible, James took stock of his situation and fled into the security of traditions elsewhere; also potent but awkward and insecure, Twain stumbled wastefully toward a new American tradition. Lacking both power and a feeling of security, however, Howells could do no more than hang on and carry on in the situation bequeathed him by Hawthorne in *The Marble Faun* and the last abortive manuscripts, and Melville in *The Confidence-Man* and *Israel Potter*.

III

Ah! poor Real Life

After this cold recitation of what's wrong with Howells, I must turn right around and say that there is more to Howells than flaws—a point that I have made implicitly many times over in my analyses of his novels (and one that is implied in the decision to analyze). Howells' flaws are in fact one set of characteristics among many others; and if all these characteristics are examined objectively, Howells emerges as an important figure in the major American literary traditions and as an author reflecting the important philosophical stances of the modern world. Because I have deliberately fixed my attention on Howells' novels, considered in isolation, I can do no more than sketch his connections to literary and intellectual traditions. As one might infer from the evasiveness revealed in his novels, he is not squarely or overtly in one tradition, but stands between the various romanticisms and late neoclassicism of roughly 1750–1850, and the naturalism and existentialism of the period from the late nineteenth century to the present. His famous phrase "Ah! poor Real Life" is, in perfect sincerity, a plea for "realism," for the serious literary study of phenomena that had been neglected and despised. But that adjective "poor" also suggests the patronizing pastoralism of Crabbe, Cowper, and Gray, just as the jocular or meditative *flaneur* of *Suburban Sketches* suggests the slumming narrator of "The Deserted Village," and the occasional cold elegance of Howells' style recalls the lesser achievements of neoclassic prose. Howells did come to reject in some ways this "literary" inheritance (recall his harsh treatment of "the contributor"); but he could not destroy an attitude that went much deeper than mere fashion, and the Marches and Westovers of the late novels are still, despite their anxious concern and their desire to identify with what they observe, the offspring of the eighteenth century.

Another tradition reflected in Howells is gothicism. It would be absurd to call Howells a gothic novelist and try to assimilate him to the "black" tradition of Charles Brockden Brown, Poe, Hawthorne, and the mature Melville; but gothic elements inform his novels, and, appropriately for anatomy-fiction, also appear as subjects for discussion. Alienation from society, sinister "demons," the eruption of ineffable horror into the pastoral calm of everyday existence, the emphasis on unconscious drives, the pursuit of innocents by devils as a basic action, the sense of a charged natural background, blackness as the symbol of the unthinkable and unavoidable —these stock qualities and devices of the Gothic novel (and of Eric Bentley's melodrama) are all found in Howells. Recall, from *A Modern Instance,* the inexplicability of the source of Bartley Hubbard's downfall in Equity, Bartley's charm and ruthlessness, his devilish qualities, the inhumanly savage animus of Squire Hubbard toward Bartley, Marcia's pursuit of Bartley (a modern reversal of the usual gothic situation), the nightmare journey to Indianapolis. Consider Rhoda Aldgate's walk into the Negro district of Boston in *An Imperative Duty:* she is overwhelmed by the universal blackness; she loses all sense of time; she feels as if she were in a dream; she has visions. The passage suggests Poe, and strikingly resembles the account of Joe Christmas' nocturnal roamings in the Negro district of Jefferson (*Light in August,* Chapter V). Consider also *The Kentons,* which resembles the post-Richardson and Radcliffean melodramas analyzed by Leslie Fiedler in *Love and Death in the American Novel.* Here, innocence incarnate is harried from its home and turned out of one refuge after another; Ellen Kenton, another Clarissa Harlowe, is driven into hysterics and neurotic illness by uncontrollable unconscious forces; the devil pops up in one grinning avatar after another. In *The Shadow of a Dream,* the universe itself partakes of the demonic, and the characters, like those in Walpole's castle, are bewildered and assaulted at every turn. In Howells' final major work, *The Leatherwood God,* he uses more extensively and with more variety than ever before the image of blackness; the major scenes occur at night in a torch-lit church, and the devil-villain hides in a swamp away from the light.

What links Howells to a more immediate tradition, the great American one of Hawthorne and Melville, is his "tragic Humanism." The term is Leslie Fiedler's; in itself it is rather awkward and ambiguous, but when defined it becomes valuable. Fiedler defines it in terms of certain assumptions of Melville and Hawthorne:

> . . . That the world of appearances is at once real and a mask through which we can dimly perceive more ultimate forces at work; that Nature is inscrutable, perhaps basically hostile to man, but certainly in some sense alien; that in man and Nature alike, there is a "diabolical" element, a "mystery of iniquity"; that it is impossible to know fully either God or ourselves, and that our only protection from destructive self-deceit is the pressure and presence of others; that to be alone is, therefore, to be lost; that evil is real, and that the thinking man breaks his heart trying to solve its incompatibility with the existence of a good God or his own glimmering perceptions of goodness. (*Love and Death in the American Novel,* pp. 417–18)

"From this it follows," reasons Fiedler, "that the writer's duty is to say, 'Nay!'; to deny the easy affirmations by which most men live, and to expose the blackness of life most men try deliberately to ignore" (p. 418). Clearly, even if we discount Fiedler's vigorous language, Howells is no Melvillean thunderer, but the link is nevertheless there, and it extends to the unpopularity of the two writers. Neither would continue to give the public what he had habituated it to expect (South Seas romance from Melville, sweet young things from Howells); both tried to disturb the complacency of an audience that was ready to be hostile, and Howells did so not only in fictions, but in his ceaseless advocacy of what he innocently called "realism." The existence of characteristics of this "tragic Humanism" in Howells need hardly be documented if one recalls my discussions of his sense of alienation, his demonic characters, and his anxious narrators. In the light of such a doctrine, much more of Howells becomes meaningful. The Howells characters' endless and wearying social life is seen to be not just a meaningless round but an attempt—of course doomed to failure—to huddle people together and reduce the endemic loneliness. A similar device is the pairing of observers to reduce anxiety (and talk about it), or the use of lone observers to increase the impact of difficult situations (in *The Landlord at Lion's Head* and the crisis of *The Shadow of a Dream,* for instance).

Although Howells was not educated as a philosopher and was in no sense a philosophical novelist, he reflected some of the major concerns of modern philosophy and intellectual life: the various currents that came together in literary naturalism, the Kantian focus on epistemology and mind, and the existentialists' concern with what Heidegger calls "Being-in-the-world." The first two I will not discuss here. Howells' connections to naturalism are well explored in Chapter V of Carter's *Howells and the Age of Realism,* and I would only add that Howells is more truly pessimistic and determinist than the naturalist writers (who, as Carter points out, stand for reform). I have devoted a chapter to Howells' fretting over perception, the reliability of phenomena, the meaning of phenomena, and the habits of the mind. This side of Howells also links him to Hawthorne and the mature Melville. The other philosophical strain requires more discussion. It is no use trying to link Howells to political existentialists like Camus and Sartre, though Howells' courageous commitment in the Haymarket case and his interest in Christian Socialism do him credit and foreshadow the activism common among literary men and intellectuals in our time. Neither does Howells parallel Kierkegaard, another modern ideal; for Howells is not a religious writer, despite his frequent and rather wistful allusions to God. Nor does Howells have any but negative links in doctrine and in temperament to Nietzsche, whose ruthless pragmatism and Dionysian energies are assigned in the Howells novel to the villain. Howells does fall in line most of all with the phenomenological and Heideggerian concern with the world as a real and dynamic place around and beyond the mind. For Howells, as for Heidegger, truth is a quality of being; being is in the world, and man is in the world of being—thus Howells' impassioned devotion to "realism," which, being a working writer and not an intellectual, he thought of only in practical literary terms. When Howells capitalizes the *R* and the *L* in his classic apostrophe "Ah! poor Real Life," he is revealing much more than the reflex coyness of his apprenticeship; he is performing an act of piety toward Being. Although the word "Poor" is patronizing, it is also a sincere apology for the neglect suffered by Being in the century of Kant, Hegel, and Graustark.

Howells also shares Heidegger's sense of a fluid, dynamic world free of, and incapable of being bound by, man's ordering intellectual projections (such as the Hegelian dialectic). Given such a world, and man in it, Heidegger derives various qualities of human life.[9] The content of the Howells novel anticipates several of these qualities: man's basic free-floating anxiety, dependent not on immediate problems but on the human condition of existence in the world; *Alltäglichkeit*, the banal daily round that man first uses as a means of ordering the world and that eventually turns back and orders *him;* "chatter," an aspect of *Alltäglichkeit*, the formal social

[9] A widely available analysis of Heidegger's ideas and terms is William Barrett, *What Is Existentialism?* (New York, 1964), to which I am indebted.

behavior meaningless in itself but useful as a momentary cure for anxiety. In scene after scene and comment after comment (by author or spokesman), Howells presents this vision of modern man existing, getting along, not getting anywhere in particular, worrying about the world (the world that he knows and in which he exists), diverting himself to little avail. Consider Mrs. Horn's soiree in *A Hazard of New Fortunes,* Howells' greatest examination of human existence. It cannot be said that the Marches enjoy themselves at the party. They can never abandon themselves and their anxieties to the moment; but they do know how to behave well and pass the time, and how to help others do the same. The Dryfoos girls, on the other hand, are part of the world, for all their boorishness. They are not yet part of *le monde,* the world of society, but they are part of the real world, the world of existence; they *are,* with no qualifications. The Marches know that, and accept with weary amiability the truth that simply by being, without doing anything, the Dryfoos girls must eventually be accepted into *le monde.* As the Marches leave the artificial world, literally a made world, of society, and re-enter the real world of human society, the latter teaches them a lesson: the prostitute, symbol of human helplessness before the givens of instinctive drives and the pressures of reality, rushes madly across their path and shatters their dream (they are thinking of the exquisite Margaret Vance) that people can be built and kept tidy in the world of flux.

Howells' philosophical side, like his others, is not simple, but the resultant of more than one force, and less in effective sum than any one of them. The simple Heideggerian reverence for being is blunted by the Kantian worry over the perception of being; the profound sense of man's existential situation and of his silly but essential efforts to avoid it is blunted by an inability to squarely face the situation or to reject the consolations of social life and other diversions. Like his mouthpieces the Marches, Howells tries to have it both ways, and as a result, is neither a Jeff Durgin nor a Mrs. Horn, a happy clear-eyed demon or a happy fool. The tensions in the phrase "Ah! poor Real Life" are not fruitful or useful; they pull in opposite directions, so that the Howells novel, as I have said in another context, seems to be the logical successor in tone as well as time to Hawthorne's last manuscripts (*The Ancestral Footstep, Dr. Grimshawe's Secret*) or Melville's novels after *Moby-Dick*.

I am not returning to the discussion of Howells' flaws; I am not attacking him for not using his many tensions in a multi-ironical art. It is no use attacking a man's nature; one can only describe it and then discuss its implications. Howells, I believe, in the final analysis must be approached as a neurotic artist—not as a neurotic only (this is the easy or Lewisohn-Fiedler way of disposing of him), but as a neurotic *artist;* a romantic trying to project his sense of things into his personal combination of anatomy and lyrical drama; a writer harmed but not wholly controlled by defects in his psychic economy. Despite his evasions and failures in the act of revelation, despite his wasting most of his time on hack writing (from our point of view), Howells still has strong claims on our attention. He had an intuitive sense of man's existence in the modern post-Nietzschean world; he had a much better grasp of his immediate existential situation (the nineteenth-century urban world). Through his satire he steadily attacked harmful systems of thought and behavior based on a non-existential (that is, rigid and unobservant) approach to reality, man, and the perception of the two. In his complex way, however, he realized man's immediate need for a working system of conduct, and he tactfully presented one: a combination, roughly speaking, of Christian Socialism and good manners. I think that Henry James was more nearly correct than he knew when he said, "Other Americans have considered and discoursed upon American life, but no one, surely, has *felt* it so completely as he."[10] Certainly, Howells had little of Fitzgerald's artistic feeling for the very rich (the second generation and after), of Dreiser's for the very shabby, but he "*felt,*" he *knew,* the central American group, the middle-class administrators and professional men; and he knew the central modern American situation: the endlessly renewed attempt to plug along, with honor, in a chaotic world. No other American author has ever done this so well as Howells. Few have tried, or do try. Among recent novelists, Cozzens and Marquand sometimes explore the subject, and do so with more controlled artistry than Howells; but Marquand is hampered by his facility, and Cozzens has been inconsistent. Only occasionally, as in *Guard of Honor* and *So Little Time,* or in the recent mature work of Updike and Bellow, do present-day novelists catch the note of an anxiety that will not let itself degenerate into neurosis or surrender. "They endured," Faulkner's tribute to the American Negro, applies also to the Marches, Silas Lapham, the Kentons, and Hope Hawberk. In Faulkner it is only the folk who endure and must endure; in Howells, all of the mankind that he knows is brought down to this level of troubled day-to-day existence on the thin surface that hides violence and pain. It is no wonder that the generations after Howells rejected him for more exciting, even if more pessimistic, versions of the human condition, and that Howells himself had trouble facing the vision that he was putting down, as if he were one of us trying to face our world of Dachau, Birmingham, and napalm.

[10] "William Dean Howells," *Harper's Weekly,* XXX (June 19, 1886), 394, in *Howells: A Century of Criticism,* ed. Kenneth E. Eble (Dallas, 1962), p. 44.

Bibliography

I. Works by William Dean Howells

Annie Kilburn. New York, 1889.

April Hopes. New York, 1888.

A Boy's Town. New York, 1890.

A Chance Acquaintance. Boston, 1873.

The Coast of Bohemia. New York, 1893.

Criticism and Fiction and Other Essays by William Dean Howells, ed. Clara M. Kirk and Rudolf Kirk. New York, 1959.

The Daughter of the Storage. New York, 1916.

The Day of their Wedding. New York, 1896.

Doctor Breen's Practice. Boston, 1881.

A Fearful Responsibility, and Other Stories. Boston, 1881.

A Foregone Conclusion. Boston, 1875.

A Hazard of New Fortunes. Two volumes in one. New York, 1890.

Heroines of Fiction, New York, 1901.

An Imperative Duty. New York, 1892.

Indian Summer. Boston, 1886.

The Kentons. New York, 1902.

The Lady of the Aroostook. Boston, 1879.

The Landlord at Lion's Head. New York, 1897.

The Leatherwood God. New York, 1916.

The Minister's Charge. Boston, 1887.

A Modern Instance. Boston, 1882.

Mrs. Farrell. New York, 1921.

My Literary Passions. New York, 1895.

My Mark Twain. New York, 1910.

The Parlor Car. Boston, 1876.

The Quality of Mercy. New York, 1892.

Questionable Shapes. New York, 1903.

The Rise of Silas Lapham. Boston, 1885.

The Shadow of a Dream. New York, 1890.

The Sleeping Car. Boston, 1883.

The Son of Royal Langbrith. New York, 1904.

Stops of Various Quills. New York, 1895.

The Story of a Play. New York, 1898.

Suburban Sketches. New and Enlarged Edition. Boston, 1872.

Their Wedding Journey. Boston, 1872.

Their Silver Wedding Journey. New York, 1899.

Through the Eye of the Needle. New York, 1907.

A Traveler from Altruria. New York, 1894.

The Vacation of the Kelwyns. New York, 1920.

The World of Chance. New York, 1893.

Years of My Youth. New York, 1916.

II. Selected Bibliography of Howells Criticism and Critical Theory

Arms, George. *Explicator,* I (1942), p. 14.

———. "Howells' New York Novel, Comedy and Belief," *New England Quarterly,* XXI (1948), 313–25.

Auerbach, Erich. *Mimesis: The Representation of Reality in Western Literature.* Garden City, N.Y., 1957.

Barrett, William. *What Is Existentialism?* New York, 1964.

Bennett, George N. *William Dean Howells: The Development of a Novelist.* Norman, Okla., 1959.

BENTLEY, ERIC. *The Life of the Drama.* New York, 1964.

BERTHOFF, WERNER. *The Example of Melville.* Princeton, 1962.

BROOKS, VAN WYCK. *Howells: His Life and World.* New York, 1959.

CADY, EDWIN H. *The Road to Realism: The Early Years, 1837–1885, of William Dean Howells.* Syracuse, 1956.

———. *The Realist at War: The Mature Years, 1885–1920, of William Dean Howells.* Syracuse, 1958.

——— (ed.). William Dean Howells, *The Shadow of a Dream* and *An Imperative Duty.* Introduction, n.p. New York, 1962.

———, and DAVID L. FRAZIER (eds.). *The War of the Critics over William Dean Howells.* New York, 1962.

CARTER, EVERETT. *Howells and the Age of Realism.* Philadelphia and New York, 1954.

CARTER, EVERETT S. "The Palpitating Divan," *College English,* XI (May, 1950), 427–28.

CHARVAT, WILLIAM. *The Origins of American Critical Thought, 1810–1835.* Philadelphia, 1936.

CHASE, RICHARD. *The American Novel and Its Tradition.* New York, 1957.

COOKE, DELMAR GROSS. *William Dean Howells: A Critical Study.* New York, 1922.

COWIE, ALEXANDER. "William Dean Howells," in *The Rise of the American Novel.* New York, 1948.

CRANE, RONALD SALMON. *The Languages of Criticism and the Structure of Poetry.* Toronto, 1953.

CRONKHITE, G. FERRIS. "Howells Turns to the Inner Life," *New England Quarterly,* XXX (1957), 474–85.

EBLE, KENNETH (ed.). *Howells: A Century of Criticism.* New York, 1962.

EBLE, KENNETH E. "Howells' Kisses," *American Quarterly,* IX (1957), 441–47.

EKSTROM, WILLIAM F. "The Equalitarian Principle in the Fiction of William Dean Howells," *American Literature,* XXIV (1952), 40–50.

FALK, ROBERT. *The Victorian Mode in American Fiction, 1865–1885.* East Lansing, Mich., 1965.

FIEDLER, LESLIE A. *Love and Death in the American Novel.* New York, 1960.

FIRKINS, OSCAR W. *William Dean Howells: A Study.* Cambridge, Massachusetts, 1924.

FOSTER, RICHARD. "The Contemporaneity of Howells," *New England Quarterly,* XXXII (1959), 54–78.

FOX, ARNOLD B. "Howells' Doctrine of Complicity," *Modern Language Quarterly,* XIII (1952), 56–60.

FRIEDMAN NORMAN. "Point of View in Fiction: The Development of a Critical Concept," *PMLA,* LXX (1955), 1160–84.

FRYCKSTEDT, OLOV W. *In Quest of America: A Study of Howells' Early Development as a Novelist.* Cambridge, Mass. 1958.

FRYE, NORTHROP. *Anatomy of Criticism: Four Essays.* Princeton, 1957.

GIBSON, WILLIAM M. "Materials and Form in Howells' First Novels," *American Literature,* XIX (1947), 158–66.

GIFFORD, HENRY. "William Dean Howells: His Moral Conservatism," *Kenyon Review,* XX (1958), 124–33.

HAIGHT, GORDON S. "Realism Defined: William Dean Howells," in *Literary History of the United States,* Vol. II, ed. ROBERT E. SPILLER *et al.* New York, 1948.

HOUGH, ROBERT L. *The Quiet Rebel: William Dean Howells as Social Commentator.* Lincoln, Neb. 1959.

KAZIN, ALFRED. "The Opening Struggle for Realism," in *On Native Grounds.* New York, 1942.

KIRK, CLARA M. "Reality and Actuality in the March Family Narratives of William Dean Howells," *PMLA,* LXXIV (1959), 137–52.

KIRK, CLARA MARBURG. *W. D. Howells: Traveler from Altruria, 1889–1894.* New Brunswick, N.J., 1962.

KIRK, CLARA M. and RUDOLF. *William Dean Howells.* New York, 1962.

KIRK, CLARA MARBURG, and RUDOLF. *William Dean Howells: Representative Selections.* New York, 1950.

LANGBAUM, ROBERT. *The Poetry of Experience: The Dramatic Monologue in Modern Literary Tradition.* New York, 1957.

LEWISOHN, LUDWIG. *Expression in America.* New York, 1932.

MCMURRAY, WILLIAM. "Point of View in Howells's *The Landlord at Lion's Head,*" *American Literature,* XXXIV (1962), 207–14.

MATTHIESSEN, FRANCIS OTTO. *American Renaissance.* Cambridge, Mass., 1941.

MAYER, CHARLES WRIGHT. "Satire and Humor in William Dean Howells' Fiction." Unpublished Master's thesis, Ohio State University, 1954.

PARRINGTON, VERNON L. *The Beginnings of Critical Realism in America, 1860–1920.* New York, 1930.

REEVES, JOHN K. "The Way of a Realist: A Study of Howells' Use of the Saratoga Scene," *PMLA,* LXV (1950), 1035–52.

REILLY, CYRIL A. "William Dean Howells: A Critical Study of *A Modern Instance* and *Indian Summer.*" Unpublished dissertation, University of Notre Dame, 1954.

SCHORER, MARK. "Technique as Discovery," in *Essays in Literary Criticism,* ed. RAY B. WEST, JR. New York and Toronto, 1952.

SOKOLOFF, B. A. "William Dean Howells and the Ohio Village: A Study in Environmental Art," *American Quarterly,* XI (1959), 58–75.

TRILLING, LIONEL. "W. D. Howells and the Roots of Modern Taste," *Partisan Review,* XVIII (1951), 516–36. Reprinted in *The Opposing Self,* New York, 1955.

VANDERBILT, KERMIT. "Marcia Gaylord's Electra Complex: A

Footnote to Sex in Howells," *American Literature,* XXXIV (1962), 367–74.

WAGGONER, HYATT H. *Hawthorne: A Critical Study.* Revised edition. Cambridge, Mass., 1963.

WASSERSTROM, WILLIAM. "William Dean Howells: The Indelible Stain," *New England Quarterly,* XXXII (1959), 486–96.

WELLEK, RENÉ. *Concepts of Criticism,* ed. STEPHEN G. NICHOLS, JR. New Haven, 1963.

———, and AUSTIN WARREN. *Theory of Literature.* New York, 1956.

WIMSATT, W. K. JR. *The Verbal Icon: Studies in the Meaning of Poetry.* New York, 1958.

WOODRESS, JAMES L., JR. *Howells and Italy.* Durham, N.C., 1952.

Index

INDEX